RIGHT TIME, RIGHT PLACES

Right Time, Right Places

One Teacher's School Reform Journey

A memoir
by

BIL JOHNSON

BOOKS

Adelaide Books
New York / Lisbon
2020

RIGHT TIME, RIGHT PLACES
A memoir
By Bil Johnson

Copyright © by Bil Johnson
Cover design © 2020 Adelaide Books

Published by Adelaide Books, New York / Lisbon
adelaidebooks.org

Editor-in-Chief
Stevan V. Nikolic

For any information, please address Adelaide Books
at info@adelaidebooks.org
or write to:
Adelaide Books
244 Fifth Ave. Suite D27
New York, NY, 10001

ISBN: 978-1-953510-61-7

Printed in the United States of America

None of this would have been possible without
the unfailing love and support of my wife,
the Lovely Carol Marie.

Our journey, started in 1991, in the fires of school reform,
imbues these pages. Always my first editor and,
more importantly, loving partner,
this could not have happened without you.

Thanks always and forever.

Contents

That 5 a.m. Alarm

Zzzzzzzzzz. Zzzzzzzzzzzz. Zzzzzzzz. That damn alarm! 5 a.m

Time to get up. S*it. Shower. Shave. Get ready for a new day.

OMG. 42 years. Get up, get ready, get dressed. Take the bus, take the subway, drive the car. Whatever. This is what teachers do. Day after day. Teachers ignore their aches and pains, their personal problems, their lives. For their students, each day.

No one who hasn't done it, doesn't get it. Arne Duncan never did it. Betsey DeVos didn't. Michael Bloomberg didn't. But those are whipping boys. The lawyers, the financial consultants, the bankers, who send their kids to school each day have *no idea*. They think it's kind of an elaborate Day Care system and hope their kids can go to the college of "their" (whose?) choice.

Of course, if you're white, privileged, and in a suburb or private school, it's not much of a problem. If you're poor, black, Latino, Asian, or an immigrant, it might be more problematic.

But, if you buy into the American Dream, it's all okay, right?

Who is so cynical that they don't see there's an American Dream for one group and an American Nightmare for the other?

BUT

we continue to say *"EDUCATION"* will make the difference and resolve the inequities.

Education will compensate for the exceptional pre-K that suburban white kids get?

Education will compensate for the economic inequalities that are clearly racially divided in this society.

Education will make the difference.

Hardly.

Let's stop using the "exception that proves the rule" with kids of color and *urban youth* and be honest.

I made the mistake of believing Jack Kennedy when he said, "Ask not what your county can do for you, but what you can do for your county."

I bought it. Whole hog. I took a Yale education and became a public school teacher. I believed I could *make a difference.*

And, when I taught in a nice suburban NYC school, woohooooooo, did it ever work!

Pulitzer Prize winner. Executive Editor of Rolling Stone. President of Bard College.

My influence on any of that? Probably negligible.

Teaching in New York City. No prize winners. No college presidents. No editors. (Yet.)

There is NOT an even playing field in America. Not in education. And anyone who doesn't own up to that has not been out there.

How many hours have ANY of our Secretaries of Education spent in classrooms?

How many Chancellors of Education in any city have?

The system is set up wrong. The incentives are wrong. Inappropriate.

Want to make more money in education? Become an administrator.

Not good at teaching? Or, don't like it? Don't want to spend each day with 20 to 30 kids? Easy. Become an administrator or guidance counselor. Deal with one or two at a time. Have your own office, maybe a secretary. Not like a teacher.

Bad system. Bad design. Bad results.

I'm supposed to listen to an administrator who has less than 5 years in the classroom *assess MY performance* in a classroom?

Here's the flaw in democracy, regarding school. Just because you *went* to school, doesn't mean you understand what *teaching* and *learning* is about.

Yet, we operate on that principle. Can anyone be reflective, thoughtful, and caring about school? Can *we*, collectively, begin to understand what it would take to actually make this system work effectively?

That may be a new question or idea for some folks.

For others, we get up at the 5 a.m. alarm each day and try to *make a difference* in the way schools run.

Introduction

This book sneaked up on me. It started simply enough, as a Blog post, a reflection on the texts I thought had impacted my career as a reform-minded public-school educator. It wasn't hard to get that going. But what followed, day-after-day, was an accounting of my career, a memoir. It quickly departed from its original organizing concept and took on a life of its own, as a collection of stories, situations, people, and places. It focused on my professional life as a teacher/teacher-educator. This story chronicles what it was like for one teacher navigating the territory of school reform over 45 years, from 1969 to 2014.

There has always been an ebb and flow to school reform in this country, going back to Horace Mann's work in 1837. While the United States has promoted the idea of free, public education to insure its informed, democratic electorate, much of the support has been half-hearted and often failed to help those most in need. That's true right up to our present day. There are a couple of shelves of books you could read to study the history of school reform in this country (see Bibliography, p. 328).

I got on the reform rollercoaster in the late Sixties and rode its ups and downs until 2014. It wasn't always a smooth ride, but it was *always* educational. Teaching is a difficult profession, even under the best of circumstances. Few "civilians" have an appreciation of what being a good teacher requires. Nobody gets into teaching *for the money.* You can make a "decent" living, particularly if you work in the affluent suburbs of this country but, overall, it is *not* a profession where you're rolling in dough. Contrary to ruthless mythology, very few teachers go into the field because of all the "vacations and time off." And I'd bet that if someone did a study of those time-off seeking-folks, you'd discover they left the profession *within five years* (almost 20% of teachers do). The other inaccurate myth, of course, is that *anyone* can teach. What *anyone* can do is stand in front of a room full of children. Whether they can actually *teach* or not is an entirely different proposition. When I was preparing teachers at Brown and Yale, I used to give them a Xeroxed handout of this Donald D. Quinn quote:

> *If a doctor, lawyer, or dentist had 30 people in his/her office at one time, all of whom had different needs, and some of whom didn't want to be there, and were causing trouble, and the doctor, lawyer, or dentist, without assistance, had to treat them all with professional excellence for 9 months, then he/she might have some conception of the classroom teacher's job.*

Teaching is an art, a craft, a science, and not everyone can do it well. What I'd like to convey here is that trying to be a great teacher is an awesome challenge in and of itself. If you don't believe that's enough, however, if you sincerely commit yourself to actually trying to *change the system*, to make it work better for more students, you've got your hands full! School reform icon Theodore Sizer used to say "It's like trying to change the tires on a car moving 60 miles an hour." Schools are resistant to change. Other teachers are resistant to change. "If it ain't broke, don't fix it," is a common refrain from too many who refuse to face up to just how broken it is.

What *this* story focuses on is how *one* teacher, with the support of many others, spent a career *trying* to change that system. There were some significant accomplishments. There were some dismal failures. The system hasn't changed but it has been altered in distinct ways, and for the better, in some places. We all take a journey when we embark on a career. For some, it is in the private sector, a world I assiduously avoided. For others, it is simply *making a living*. But there are certain professions which allow practitioners to try to *make a difference* for those they serve. Public school teaching is one of those professions — a calling.

Like the old *Mission Impossible* opening segment, *teaching for change* involves a commitment to a task not everyone wants to take on. It is definitely a *"Your mission, should you choose to accept it"* scenario. I accepted the Mission and, like that old Robert Frost chestnut, *"that has made all the difference."*

Chapter 1

What It's Like
(Being a Teacher in the U.S. of A.)

For those who have taught public high school here in the United States there are several "givens." Topping that list are the realities that #1. – you will not make a lot of money, and #2 – you will not get much respect. As we all know, *everyone* has gone to school and, therefore, believes they *know* what teaching is: you stand at the front of the room (with the big desk!) and talk about the subject you are assigned to teach. In the broadest sense that may be true, but I would contend that the reason most people remember *so little* about their *academic* high school life, in particular, is because that model of teaching is *grossly ineffective*. Indeed, if you ask most folks what they really remember about high school the conversation will immediately turn to the social (friends, proms, etc.) or the athletic (sports!) or the dramatic/musical (shows!). There will be occasional mention of a special *teacher* but that often has to do with a *personality* and, in fact, little is remembered about what was actually *learned* from that teacher. Most people, by virtue of having *attended* a high school (be it public, private, parochial, charter, whatever), believe they *know* what teaching is — and, therefore, understand (and accept) why teachers are not well-paid or respected.

To try to dispel these notions I would begin by pointing out that #1 – *teaching is not "telling"* and, in fact, *good teachers* inspire, compel, and, most significantly, *engage* their students. As Ted Sizer, a man who should be on the Mt. Rushmore of Teaching (along with John Dewey, Francis W. Parker, Rousseau, and Foucault), noted in his 1984 *Horace's Compromise*, students must learn "to use their minds well." Few adults live in a world where rote memorization and multiple-choice tests are "usual" (the only adults who do, in fact, are *teachers*) so it becomes problematic, if we examine our educational system closely, we see that much of it— even in 2020 — relies on antiquated notions! And here's where re-reading James Herndon's 1971 *How to Survive in Your Native Land* struck a responsive chord for me. Some of my most deeply held tenets about teaching/learning were formulated in the Spring of 1971, as a college senior, when I first read *How to Survive* — even if I didn't realize it at the time.

Two important realities Herndon drummed into my embryonic teacher brain were these: school is *compulsory* and institutions *adapt to change* without altering what they do and how they do it. In the middle of *How to Survive*, Herndon has a section called "Explanatory Notes" (pages 88 to 121). While they are all informative (and remain so, almost 50 years later!) it is *"Explanatory Note #2 – Jail"* that puts *compulsory education* in clear perspective. Using the term "jail" as a substitute for "juvenile detention," Herndon notes:

If kids in America do not go to school, they can be put in jail. If they are tardy a certain number of times, they may go to jail. If they cut enough, they go to jail. If their parents do not see that they go to school, the parents may be judged unfit and the kids go to jail. You go to jail. All of the talk about motivation or inspiring kids to learn or innovative courses which are relevant is horseshit. It is horseshit because there is no way to know if students really are interested or not. No matter how bad the school is, it is better than jail . . . As long as you can threaten people, you can't tell whether or not they really want to do what you are proposing they will do . . . All you can tell is, they'd rather come to your class than go to jail. (pp. 97-98)

That is harsh, and a bit exaggerated, but it does sum up a reality of public schooling — kids *have to be there*, like it or not. And you, as a teacher, if you're trying to be a *good* teacher (and not simply a "deliverer of information") have to face that reality. Combine that with what the kids "expect" when they show up (that you will stand there, near the big desk, and "deliver" a subject to them) and it's a dilemma and a challenge. As Herndon noted earlier:

I could have brooded about the gulf between something called learning and something called achieving in school, about the teacher as authority or entertainer or provider of work — about the razor's edge you must walk between the expectation of the kids (one to which they cling firmly, even though they may despise it) about what school is and your own conviction that most of that is worthless at best. (p. 67)

But one of your goals is, as he says, to live "easily in the classroom." Before I ever set foot in a classroom, these ideas were roiling around in my brain, trying to imagine what it would take for me to become a *really good teacher*.

1970

In the wake of the May Day demonstrations in New Haven in the Spring of 1970 I was determined to do something to *make a difference*. We were living in a crazy age. While our three days of protest, May 1st, 2nd, 3rd (a Friday, Saturday, Sunday), had passed without a violent incident, we *did* have armed National Guard troops on the streets surrounding the campus. When I woke up on Friday morning, May 1st and opened the shutters to my single room in Morse College, I was shocked to see the Yale Power Plant parking lot filled with Troop Transport trucks and *armed* soldiers lining the street!

All the more frightening, then, was the news Monday night, May 4th, that four students had been *killed* by the Ohio National Guard during demonstrations at Kent State University. "Holy Shit! They had *real* bullets in those carbines?" Had we, in fact, literally "dodged a bullet" during the May Day weekend?

In the aftermath, I was more resolved to stay in New Haven and do *something* that would further the *cause*, however that might manifest itself.

Chapter 2

School Change/School Reform

It's fairly common knowledge that "the Sixties" was a period of social and political ferment in the United States. *Movements* dominated the period: Civil Rights, Anti-War, Women's', and Gay Rights are the ones the textbooks "cover." The desire for *change* was pervasive and, led by the college-aged *Baby Boomers*, there was also an energetic, if inchoate, "school change/school reform" movement. The *Free School* movement was most prominent among these. As defined in Wikipedia:

> *The free school movement, also known as the new schools or alternative schools movement, was an American education reform movement during the 1960s and early 1970s that sought to change the aims of formal schooling through alternative, independent community schools.*

The best-known public-school alternative at that time was the Philadelphia Parkway Program. According to the Education Research Information Center (ERIC) in April of 1973:

The Parkway Program is the prototype school-without-walls created by the School District of Philadelphia in 1967. The program presently consists of four units of approximately 200 students (chosen by lottery from throughout the city), ten teachers, ten to 12 interns, and a Unit Head and administrative assistant housed in four separate non-school locations around the city. The students attend classes in: (1) conventional subject matter areas, the bulk of which are taught by the Parkway teachers, and which usually take place in sites around the city contributed by agencies and institutions, and (2) subject fields not ordinarily available to high school students, offered by volunteers (many from institutions) whose courses are monitored by Parkway staff. To provide intellectual and interpersonal coherence to the program and to offer counseling and basic skill development to all students; Parkway offers a period each day called tutorial.

The idea of "schools-without-walls" was to use community resources/people to educate "at-risk" students. The other popular alternative that evolved were "schools-within-schools" (SWAS)— programs that did not follow the mainstream curriculum but were housed in traditional junior and senior high school buildings and designed for kids who didn't find "regular" school particularly effective. All of this fit right into the *counterculture movement* of the late 1960's/early 1970's (see: Theodore Roszak, Philip Slater, Charles Reich). This was the movement that influenced me as I began considering a career in education.

Before I ever read James Herndon's *How to Survive in Your Native Land,* my first immersion in school change/reform was the result of my organizing activities during the May Day Demonstrations in New Haven. Black Panther co-founder Bobby Seale was on trial on (trumped-up) murder charges, and thousands of people descended on New Haven to protest what was clearly another Nixon/Hoover attempt at destroying the Panthers. Determined to "do something" beyond May Day, I landed a summer job with the Yale Council on Community Affairs and my assignment was to catalogue resources for a proposed New Haven Parkway Program — the *New Haven High School in the Community*, an alternative high school.*

That was my first experience working with an "alternative" school and it set my course regarding school change/school reform. I knew the system I had gone through "worked" for me (there I was at Yale, after all) *but* it hadn't engaged me or inspired me and, quite honestly, my first year and a half at Yale (when it was still an all-male bastion) was a struggle. I was far behind my classmates who had gone to prep schools or elite public high schools (Great Neck, Bronx Science, Stuyvesant, New Trier). I didn't blame Bay Shore High School so much as I saw the larger system as flawed. My political activity and mindset made me a natural for the "alternative school" movement. And that's where Herndon re-enters the picture.

In reviewing *How to Survive in Your Native Land*, I can see how it, along with my experience in helping to create the New Haven High School in the Community, set my mind to thinking about working in an "alternative" school setting, if not creating my own school. Two significant pieces of advice from Herndon were *Explanatory Note #3 (No Man)* and *Explanatory Note #5 (Four-or-Five-Minute Speech for a Symposium on American Institutions and Do They Need Changing Or What?)*. The sarcasm in the second note's title is obvious. What makes Herndon's writing so effective is that he never fails to see the humor in all this. "No Man" is based on the simple notion that teachers *"feel we have nothing to do with it (educating children) beyond the process of managing what is presented to us."* As he explains it:

> *Teachers imagine that they determine nothing. After all, who built the school? Not the teachers. Who decided there would be 38 desks in each room? Not the teachers. Who decided the 38 kids in Room 3 ought to learn about Egypt in the seventh grade from 10:05 to 10:50? Not the teachers. Who decided there ought to be 45 minutes for lunch and that there ought to be stewed tomatoes in those plastic containers? Not the teachers. Who decided about the curriculum and who decided about the textbooks? Not us. Not us!* (p.100-101)

Indeed, too often those who are closest to the kids on a daily basis — the teachers — have the *least input* as to what goes on in schools (and this is true even today). As Herndon continues:

> *Nobody, it seems, made any of these decisions. Noman did it. Noman is Responsible for them. The people responsible for the decisions about how Schools ought to go are dead. Very few people are able to ask questions of dead men.* (pp. 101-102)

"No Man" is a serious problem teachers need to confront from *Day One* when they enter the profession.

I believe Herndon's *Explanatory Note #5* was the most impactful advice I gleaned from *How to Survive*. I can see, in retrospect, how it colored my approach to changing/reforming schools during my entire career. Initially, my efforts were scattershot, as so much of the late '60's/early '70's "movements" were. It takes time for seminal ideas and philosophy to take root, requiring deeper thought and articulation to clarify ideas, to winnow out the excesses, to focus the task. In the Spring of 1971 I was really only armed with Herndon's notion of change but it was, for me, powerful and exciting.

Explanatory Note #5: Four- or Five-minute Speech for a Symposium on American Institutions And Do They Need Changing Or What?

> *The first characteristic of any institution is that no matter what the inevitable purpose for which it was invented, it must devote all its energy to doing the exact opposite. Thus, a Savings Bank must encourage the people to borrow money at Interest, and a School must inspire its students toward Stupidity. The second characteristic is that an institution must continue to exist. Every action must be undertaken with respect to eternity.* (p. 109-110)

By the time I graduated from college, I had experienced seventeen years of formal education. Because I attended Yale between 1967 and 1971 I was able to view, first-hand, how a venerable institution dealt with change. During my four years Yale changed its grading system (from a 0-100 scale, with 70 as the "fail" line, to a "modified" Pass/Fail system, which included "Honors" and "High Pass" — essentially an A,B,C, F scale), it also reduced the number of courses required for graduation (from 40 to 36) and, halfway through my time there, *admitted women* — making *my* graduating class the first co-educated undergraduates ever! Those are significant changes. I'm sure, to the "Old Blue" alumni, Yale did seem to be a different place.

Being in the midst of it all, we simply believed we were the "wave of the future" and that Yale would be forever "different" (and better)because of those changes.

Yet, when I worked at the University in 2007-2008, co-education was something the students thought had always been there and the grading system was a fairly common A,A-, B+, B, B-, etc. The course requirement for graduation was now 32. More shocking, and distressing was how *conservative* the student body seemed, all "nose-to-the-grindstone" and depressingly competitive. Having spent 12 years working at Brown University, where the undergraduate atmosphere strongly resembled my Yale late '60's/early '70's vibe, I was taken aback in New Haven. But then I remembered what Herndon had told me in *Explanatory Note #5:* "An institution loves change and criticism. It adapts. It endures. (p.110)" By 2007-2008 Yale's retreat to a former incarnation (an earlier version of the more conservative institution) *proved* Herndon's idea that "institutions" endure and adapt. It also spoke to another part of *Explanatory Note #5* that had informed my career as an educator — and proved equally important in my work. In looking at the ability of institutions to change and adapt, Herndon said:

> *The public school is the closest thing we have in America to a national established church. Getting-An-Education the closest thing to God, and it should be possible to treat it and deal with it as the church has been treated and dealt with. The treatment has not changed the existence . . . but it has allowed the growth of alternatives to it.* (p. 112)

It *is* so. The American Public School (and even old private Universities) require legitimate *alternatives* if we are to create genuine change. As my career progressed, I realized we could never topple *The Public High School* but we could, if we were creative and courageous, create *alternatives* that were more effective and humane than the current system, just as Luther and other Protestants created *alternatives* to the Pope and Roman Catholicism. Luckily for me, as has so often been the case in my life, I was in the *right places at the right time.*

Graduating on Flag Day (June 14th) 1971 with an American Studies (Intensive) degree (Area of Concentration: Literature), I spent several months casting about as a vagabond house painter and then a carpenter's apprentice on Long Island before the weather turned wintry and I visited the Main Office at Bay Shore High School where Mrs. Eileen Swital (who had been the Principal's secretary when I was there, 1963-1967) assured me I could substitute teach (for $25.00 a day) *without* certification because (wink, wink) she wouldn't be able to find a "qualified" certified teacher for that day. As a result, I worked almost daily from Pearl Harbor Day (December 7th) 1971 until about June 1st 1972, when I left for Hamilton, New York, and Colgate University's Master of Arts in Teaching Program.

While substituting at my old High School and Junior High there was little of Herndon's advice I could readily implement *but* what I did learn was that I *loved* being in the classroom, I related well to adolescents, and everything felt *natural*. It sealed the deal, regarding going to graduate school in 1972-1973 to get a Master's degree in teaching (I had already applied to Harvard and Colgate). Harvard admitted me with *zero* financial aid and Colgate gave me a boatload of money (including a *paid internship!*) so there was no question as to where I was going. And, once again, *right place, right time.*

Three factors at Colgate perfectly integrated my Herndon ideas with my classroom practice and budding school change/school reform crusade. First and foremost was my Social Studies Methods course professor, the late Bill Moynihan. Tall, thin, bespectacled (he always reminded of Syracuse's basketball coach, Jim Boeheim) Bill was a low-key, brilliantly thoughtful educator. He knew what was important about teaching in secondary schools and he transferred that knowledge in a seamless, supportive way. It was Bill who contributed the second crucial building block to my career: he assigned Paolo Freire's recently published *Pedagogy of the Oppressed*, one of the first books that began to clarify a process for harnessing the entropic energy the Sixties brought to school change. Freire's notion of *critical pedagogy*, student-centered classrooms, and active learning built logically and incrementally on John Dewey's *progressive education* philosophy. Finally, my first semester (paid) teaching internship placement was at Greenwich High School in Connecticut, an affluent New York City suburb where the 2800 student high school was divided into 4 Houses (creating four smaller, 700-student schools, each with its own Housemaster/Principal and teaching staff). The school operated with a "modified-block" schedule (not your usual 7/8 period day): teachers met classes *four* times a week (not five) and two of those meetings were *66 minutes* (the other two were 44 minutes each), providing a chance to do far more than *squeeze in* subject content. It provided me space to learn how to apply Freire and Herndon with real students and it was great!

All this set the stage for the beginning of my career in September 1973 at a newly created school in Rye Brook, Westchester County, New York: Blind Brook Jr./Sr. High School. That began in the Spring of 1973 with an ad I saw in "The Teacher Drop-Out Newsletter," a publication that advertised teaching positions in "alternative" schools around the country. Blind Brook had placed an ad. I called and got an interview. That was April of 1973 and it changed my life.

See Endnotes (page *for description of the New Haven High* *School in the Community*

1973

1973 was the year Watergate heated up, big time. By the time school was scheduled to open we were all eagerly awaiting the publication of the infamous Nixon Tapes. At the same time, those of us who were going to inaugurate the opening of the Blind Brook Jr./Sr. High School, were *picketing* before and after school: a "job action" in response to contract negotiations. And the building wasn't ready.

I walked on a picket line before I ever taught one minute of school in the Blind Brook-Rye U.F.S.D. Along with many of my other newly-hired colleagues, flaunting our long hair, beards, and hip attire, we must have been quite a sight for the residents dropping their kids off. We were squeezed into the Ridge Street Elementary School for several weeks. Makeshift classrooms were created in the auditorium, the multi-purpose room, the gymnasium. What a scene.

Once the Blind Brook building opened, around the corner from Ridge Street, the construction was not complete. I halted a class one day so we could observe two men install my white board. As they drilled (loudly) into the wall, I told my students to watch closely and appreciate how our board would be securely fastened for the rest of our time at BBHS. The work guys laughed and hung the board without comment, moving on to Steve Jones's area to install the next one.

We had moveable walls. Dividers on wheels, so we could open up areas to team-teach, if we so desired. It was an interesting, unique environment. As far as the contract went, our Union leaders had the School Board visit the UFT headquarters in Elmsford for a negotiating session. About a dozen of us showed up before the Board and were busy Xeroxing, typing, and scurrying around when they arrived. We weren't doing *any* work associated with our "job action" but I'm sure it looked like we were deep into Strike preparations. The contract was settled by the end of the week and I was ecstatic to be making $12,766 a year with my Master's degree (more than my parents made *together* that year. That's what getting-an-education does for you).

By October, the construction was completed, the contract was signed, and we were happily working with students in our *New World* school.

Chapter 3

Find a Good School

Herndon's first "Explanatory Note" in *How to Survive* proved prophetic regarding my arrival at Blind Brook Jr./Sr. High in September of 1973.

> *Explanatory Note #1: Find A Good School And Send Your Kid There It is a good school because of the principal, and because of the teachers whom he collected together . . . It is a good school because a district superintendent tried to get intelligent, serious people to come to work in the district and, once they did, allowed them to work. . .. they (teachers/administrators) like and respect kids.* (p. 89-90)

The unincorporated Village of Rye Brook existed within the Town of Rye and was bounded by Port Chester, New York, and Greenwich, Connecticut, until it became an incorporated village in 1982. In September of 1973, when I began teaching in Rye Brook, the town had recently passed a bond to construct its own

Jr./Sr. High School. There already was an elementary school (The Ridge St. School) but senior high school (10th-12th) students were sent to other area high schools — Port Chester, Valhalla, Rye Neck, and Mamaroneck. The community had decided to not only to create its own school, but also bought into a radical architectural design for their new facility. Featuring an array of floor-to-ceiling windows, the school's interior had *no walls!* Remember, this was the early 1970's and the concept of the "Open Classroom" was in vogue. According to Wikipedia:

> *An open classroom is a student-centered learning space design format which first became popular in North America in the late 1960s and 1970s . . . The idea of the open classroom was that a large group of students of varying skill levels would be in a single, large classroom with several teachers overseeing them. It is ultimately derived from the one-room schoolhouse.*

The Rye Brook community had bought into the "open classroom" concept but didn't realize, until the school was actually built, that their budget only allowed about *half* the square footage for classroom space a true "open classroom" design required. The initial idea was that there would be *at least* one open area (the size of a classroom) *between* classes that were in session. With *half* the square footage, those "open" areas disappeared and the first few years were a genuine challenge for teachers and students alike. As noted in Wikipedia: *"If poorly planned or laid out, open classrooms can sometimes lead to problems with noise and poor ventilation. Classrooms that are physically open are increasingly rare, as many schools that were built 'without walls' have long since put up permanent partitions of varying heights."*

The school started with grades 7, 8, 9, 10 and a plan to add 11 and 12 in the succeeding years. *Open space* (no walls) with 7th and 8th graders mixed among 9th and 10th graders could easily be a recipe for *disaster*. But it wasn't — and it wasn't because Herndon's *Explanatory Note #1* proved to be exactly correct. The Blind Brook Rye Union Free School District was led by a Superintendent with the curious moniker, Harley Dingman. In his infinite wisdom, Harley hired Irvington High School's Principal, David Schein, to lead our new school. Dave inherited some staff — Ridge Street veterans who had taught 7th, 8th, or 9th grade and wanted to become High School teachers. But he had carte blanche to assemble the rest of his new staff. With a small school like Blind Brook (about 100 students per grade) and only a half dozen or so holdovers from Ridge Street, Dave was able to "*get intelligent, serious people to come to work in the district and, once they did, allowed them to work.*" As it happened, Dave, along with Curriculum Coordinator Elmer (*Bud*) Moore, recruited a staff they believed could implement a "*humanities curriculum that included interdisciplinary studies.*" (wiki)

What this led to, as the first few years unfolded, was the hiring of TEN teachers from the Colgate Master of Arts in Teaching program and another half dozen from Columbia's teacher prep program (which was, philosophically aligned with Colgate's). By the time the High School graduated its first full class in 1976, *half* the teaching staff were products of Colgate and Columbia, with Paolo Freire and John Dewey center stage!

It's hard to describe the first few years at Blind Brook without wondering "How did we do it?" *and* "What were we thinking?" Quickly realizing the "no walls" thing was a problem (imagine trying to teach your 7th grade Social Studies/

English group next to — remember NO WALLS! — a *MUSIC* class full of 7th graders who were just given *tonettes*!), we soon ordered movable dividers and rolling bookcases/closets that served as physical barriers between teaching areas. Students moved around *behind* classrooms, so anyone who was free might well amble past your class in the middle of some lesson, invariably distracting *someone*. It was a kinetic and energetic place, to say the least.

It was also one of the most exciting, interesting, and educational places *any* of us could ever have hoped to experience. The faculty I worked with in those early years were among the brightest, most creative, most dedicated *people* I have ever known. Some are still close friends and we often marvel at what those years were like, and how important it was to know that Dave Schein, our Principal, *always* had our backs. Dave's priorities were simple and straightforward: #1 – the kids; #2 – the teachers; #3 – anything else that happens in and around the school. He never wavered in his commitment to those priorities and he instilled a great sense of dedication in the staff, particularly around the idea that "the kids come first." He was a great supporter of "go for it" with the teachers — which was good and bad. It was great for those of us Dave had hired, but less so for the veterans who had already put years in the District. Blind Brook was great, it was not perfect.

As new, young teachers (full of ourselves, for sure) we undoubtedly came off as arrogant assholes to the veteran teachers. We, of course, saw them as hopeless old dinosaurs who weren't familiar with Freire and didn't see that we were the Vanguard of the Future ("*Teenage Teachers from Outer Space!*" was the brilliant Peter Tarshis's nickname for us). *We* were going to upend Public Education and make it work (despite having read Herndon, I was still sure *we* at BBHS *could* "change the system"). Dave did his best to smooth things over between the old/young factions, but it was pretty clear which group was in the driver's seat. I already had a history with my Colgate housemate, Steve Jones, an English teacher hired with me as part of the initial "Dirty Dozen" Dave brought on board. We arrived at Rye Brook thinking we were "the Pro's from Dover," like Hawkeye Pierce and Trapper John in the original Robert Altman *M*A*S*H* movie. There's a thin line between confidence and arrogance, and I'm not sure we always knew the difference.

Nonetheless, it was a unique and special group that forged indelible relationships with students and families in the Rye Brook community. I lived in an old carriage house on the property of the Ridge St. School and played recreation softball with fathers of my students in the summer. Teachers, old and young, put in countless hours at the school in those early years, coaching teams, directing plays, leading the choir, tutoring math and writing, supervising the school newspaper and yearbook. And *everything* was being created *on the fly* and *from scratch*! It was amazing, invigorating, exhausting and debilitating at times. But it always felt like we were *doing something important.*

Five years in, when we had to be reviewed for accreditation, we did all the paperwork, met in committees, and spruced the place up for our three-day visit, generally feeling anxious, even though *we* believed we were a *really* good *school.* It was gratifying, then, when we met with the Review Team for their "Executive Summary" and were told Blind Brook was a "House of Joy" and we *were* hitting all our marks academically! It made all the work, all the hours, all the "dealing" with problem kids (and problematic parents!)

more than worthwhile. *We* were on the right track. *We* were doing school the right way. Like Herndon, I believed *we,* at BBHS, were Columbus discovering the New World. I forgot what Herndon said about change and institutions and, slowly but surely, the earth shifted, the sky changed, and the New World sunk below the horizon.

Chapter 4

*Winners and Losers
And 10 Crucial Questions*

What I didn't mention, head-on, when discussing *"Find a Good School"* and those early years at Blind Brook is what you may have already thought: Rye Brook is an almost exclusively white, *upper* middle-class neighborhood. If you can't create *The New World* at a place like that, where can you? There's truth to that, of course, but schools, like life, are far more complicated. As Herndon further notes in *Explanatory Note #1*: *"an American school must have winners and losers"* (p. 91) and *"winning is never permanent." (p.93)* He also says, *"The fundamental act of the American School is to deal with children in groups"* (p. 94) and *"The school's purpose is not teaching. The school's purpose is to separate sheep from goats."* That's a lot to consider but, if you have spent forty plus years in and around public schools, you know Herndon is *exactly* right.

While it would seem *all* the kids who attended Blind Brook Jr./Sr. High School could be seen as "winners" (by virtue of simply *going* to that school), once classes began meeting, the *winning/losing* ensued. Right from the start, when I was teaching *7th Graders*, parents wanted to know if their child would get into "the college of their choice" (I, of course, would respond by saying, "The college of *their* choice or the college or *your* choice?" My belief was that too many parents chose colleges for their child based on the status of putting an Ivy League sticker on the back window of their car). The pressure on the kids was palpable. We did avoid "tracking" (with the exception of Math, of course, where *accelerated* classes existed). When we finally had an 11th grade and could offer Advanced Placement courses, there was a fight because I proposed *A.P. for all*. The compromise we reached was that there would be *no* "requirement" (i.e. Grade Point Average) for taking A.P. U.S. History but a "regular" section of United States History would also be offered. Most kids opted for the A.P. class, figuring it would look good on their transcript.

As anyone who has spent time in a school with adolescents knows, *everyone* is aware of who the smart kids are (the winners) and who aren't (the losers). We worked hard at fighting labeling, celebrating all kinds of achievement by our students (Mr. Tibbs's shop projects *were* incredible, and Mr. Trautwein's & Mr. Tarshis's musical and drama productions *were* exceptional. The artwork from the studios of Mr. Marlis & Ms. Van B was *stunning*). Nonetheless, there were still kids who felt like "winners" and others who saw themselves as "losers." And, as anywhere else, some of that was carried with those people into their adulthood, one of the curses of the school process.

What you also need to know is that if you were to visit Blind Brook Jr./Sr. High School in 2019 it would look a lot like the high school *you* probably attended, whether that was in the 1960's (like me), the 1980s, or the early 2000's. Today, BBHS is enclosed, a rabbit warren of classrooms, with a "standard" curriculum that separates A.P. classes from Honors and College groups. The daily schedule features *nine* forty-minute class periods with a 23 minute "Activity Period" at the end of the day. Pretty standard stuff and a world away from the Blind Brook that existed from 1973 until Dave Schein left (driven out by several short-sighted School Board members) in the early 1980s. As Herndon noted, an enlightened superintendent and a good principal can make all the difference in the world and, at Blind Brook, they did. But with Harley Dingman retired and Dave Schein driven away, BBHS started shifting back toward the mainstream, clearly sailing toward a port I had no interest in visiting. I lasted until 1984 but, like some kind of addict, I needed that *rush* of excitement that a *new* school or an *innovative* school might provide. It took three years of wandering in the wilderness before I found that next adventure, in an unlikely setting back in Westchester County. Before examining that story, though, I'd like to assign some homework.

In 2003 I published a book about teaching Social Studies/History. It was designed for my students at Brown University who were preparing to be Secondary School teachers. The first Chapter raises questions which are important for *everyone* who cares about our schools. The title of that Chapter was: *Why Do We Do What We Do The Way We Do It?* That question, when applied to high schools is crucial and engenders *ten* other questions I am assigning to you for *homework* (answers will be provided in the next Chapter).

Here are my *questions about school assumptions*:

#1. *What's the educational philosophy behind the 7 or 8 period day that most secondary schools use?*

#2. *Why is the curriculum arranged and sequenced the way it is? (e.g. "Algebra, Geometry, Trigonometry" "Biology, Chemistry, Physics")*

#3. *If we truly believe "all students can learn" is sorting and tracking the best way to help students attain that goal?*

#4. *Why are students grouped according to their date of birth rather than their stage of development?*

#5. *Why does multiple-choice (and "objective") testing dominate schools when it is barely present in the rest of society?*

#6. *If students took their final examinations one year later, without their courses "in front" of the test, how would they do?*

#7. *Why are external (state/national) tests necessary to create "high standards?*

#8. *Why don't teachers know what their colleagues do (in their classrooms)?*

#9. *Why are novice teachers given the most difficult assignments/ schedules?*

#10. *Why are there significant numbers of educators in schools who are almost never in classrooms?*

That's your assignment. Take some time to reflect on them. Jot down your answers. The Answer Key is in the next Chapter

Chapter 5

Answer Key

As my career as an educator progressed, I became more and more interested in *assessment* (testing/evaluating, etc.) and fixated on trying to get students to ask "wadja learn?" rather than "wadja get?" Regarding the 10 questions I assigned as homework, I will ask: *What did you learn?* I'm guessing that, with no grade or homework check hanging over your head, you didn't "look up" answers to the questions, particularly knowing the results would be revealed (which says something else about compulsory education and our evaluation system). Without further ado, let's take a look at the answers.

#1. *What's the educational philosophy behind the 7 or 8 period day that most secondary schools use?*

At the end of the 19th century, U.S. universities wanted to make high school curricula more uniform so they could better assess their applicants. They created the Committee of Ten in 1892, headed by the President of Harvard University, Charles

Eliot. The Committee was charged with *standardizing* the high school curriculum (there were competing philosophies being promoted and implemented around the country). *That* Committee's report (published in 1893) became a blueprint for American secondary schools *right up to the present day*. Regarding the 7 or 8 period day: the Committee recommended that *all* high school students take courses in Literature, History, Mathematics, Science, and foreign language (Latin & Greek were favorites at the time). That's *five* main/core subjects. Add physical education, art/music, plus lunch and you get 7 or 8 classes per day (Phys. Ed./Art/Music might alternate days). The standard time allotted for high school was, generally, 8 a.m. to 3 p.m. If you take your 7 or 8 periods and *divide* that into your 7 hours, you get 52.5 or 60 minutes. Consider that you need to allow "passing time," homeroom (for attendance), and you can see how the 40/42/45/47/49/52-minute period became (and remains!) the standard for high schools.

To answer our question: there is *NO* educational *philosophy* behind the 7 or 8 period day! There is only arithmetic. This reflects the influence of the Industrial Revolution in the U.S. and a man named Frederick Taylor, who led an "efficiency" movement in the early 20th century. Beyond separating sheep from goats (managers from workers, in Industrial parlance), students were taught some basic skills for good workers (Follow directions, move at the bell, defer to authority). *Moving* large numbers of people *efficiently* was as much a part of the 7/8 period day as the arithmetic. Grant Wiggins, my late colleague who was a leader in school (re)design and assessment in the late 20th century, posed a simple scenario to assess the educational value of this system:

Imagine if Bill Gates asked his engineers at Microsoft to get up every 45 to 50 minutes and move to a new workstation with a new supervisor, to work on a totally unrelated task (from the last supervisor's) five or six times a day. How effective would the company be?

The answer is obvious: "not very effective." Yet we expect adolescents not only to do this *every day* but to master *all those subjects!* It's amazing, really, that so many people come away from it with *any* reasonable skills and competencies!

#2. Why is the curriculum arranged and sequenced the way it is? (e.g. "Algebra, Geometry, Trigonometry" "Biology, Chemistry, Physics")

This one is simple but stunning. While the Committee of Ten made recommendations as to what subjects should be taught, they firmly believed *Local Districts*, knowing their students, should determine not only *what* specific subjects be taught (English Literature? World History?) but also recommended that the *Local District* should determine *the sequence* the courses be taught in.

As a guideline, they listed possible courses *alphabetically* (Algebra, Geometry, Trigonometry; Biology, Chemistry, Physics).

Those courses have become *embedded* in U.S. curricula everywhere and there are administrators and teachers who will *fight you to the death* if you try to change the order, even though there's *no research or philosophy* to support that *alphabetical order!*

#3. If we truly believe "all students can learn," is sorting and tracking the best way to help them attain that goal?

We talk a pretty good game in the U.S. of A. about equality for all and equal opportunity but our schools, from

Day One begin *sorting* the "winners" and "losers" (often based on objective testing or some other kind of achievement-based or anecdotal tool). While grouping students with similar aptitudes or skills for some *portion* of a school day can be productive, the *rigid* tracking that we see in most high schools is deleterious to an *overwhelming majority* of students. There is tons of research about this (I'd recommend Jeannie Oakes's classic *Keeping Track* as well as Anne Wheelock's *Crossing the Tracks* as evidence) and a factor that adds to the winner/loser mentality is often generated *from teachers*. There is a boatload of research that proves teacher *expectations* (based on a belief their students are gifted/honors or challenged/below-grade-level) directly correlates to student achievement (see Rosethal, 1968 & Brophy & Good, 1970). This *totally* works *against* trying to create a school that is a genuine *Learning Community*. As I wrote back in 2003:

The balkanized curriculum taught in short blocks to tracked students has managed to serve only a small percentage of "winners" in the system. Yet these assumptions remain unquestioned and are seldom, if ever, discussed in school districts. (p.6, The Student-Centered Classroom)

It's never too late to engage in that discussion in your school or school district. We certainly don't need any more first or second grade readers being told, "You guys are the *Bluebirds* and you guys are the *Vultures.*" Kids *know!*

#4. Why are students grouped according to their date of birth rather than their stage of development?

This question is fun because it is one where the school (particularly *secondary schools*) regularly contradicts itself. Because of a slavish commitment to grouping people by *birth date*, an easy way to organize people but not necessarily a truly effective one when we consider intellectual and cognitive growth, schools trap themselves in untenable situations, *except* when sheer *performance* is the major criteria for success. Simply put: the naturally gifted sophomore running back is not told he has to remain on the Junior Varsity *because* that's his age group. The brilliant freshman cellist is given the first chair in the school orchestra because no one questions she is the best and deserves it. Whenever students can *show what they know or can do*, *birth dates* magically fly out the window! In sports and the arts/music, we don't care about *when they were born!* My challenge to schools is, "When are you going to start creating *performance-based assessments* to gauge what students actually *know and can do* ?»

#5. Why does multiple-choice (and objective) testing dominate schools when it is barely present in the rest of society?

Given what we've already looked at, the pervasiveness of multiple-choice testing (as well as other "objective" measures, like fill-in-the-blank) fits perfectly into a system that requires sorting/tracking and *short periods* of instruction. (It also ensures that classes will *have to be* teacher-centered. It harkens back to what is referred to as the *"mug-jug"* approach to education. Students are empty vessels (mugs) who need to be filled with knowledge from the all-knowing teacher (jug).) The problem with all of this is pretty evident. Did the student *really* know the answer ("c") or is (s)he a really good guesser? If we ask the same question a month from now (without review) will they still answer correctly? And, just for the hell of it, where in *real life* do you *ever* encounter a multiple-choice test where you have to answer "on-demand" questions (aside from the DMV or the tv show *Jeopardy* or, maybe, in an Emergency Room, where you can *consult* with others)? Nonetheless, our schools are still *rife* with these tests, not to mention the SATs, ACTs, Law Boards, and so on. They are quick, they are convenient, they are an easy way to *process* large numbers of people and, while some believe it shows how smart you are it doesn't at all show *how* (in what ways?) *you are smart!*

All these questions, of course, are based on *assumptions* about how schools work and, sadly, they are questions which are *never* asked. That these were first published in a book released in *2003* and *are still relevant* today speaks volumes.

#6. *If students took their final examinations one year later without their courses "in front" of the test, how would they do?*

This was another question the late Grant Wiggins often asked in professional development workshops and, for anyone who is (or was) a teacher, the response is easily predicted. People nod, eyes roll, heads shake, and sheepish smiles unfold — because everyone knows that, too often, teachers spend 179 days preparing students for a one-day *Brain Dump* in late May or June. Yet we persist. While the New York State Regents examinations may well establish some broad standards, do students actually remember much (if anything) they learned in their classes? What we are questioning here is one of the most basic *flaws* in our system: it is based on *input* and not focused on *output* (beyond a single, Final test grade!). This means that what becomes important in a classroom is that the *teacher teaches*, not that the students *learn*. And this gets us back to Herndon's *Explanatory Notes*, that an *institution* must devote all its energy to doing the exact opposite (of its stated purpose) and "an institution must continue to exist." (pp. 109-110, *How to Survive*)

#7.   Why are external (state/national) tests necessary to create high standards?

There is a Testing Industry in this country that strikes genuine fear into administrators and teachers ("Test results will be *published /posted online* in the local newspaper!"). This industry has steadily grown in the last half-century as cries rose for Standards and Core Curriculum Goals. The reason for this is one that we all know but, again, *never talk about*. In most schools *there are no standards* to speak of. What do I mean by that? Quite simply, in any given school, in any given *department*, Teacher #1's "A" may be quite different from Teacher #2's "A." Do teachers, whether as a school faculty *or* as a Departmental cohort, ever sit down and develop a *criteria*, with clear indicators and exemplars, that create a school *standard* for that department? Presently (and historically) the focus in secondary classrooms has been on *covering content*. The verb there (*covering*) is important. We're not "revealing" or "exploring" or "engaging" *with* students, we are *covering content,* which means the classroom has to be *teacher-centered* and *content-driven.* When you bring in an external standardized test, teachers then begin to *teach to the test* and, once again, lose sight of far more important *learning goals* (as well as valuable time). A test score *is not* very *reliable* evidence of learning. It is *valid* (all the students took the same test at the same time under the same conditions), but it is not *reliable* (how do we know *why* Bobby chose answer "c" on question #4 or Loretta chose "b" on question #8?). The combination of a lack of Local Standards with a large-scale Testing Industry perpetuates a system of *teacher centered* classrooms that focus on covering content, not on genuine *student learning.*

*#8. Why don't teachers know what their colleagues do (in their
classrooms)?*

Teaching can be a terribly lonely profession. At the secondary level, most teachers are *independent contractors*. While
there is a need and desire for teacher autonomy, there is too
little conversation *between* teachers about *professional practice*.
While there are always a certain number of professional development days set aside for the teaching staff each academic year,
many teachers would tell you those days are seen as a "joke" or
"useless." (I am, of course, generalizing here. I worked in several schools where excellent, *regular* professional development
was *built into* weekly meetings but those were *exceptions*, not
the rule). There are very few schools where teachers actually
visit each other's classrooms to observe a colleague's practice
(and then discuss it). A visit from an administrator (*evaluation*) can strike fear into veteran teachers. Why? Because
School Culture is seldom, if ever, focused on the notion of
Group Learning, neither for kids nor adults. The idea that
"It's my classroom. I'll shut my door and do what I do and
it's nobody else's business" is another deleterious baked-in
characteristic of too many schools. If we (as teachers) take a
look at other *professions* (law, medicine, architecture) we see
professionals who *consult* with one another as a *regular part
of their practice*. Once again, because of the history of school
culture (a book unto itself), the schedule, and a paranoid fear
of being "evaluated/judged," teachers *do not work collegially*,
and the profession is worse for it. (A quick note about those
early years at Blind Brook High School: because of the *no
walls* design *no teacher* could hide out in a classroom. We
were on public display for *everyone* to see/hear and it made
us better teachers.)

*#9.   Why are novice teachers given the most difficult assignments/
schedules?*

All of these questions are naturally connected and this one
directly speaks to the grouping/tracking of students *and* school
cultures that do not foster *collegiality.* Simply put, many of our
newest teachers are given the *most difficult students* to work
with at the *beginning* of their career. This contributes to why
20% of teachers *leave the profession* within five years. *Seniority* is
a factor here but the public's inability to truly understand how
complex and difficult it is to be a teacher also contributes to it.
Because of the pervasive sense that "anyone can teach" and the
low $tatu$ of the job teaching: #1 – does not necessarily attract
"the best and the brightest" candidates and #2 – drives out
young practitioners because of a system that does not provide
a *mediated entry* into the profession. There has been extremely
slow progress in the development of assigning new teachers
a Mentor, a veteran teacher who regularly observes and con-
sults with the new teacher. That the profession needs large
numbers of people creates even more complications (as well
as programs like *Teach for America*, the stopgap band-aid that
does not improve schools or help students). Bringing teachers
into the profession in a thoughtful and *educational* fashion is
what we truly need in school cultures.

*#10. Why are there significant numbers of educators in schools who
are almost never in classrooms?*

A *huge* problem faced in schools has to do with the fact that
most Districts are designed to replicate a business/corporate
model. There is a Board of Directors (your School Board), a
CEO (The District Superintendent), Senior Vice Presidents

(Principals and Vice Principals), Managers and Directors (Counselors and Department Chairs) and then your Workers/Labor Force (classroom teachers). What most schools have is a *significant* number of adults who are almost *never* in classrooms *with students*. A contributing factor to this top-heavy system is that the *incentives* in schools are upside down. If you are not a particularly good teacher, or if you *do not like* being in classrooms with kids (because you may not be a good teacher), you can *make more money* by becoming an administrator. Not only do you *get your own office*, you seldom deal with more than one/two/three students at a time. You are also charged with *observing* and *evaluating* teachers. There are a barrel full of problems here. People who are not good teachers or who do not want to work with large groups of kids can not only *get out* of the classroom but actually *make more money* if they do so. I do not want to tar all administrators with the same brush. Some are genuine *leaders* (the title "Principal" comes from the 19th century designation "principal teacher") and I had the good fortune to work for a few of those. The system, though, often overburdens administrators with too many balls to keep in the air (the School Board, Parents, Teachers, Students, Coaches, Music Directors, Counselors, the PTA) and *does not* create a culture that engenders *professionalism* for any of the adults in the school. There are "redesigned" schools that have drastically reduced those upper layers of management and created places that are, indeed, *Learning Communities* where *teachers* not only have input but are present in *significant numbers* (and if you don't believe *smaller* class size makes a difference, you have never been a classroom teacher!).

After examining the Ten Answers to our questions, we can not only see all the reasons our school system is ineffective but also why it is so hard to reform. The majority of parents (whether public, parochial, private, or charter) are "satisfied" with their local districts, despite the dire reports we receive about student achievement, poor attendance, or student alienation. The notion that "other people's" schools (particularly urban/minority-majority) are the ones that need reforming is pervasive and, in general, there is *no* groundswell reform movement or strong political will to change the system that exists.

Having been involved in school reform since the late 1960's I have witnessed the shifting philosophical tides, the advancing and receding of political agendas, as well as schools being used more and more as the battleground for bitter Culture Wars. No matter what the headlines or Presidential "program," the schools have remained relatively unchanged not only since the late 1960s but actually since the 1930s. Despite that, I still believe we should continue to work for change. The Parker School (in Massachusetts) and Blackstone Academy (in Rhode Island) are just two lighthouses in a dark education landscape — but they are not alone and they do shine a light on *how* schools can, in fact, serve as *Learning Communities*, as partnerships between the Community and the Education Professionals who work together to provide our students with an engaging and enjoyable learning experience.

1984

In the Year of Orwell, I left Rye Brook and Blind Brook High School and headed north, to Boston. It was a city I was very familiar with, having been there countless times since my college days, and it would now become my *practice city*. As I saw it at the time, Boston was more manageable than New York, a place I still found a bit intimidating. And I definitely felt the need for a geographic, a *physical* move to reflect the *spiritual* move I believed I was making.

There was no teaching job in Boston, which was fine with me. The Reagan administration had just issued its *A Nation at Risk* report from the Commission on Excellence in Education, painting a bleak picture of the state of education. Their recommendations were simply that *proficient* students take *more* courses, particularly in math and science. There was a passing mention of increasing teacher salaries and improving teacher preparation but, at only 36 pages, the report was not exactly comprehensive. In the spring of 1984, I took a Bartending Course (& earned a Certificate), entertaining some romantic notion that I would become a *writer* in Boston while serving drinks, hearing stories, and fulfilling a Hemingway/Kerouac notion pulsing in my brainstem. Having secured an apartment right on Commonwealth Ave. in Brighton, I could conveniently catch the *B/Green Line* into downtown Beantown, where I literally went from bar-to-bar, looking for a job.

Within a week I had a job on Boylston Street, across from the Boston Public Library (where, years later, a bomb would go off at the Boston Marathon!) at a little boutique, chi-chi restaurant called *Annie B's*. It was a fun job, providing me with some interesting experiences, but it failed to adequately meet my financial needs and, by the end of August, I was looking for a teaching job. *The Boston Globe's* Sunday edition ran ads for teaching positions and I quickly got a couple of interviews. The first was in East Boston, right next to Logan Airport, and I hit it off well with the Superintendent. All but assuring me a job, he simply had to wait for a certain teacher to put in *transfer* paperwork and I'd get a call.

Despite that, I went to my second interview, in Winchester (where Yo-Yo Ma & CIA Director William Casey both lived) and the English Department Chair, Fran Russell, *loved* that I had gone to Yale and, after a brief interview, ran me down to meet the Principal. Like the East Boston Super, Fran assured me I'd get a call within days about the position. I thanked her but, at that moment, was pretty sure I'd be working in the city.

The Friday of Labor Day weekend I got a call from Winchester, asking if I wanted the job (starting the following Tuesday!). An earlier call from the East Boston Superintendent informed me that no papers had been filed yet, so there was still no job. Winchester was actually offering *more money*. Accepting the Winchester job, I began readjusting my thinking, about driving North, not East (the commute was about the same), and working in a suburban, not urban, district.

While watching the U.S. Tennis Open on Monday, Labor Day afternoon, September 3rd, my phone rang. I hadn't planned on doing anything that day and thought it might be a friend. It turned out to be the East Boston Superintendent. The job was now available. He expressed deep disappointment when I told him I had taken the job in Winchester. I was grinning as I hung up the phone and hummed a Joni Mitchell tune.

You don't know what you've got 'til it's gone . . . .

Chapter 6

(First) Pause

My first year in Boston was a blur. Despite getting the teaching job in Winchester, I kept my bartending gig, usually working Thursday night, Friday and/or Saturday night, and Sunday brunch. Even though that would be a full plate for any normal person, I also took a part-time position at Hellenic College, a Greek Orthodox institution in Brookline, teaching United States History on Monday, Wednesday, Friday afternoons from 3:00 to 5:00 p.m. (with the fringe benefit of watching the Larry Bird-led Boston Celtics practice in the Hellenic gym.) I'd be less than honest to not note here that my weekends (following a *strict* Friday night through Sunday night regimen) were classic examples of drug/alcohol excesses. Like any good addict, I denied having a problem and it was a crazy, careening three years that, naturally, ended with a (rather anticlimactic but predictable) crash and burn. In spite of my *bad behavior*, my time at Winchester was wildly successful, a veritable highlight reel while it lasted.

The first weekend I lived in Boston I took the "B" line from the stop in front of my apartment building in Brighton to Kenmore Square and walked over to Fenway Park, where I bought a bleacher seat ticket and took in a Red Sox game. It was a beautiful July afternoon and, at that point, I was still adjusting to the move. One of the most immediate challenges I faced was *understanding* the natives. The famed Boston accent required some getting used to and I spent at least three or four weeks saying, "Excuse me?" Once I began teaching I encountered the same problem with my students. "Hey, Mr. Jawn-son, are you gonna potty this weekend?" Quizzically, I'd ask, "Potty? *Potty?* Like go to the bathroom?" "No!" they'd laugh, "No! You know, *potty* . . . like drink beer, and all ..." I'd feign that I finally understood, "Ah, you mean party! Why can't you guys speak English?" They'd howl with delight and continue to make fun of me and *my* crazy accent that insisted on pronouncing the letter "R."

It was during this year that James Herndon's latest book, *Notes from a School Teacher,* was released and, naturally, I gobbled it up. The timing seemed fortuitous. *How to Survive* appeared just before my teaching career began and now, pausing to restart my career, a new Herndon book. While *Notes* echoes many of the basic ideas of *How to Survive* (particularly regarding school structure) it also reflects the shifts that had occurred across the educational landscape over those dozen-plus years . Writing in the early 1980s, as the President of his local Union, Herndon takes on the *hot* issues of the time: standards, time on task, merit pay, and teacher evaluation. The last one particularly irks the author, as it seeks to quantify what he believes is essentially *unknowable.*

Herndon frames his discussion of teacher evaluation using the merit pay issue, quoting AFT President Albert Shanker:

The idea that if you're paid more you'll work harder may apply to selling encyclopedias. If you're a lion-tamer, you're going to work any harder just because you'll be paid more. The job of a teacher is more like a lion-tamer, I think.

As Herndon describes it:

> *You begin to teach as a lion-tamer, to be sure, and if not eaten up, go on to ask other teachers what they do here and there, what "works" for them, and quite soon, by some curious amalgam, you develop a way to work in the classroom which suits you and which you think is best . . . best, considering the various and vast distances between what you must do, want to do, and can do.* (p. 83)

At Blind Brook I had been a *Humanities* teacher, a *Social Studies* teacher, an *American Studies* teacher, a *History* teacher, an *Ethical Issues* teacher, but *never* a full time *English* teacher, which is what I now was in Winchester. My teaching assignment was: lower track Juniors (U.S. Literature and Poetry); the T.V./Media course (for "low-achieving" Seniors); and one group of "challenged" Sophomores, for a writing class using our shiny new Macintosh computers. After several weeks working with my kids I realized that everything I believed about *tracking* was true, particularly about *expectations*. My students had been told they were low-achievers and therefore *became* low achievers. I wasn't having any of it. From the start I let them know that I thought they were pretty smart and could, if they put their minds to it, *easily* achieve success in my classes, *if they met me halfway and worked at it!* It took some time (lion-taming) but, in relatively short order, they were doing great work and, more important, *we* were having *fun*.

Winchester High School was a world away from Blind Brook. It was four times as big, in terms of number of students and physical size. To me it was a *throwback*, much more like the Bay Shore High School I attended in the mid-Sixties than the Blind Brook of the mid-1970s/early 1980s. Winchester seemed not to have been touched by the Sixties school reform movement — but it *was* sensitive to the Federal rumblings bubbling up in the mid-1980s. In *Notes from a School Teacher,* Herndon writes that public education has been subjected to periodic *pendulum* swings, starting with the *Committee of Ten* in 1893, followed by the *Carnegie Foundation Reports (around 1910),* then Dewey's *Progressive* movement promoted by Columbia University in the 1930's, and then the *Sputnik Revolution* shifting the educational focus in 1957. The late 1960s saw the advent of the school reform/alternative school movement and, by the mid-1980's Herndon rails about the *Committee on Excellence* and their recommendations. His point is: the pendulum swings from left (progressive) reforms to right (conservative) reforms *but very little actually changes* for the *classroom teacher*. While still deeply interested in *genuine* school reform I figured the best I could do, for the time being, was teach *as a subversive activity* (thank you, Neil Postman and Charles Weingartner), introducing Winchester High School to some new ideas *inside my classroom.*

This created some buzz at Winchester High. While I only taught about 125 kids (out of a student body of approximately 1600) they were the middle/low track students and, therefore, part of the numerical majority of the student body (AP & Honors students comprised not more than 20% of the student population). Anyone who has worked in a school knows how quickly news/gossip spreads and, before I knew it, random kids were popping into my room during free periods to check out the new guy. My students thought I was a good teacher, apparently, and pretty cool, at that (I was conversant in the popular music of the day, sports talk, movies & tv, popular culture, and would connect that to their lives and school as much as possible.) My Dad always said the only ones who could judge whether he was a good father or not were me and my brother. I figured the same held true about my teaching (only *my* students could really judge) and that brought me back to Herndon.

> *Are the great teachers more entertaining? Have they better intellectual command of their subjects? Have they greater rapport with their students? Are they more efficient, provide more time on task? Are they more aware of their students' ethnic backgrounds, social class, personal or family problems? All of the above? Well, some of the above? No one knows. Does anyone know whether students actually learn more from great teachers, if you could ever find out who were the great teachers? No one knows that either.* (pp.84-85)

I have no idea how good a teacher I *actually* was at Winchester High School, but I *did* know that focusing on my students and working at *engaging* them hit responsive chords. The first year at Winchester flew by and my whirlwind lifestyle as the hip, young (*Bartending*) *Teacher* wrapped up.

Still hoping to become a writer, I also took a couple of workshops on *screenwriting* and actually found a writing partner (a customer from the bar) and headed into the summer (and full-time bartending) hoping to write the *Great American Screenplay*, but still looking for how to get back on that school reform bandwagon. And that's when Ted Sizer's *Horace's Compromise* entered the picture.

1986

January 1986 was the exact mid-point of my time at Winchester High School (even though I didn't know it at the time). That is not a significant date in any history book. January 28, 1986, however, is.

By January 28, 1986 I had already lived through several memorable historic events. I remember, at age 8, seeing the front page of *Newsday* ("The Long Island Newspaper") declaring that *Sputnik I* had orbited the earth. On November 22, 1963 I was a freshman in an eighth period study hall at Bay Shore Junior High School when we got word that President Kennedy had been shot. It was a Friday and we were going to have our first Freshmen Dance that evening. It was cancelled. On July 20, 1969 I was working at *Flynn's Restaurant* in Ocean Bay Park on Fire Island when Neil Armstrong took "One small step for Man" and less than a month later I was *at* Yasgur's Farm in upstate New York for the Woodstock Festival. On August 9, 1974 I was home in Port Chester preparing classes for the coming school year at Blind Brook when Richard Nixon resigned. I also remember events that won't make the history books but were crucially important in my life. Sitting in Hamilton, New York on May 10, 1973, finishing up classes at Colgate, I watched the Knicks defeat the Lakers for the NBA championship. On October 18, 1977 I was sitting in my living room in Port Chester, watching Reggie Jackson hit three home runs to lead the Yankees to their first World Series win since 1963 when I was in 9th grade!

On January 28, 1986 we had set up a big television in the Common Area of the English Department so that all of our students could watch the launch of the spacecraft *Challenger*. The teachers planned this because Christa McAuliffe, a public high school teacher from nearby New Hampshire, was aboard. It was history and *a teacher* was an integral part of it. By 11:30 a.m. we had our classes assembled, with students sitting around tables and on the floor, all with a clear view of the launch. At 11:39 a.m., 73 seconds into the flight, the unimaginable happened and we all watched the spacecraft disintegrate before our eyes. There was a suspended moment of silence, a collective gasp, and then cries, shrieks, and tears. It didn't take long for *everyone* to realize what we had just witnessed: seven people had atomized. We saw it. There was no taking it back. And it *was* horrible. What do you do? What can you say?

The rest of the day was spent *processing* the event, trying to come to grips with "the horror, the horror." The *real world* had inserted itself into our school day in a most shocking and tragic way. As a teacher, you try to be supportive, you try to model how a person deals with incomprehensible tragedy and comes through intact. It's not part of the job description yet it's an integral part of being a teacher.

Chapter 7

(Second) Pause
My Boston "Album"

Dr. Gonzo meets Dr. Sizer

The second year in Boston/at Winchester High continued at a breakneck pace. As the 1985-1986 school year began, an Assistant Principal approached me, asking if I would be interested in directing the Fall play. (yes, but I insisted on producing/directing Sam Shepard's *Buried Child*). Around the same time, the Athletic Director inquired as to whether I would want to coach the boys› tennis team in the Spring (Yes, I'd love to!). All the while I was still bartending on Thursday, Friday or Saturday, and Sunday Brunch, creating a *seriously bifurcated life*! Unlike Rye Brook, where I *socialized* with my colleagues (and some of the parents in the community), my life in Boston was sharply divided between the *professional* (teaching) realm and my *personal* (non-teaching) affairs. Dr. Theodore Sizer's *Horace's Compromise* became the text that guided my classroom practice, while "Dr." Hunter S. Thompson's *Fear and Loathing in Las Vegas* provided the soundtrack for my personal life. 1985-1986 became a bizarre, self-produced *concept album*. Side One was *Dr. Sizer & Mr. Johnson* and Side 2 was *Dr. Gonzo and Mr. Bil*. And that's where we pick things up as the needle drops on 1985-1986.

Side One:

Dr. Sizer and Mr. Johnson

Track One: Horace's Compromise

Published in 1984, Ted Sizer's *Horace's Compromise* entered my life at some point during my second year at Winchester and it struck a number of responsive chords. There were philosophical echoes of Herndon while the focus was on *disciplined* school reform proposals in a manner our Sixties alternative school movement never did. Sizer creates Horace Smith, a veteran English teacher in a suburban high school, as his vehicle for examining the state of education across the United States in the early 1980s. In his introduction, he notes: *"This book urges renewed public attention to the importance of teaching in high schools and to the complexity and subtlety of that craft."* (p 4) AMEN!, I thought. Sizer echoes Herndon by declaring, *"High school is a kind of secular church, a place of national rituals that mark stages of a young citizen's life."* Needless to say, I was sold on Sizer right from the start.

The author then takes us through Horace's day, the rhythms and patterns clearly recognizable to anyone who has been a teacher. Sizer also notes this about his character:

> *Horace is a gentle man. He reads the frequent criticism of his profession in the press with compassion.*

> *Johnny can't read. Teachers have low Graduate Record*
> *Examination scores. We must vary our teaching to*
> *the learning styles of our pupils. We must relate to the*
> *community. We must be scholarly, keeping up with our*
> *fields. . . . Horace is a trouper; he hides his bitterness.*
> *Nothing can be gained by showing it. . . . He will go*
> *with the flow. What alternative is there?* (p. 19)

And that's where Sizer elucidates how Horace Smith, in order to do his job and still be able to look at himself in the mirror, *must* make *compromises*.

> *Even after adroit accommodations and devastating*
> *compromises — only five minutes per week of attention*
> *on the written work of each student and an average of*
> *ten minutes of planning for each fifty-odd minute class*
> *— the task is already crushing in reality a sixty-hour*
> *week. . . . Furthermore, none of these sixty-plus hours is*
> *spent replenishing his own academic capital. That has to*
> *be done in addition, perhaps during the summer.* (p.20)

Indeed, this was not unlike the position I found myself in teaching English at Winchester High School! Happily, as the book proceeds, Sizer makes a compelling (and persuasive) case for student-centered teaching/coaching, as well as a much larger scale school reform proposal (which would enter my life in a *big way* sooner than I expected!). Encouraged by the text, I charged ahead, holding my students to high expectations, often breaking them into small groups, and, most importantly, *listening* to *their ideas*! I was an anomaly at WHS but, like *Horace Smith* I was trying to get by with the fewest *compromises* while being able to look myself in the mirror each morning.

Track Two: In the Classroom

My degree from Yale was in American Studies (an interdisciplinary major) but my Area of Concentration was *Literature*, so I relished the opportunity to teach English. I discovered Winchester had more than enough copies of Hemingway's *In Our Time* and Stephen King's *Night Shift*, the first collections of short stories from both authors and *perfect* material for my (supposedly low track) students. I supplemented those authors with the short stories of Breece D'J Pancake (a little known but *brilliant* writer). The students ate it up. The stories were, indeed, short (*On the Quay at Smyrna*, Hemingway's opening story is only *two pages*), the language was easily accessible, and the students had lots of ideas about symbolism, character, and all the classic elements of literary analysis. What sent the class into overdrive, though, was my sharing a couple of stories by Josh L. Brounwin, an unpublished author. (If you re-arrange the letters of "Josh L. Brounwin" you get "Wilbur Johnson," a device I learned from researching Vladimir Nabokov in a course at Iona College). When the students were told this was *my* fiction, they got excited about writing *their own* short stories, and we were off.

In much the same way, my Senior Elective in T.V./Media became great fun once it was turned over to the students. We had a basic (read: primitive) television studio, with two cameras and a control board that could switch from camera to camera as well as do some limited special effects. After studying commercials, the students reveled in creating their own satiric versions of what they had seen on t.v. Fabulous and fun! At the same time, my Sophomores quickly got the hang of the Macintosh computers and were busy either writing assignments for other classes or creating their own fiction. I was beginning to really understand Ted Sizer's notion of *teacher-as-coach* as a result of the work at Winchester.

Track Three: Buried Child

Having accepted the assignment of producing/directing the Fall Play, on the condition I could do Sam Shepard's Pulitzer Prize winning *Buried Child*, I soon found myself holding auditions. Winchester had a tradition of doing Fall plays that included large casts, producing what I saw as hackneyed material (I told someone," No one needs to see *Arsenic and Old Lace* again."). I also saw using Shepard as an opportunity to make the play another class for the students. Let's be clear here, though: I had *never* produced/directed a school play before. Having gleaned a great deal from watching the work of my brilliant Blind Brook colleague, Peter Tarshis, I dived into the task with great energy and a headful of ideas. The work of Viola Spolin and Sandy Meisner proved essential to working with my young actors and the Industrial Arts teachers (Dave Miller & John Fusco) with their stage crew created a beautiful set for the play. I winnowed out the *seven* actors needed for the drama and then chose *seven* understudies (who would have their own performance in a Saturday matinee, a first for Winchester). Our numbers were small, given Winchester's Fall Play history, but the talent was enormous, and both casts provided wonderful performances.

Track Four: Tennis

As springtime rolled around, tennis season was on the horizon. Unlike the drama production, I *did* have experience coaching tennis, having served as the Boys Varsity Coach at Blind

Brook for five or six years. It goes without saying that affluent suburbs invariably have good tennis teams and, indeed, my Blind Brook teams were more than competitive (only *Bronxville* stood in the way of our League title year after year). Winchester, though, was another level altogether. There was an array of banners in the gymnasium heralding Tennis team League Championships going back to the early 1970s. I told the Athletic Director that I feared creating a blank space or a banner saying "Johnson F-ed Up" being raised if I didn't come through. Luckily for me, I was blessed with some great players. We went 13-0 in League play, 18-0 for the season, and made it to the State semifinals before losing. Led by Senior captain Shawn Herlihy and some sterling underclassmen (Joe Palumbo, Gavin Barton, Scott Herlihy) the team was a pure joy to work with, far beyond the winning.

Track Five: The Golden Apple

During my first year at Winchester someone (the PTA? Administrators? Department Chairs?) thought it would be good idea to "recognize" teachers by giving an award in the Spring. It was called "The Golden Apple" and the student body voted on it. With administrative approval, a teacher was "recognized" at the Spring Awards Assembly. It was a very well-kept secret, with even the Faculty speculating as to who the recipient might be. My first year, having created sufficient buzz, I thought it would be *very cool* to win the Golden Apple — but how many Rookies win the MVP?

In 1984-1985 the award went to a colleague in the Math Department and, to the credit of the Faculty, there was no gossip or backbiting about the winner. By my second year, the students were *assuring me* I would be the Golden Apple recipient. I, of course, knew better than to seriously consider student scuttlebutt and actually believed my Department Chair when she told me I *had to* accompany her to the Spring Awards Assembly because, as the least senior member of the department, it was *my turn*. That, of course, was a ruse and, to my delight and surprise, I actually did win the Golden Apple! It was gratifying, even if it seemed to be a popularity contest. My English Department colleagues were pleased that we had wrested the award away from those math barbarians, so that also made it a fun win.

Track Six: The NEH Application

In the Spring of 1983, as my days at Blind Brook High School dwindled, I became aware of a unique *summer experience* opportunity. William Bennett, Reagan's Secretary of Education (and staunch Conservative), believed one of the problems with high school education was that *teachers* were not well-versed in their discipline. They needed more grounding, as Bennett saw it, in the *content* they were teaching. While I may not have agreed with his philosophical stance, I was thrilled by the initiative he created as a result: *NEH Summer Seminars for Secondary Teachers*. The National Endowment for the Humanities (NEH) received a huge grant from the Department of Education to create 15 four-to-six-week summer seminars (primarily focused on the arts, literature, and history) conducted on University campuses around the country and led by well-regarded professors who were *experts* in their field. Stipends for teachers attending the Seminars would range from $2400 (four weeks) to $3600 (six weeks). Only 15 teachers would be admitted to each cohort. My eyes lit up when I saw that one of the initial offerings was a Literature Seminar at Yale. Six weeks in New

Haven studying with Professor Michael Cooke and reading Conrad, Ellison, and Garcia-Marquez with 14 other teachers from around the country — what an opportunity!. I couldn't wait to apply.

Long story short: I was accepted, sublet a lovely apartment adjacent to campus, and spent six weeks in New Haven with a wonderful group of high school teachers that included two published poets — one from Issaquah, Washington (Thomas Brush) and one from Minneapolis, Minnesota (George Roberts, who also happened to be *Prince's* English teacher). Equally important was that teachers were eligible for an *NEH Summer Seminar* every three years, meaning I could apply for one again in 1986.

As the second semester at WHS began in early 1986, I went online and found the offerings for that summer's *NEH Seminars for Secondary Teachers.* What immediately caught my eye was a seminar at Columbia University on *Modern American Drama* taught by Howard Stein, the first permanent chair of the Oscar Hammerstein II Center for Theater Studies, and the head of playwriting at the University. No-brainer. I had to wait until April to find out if I would be included in the group of 15 selected to study in New York City. My classes and tennis coaching proved a suitable distraction, though I *wanted* this second NEH more than I had the first. Happily, in early April, I was accepted, and began eagerly looking forward to what I thought would be another exciting summer, little knowing that it would actually be a life-altering experience!

Flip it over!

Chapter 8

Side Two:
Dr. Gonzo and Mr. Bil

Track One: Fear & Loathing in Las Vegas

Life away from Winchester High School from 1984 to 1987 had a definite Jekyll/Hyde quality to it, particularly over the weekends. And it was there that another formative text reared its (Ugly? Crazy? Insane?) head. If you have never read Hunter S. Thompson's *Fear and Loathing in Las Vegas: A Savage Journey to the Heart of the American Dream* (1971) I highly recommend it. As a piece of literature, it is unique and groundbreaking. As a blueprint for a lifestyle, it is borderline criminal/suicidal! Thompson was part of the New Journalism literary movement that began in the mid/late 1960s, featuring Tom Wolfe (the Electric Kool-Aid Acid Trip) and Norman Mailer(Armies of the Night, Why Are We in Vietnam?). As an undergraduate Literature concentrator, I was taken with not only the pure energy of the writing but also with the fine subjective/objective line the authors tight-roped (or fell from!). *Fear and Loathing* grabbed me from its opening sentence: "We were somewhere around Barstow on the edge of the desert when the drugs began to take hold. I remember saying something like 'I feel a bit lightheaded; maybe you should drive . . . " (p.3) The entire book reads like a novel and it is hard to distinguish what's real/true and what is the product of Thompson's (admitted) drug/alcohol addled imagination. At the heart of it, though, was this: "we're on our way to Las Vegas to find the American Dream." (p.6) The book is uniquely American and, as a product of the 1960s drug culture, there was a level of visceral, careening muscularity to its prose.

While I was not much of a drug user in college (to this day, marijuana repulses me, the aroma is gross & its effects on me were always negative: muscle aches, paranoia) I *had* experimented with LSD enough to appreciate Thompson's imagery and colorful descriptions in *Fear and Loathing*. Living in Boston my experimental tastes shifted to alcohol (Scotch & champagne) and Peruvian Marching Powder (as Jay McInerney so aptly described it in *Bright Lights, Big City*), but *only* from Friday night to Sunday night! All the discipline I had formerly used in sports and academics was now applied to my emulation of Thompson and Dr. Gonzo during my weekends in Beantown.

Track Two: Annie B's & Catering with Kayo

Those weekends, bartending at *Annie B's* on Boylston St. primarily, are a bit hazy as I look back. One interesting aspect to the job was that I was the only *straight* man on the bar/wait staff, a new experience for me, but one that certainly expanded my view of the world. Two other experiences I remember clearly are meeting Jim Koch (pronounced Kuk), the founder of the *Sam Adams Brewery*, and working with Brazilian chef Kayo (pronounced Kye-Oh) D'Olivero. In Koch's case, it was 1984 and he had just started his brewery, reviving a family business. He was actually *walking* from bar-to-bar all across Boston, trying to convince bars/restaurants to stock his new beer. Showing great foresight, our restaurant manager agreed to *feature* the new brew (thinking it might bring in business) and I actually still have a lovely ceramic stein that Koch gave all our bartenders marking the first *anniversary* of the brewery.

Kayo D'Olivero was a wiry, bearded, energetic chef, a magician in the kitchen. A quiet, kind soul, we hit it off from Day One. While he often feuded with the owners of the restaurant (they were control freaks) he loved working with (and feeding) the staff. In short order, Kayo began a catering business and, once it became popular in Boston, he left *Annie B's*. Before leaving, though, while still the head chef at the restaurant, he hired me as his bartender on catering jobs and it was some of the most fun I had in those years. We catered small parties on sumptuous boats in Boston Harbor as well as *huge* wedding and birthday parties for Russian Orthodox Jews in Brookline (where I was simply a server, because we put a half dozen bottles of alcohol on each table). Sometimes it was just the two of us, sometimes we'd recruit a waitress from the restaurant to work with us, but it was *always fun*, and profitable (something I needed to support my growing alcohol/substance abuse problem). Flashing back to "Dr." Thompson, I think Kayo and I saw what we were doing as:

> *A classic affirmation of everything right and true*
> *and decent in the national character. It was a gross,*

physical salute to the fantastic possibilities of life in this
country — but only for those with true grit.
And we were chock full of that. (p.18, *Fear and Loathing*)

Track Three: The Beantown Music Scene

In the 1980s Boston and Cambridge had a *thriving* music scene.
Growing up in the Sixties, *music* was integral to our lives. The
British invasion started by the Beatles built on the rich Mo-
town sounds we were already addicted to. *The Ed Sullivan Show*
became must-see-t.v. on Sunday nights as band after band made
appearances. I went to my first major concert on February 26,
1966 at the Island Garden in Hempstead, New York, to see
Bob Dylan (backed by the future *The Band* musicians in the
second half of the show). My brother and I (and three friends)
drove upstate on a *Wednesday* to attend *Woodstock* (which
started on Friday) in August 1969. By 1984, I was playing
the guitar a lot and had recently picked up plunking around
on the piano (Winchester had a Faculty Room that was used
as storage space for the Music Department, so I had access to
an upright piano and an acoustic double bass during my free
periods). One of my apartment neighbors on Commonwealth
Avenue was in a rock/punk band that played the local clubs and
the *Boston Phoenix* newspaper and radio station provided all the
music news anyone needed. As noted by Peter Vigneron in the
November 27, 2012 *Boston Magazine*:

> *Thirty years ago, the Phoenix was the essential*
> *paper for a new generation of readers: those interested*
> *in a smart, countercultural alternative to the offerings*
> *of the mainstream press. Its writers and editors, many*
> *of whom are now among the most distinguished in*

*American journalism, surveyed the landscape here in
the city and created an enduring body of work in culture, the arts, politics, even sports. Its music section was
read nationally, exerting—along with the Village Voice
and Rolling Stone—a powerful influence on early rock
criticism. The Phoenix helped develop an entire genre
of writing, media criticism, that is now a staple in most
papers and magazines.*

There were jazz and rock clubs all over Boston and Cambridge. Landsdowne Street had the *Avalon* and *Axis*, Harvard
Ave. in Allston featured *Bunratty's,* and there was great jazz at
Paul's Mall right on Boylston Street in Back Bay. *ManRay* in
Central Square, Cambridge (easily accessible on the "T") was
another great venue. There were also great concerts on the
Boston Common in the summer, where I saw Don Henley,
the Eurhythmics, and Howard Jones. Rock luminaries of the
time like Peter Wolf (of the J.Geils Band) and Dan Fogel-
berg were quasi-regulars at *Annie B's* and once, again, "Dr."
Thompson captures the feeling of that era in *Fear and Loathing.*

*Turn up the radio. Turn up the tape machine.
Look into the sunset ahead. Roll the windows down
for a better taste of the cool desert wind(or cool Harbor
breeze, in my case). Ah, yes. That's what it's all about. . .
Tooling around the Main Drag on a Saturday Night.*

I don't think I'm alone, as a Sixties Survivor, who recalls
much of his past by evoking a soundtrack from a particular era.
My mid-Eighties life in Boston is remembered with music from
McCoy Tyner, The Police, Joe(as well as Michael)Jackson,
Tears for Fears, Peter Gabriel, Dire Straits, and hundreds more

(remember *MTV* had just burst on the scene). There's a lot of music you have time for when you're burning the candle at both ends from Friday night to Sunday night.

Track Four: Beantown Sports

It was tough being a *New York* sports fan living in Boston. The Red Sox had *one* good season when I lived there but, happily, lost to the *New York* Mets in the 1986 World Series (I attended one game in NY and one in Boston. The Mets lost *both*. When offered a ticket to Game Seven in NY, I *turned it down*, thereby *winning* the World Series for the *New York* team). The Celtics, on the other hand, were dominant in the NBA (the Knicks sucked!) and, aside from seeing them practice at Hellenic, one of my WHS teaching colleagues got tickets to the old Boston Garden, so I saw several games over those years. Bird, Parrish, McHale, one helluva team, for sure. The Patriots were in the Super Bowl my first year in Boston and I gleefully watched their dismantling by the Bears. The Mets win was big but the New York Football Giants winning the Super Bowl on January 25, 1987 was *my* sports highlight during my exile in Boston, 1984-1987.

Track Five: Writing

Throughout my years in Boston I never lost my desire to become a writer. I cranked out short stories (which I shared with my students) and I attended *workshops*. One of the first was a two-day *screenwriting* clinic led by Syd Field whose book, *Screenplay: The Foundations of Screenwriting*, was regarded a classic. Two other participants at that workshop were Steven Wright, the comedian who went on to win a 1989 Oscar in the "Best Short Film, Live Action" category and Craig Lambert, a Deputy

Editor of *Harvard Magazine*. Despite loving Wright's comedy, I never struck up a conversation with him (he didn't seem very approachable) but Dr. Lambert and I hit it off famously and began a friendship that encompassed writing, sports, and cultural criticism — to this day. Craig, aside from being a fine journalist (*Sports Illustrated, Town & Country, New York Times*) and writer/editor for *Harvard*, has published two fine books (*Mind Over Water* and *Shadow Work*). He has always been a reliable sounding board on a range of topics, even beyond writing.

As a result of the writing workshops I managed to write *two* screenplays and one stage play (finished after leaving Boston, in an *NYU* workshop in the summer of 1988). All of that work presently sits in a file drawer (along with a 415-page novel) in our upstairs office, waiting to be discovered posthumously, as I see it.

Track Six: Coda

My life in Boston was a raucous roller-coaster of a time and, looking back, my non-Winchester life echoes with sounds of Thompson's *Fear and Loathing*. As such, it is his summary (of a different place and time) that best reflects my feelings for Boston, 1984-1987.

> *It seems like a lifetime, or at least, a Main Era — the kind of peak that never comes again. San Francisco in the middle Sixties (Boston in the middle Eighties) was a very special time and place to be a part of. Maybe it meant something. Maybe not, in the long run ... but no explanation, no mix of words or music or memories can touch that sense of knowing you were there and alive in that corner of time and the world. Whatever it meant. . .* (pp. 66-67)

Chapter 9

Reset
1986-1987

Summer 1986: Changes in Attitude, Changes in Latitude

The summer of 1986 marked the beginning of several new directions. A DUI arrest and overnight in a local lockup jolted me into sobriety and my second NEH Summer Seminar, in New York City, allowed me to quit the bartending job. The *Modern Drama* course at Columbia was scheduled for six weeks starting in late June and running through early August. I sublet an apartment on West 111th Street, between Broadway and Amsterdam Avenue, from a Manhattan School of Music teacher for two months, bookending my seminar with *two* free (extra) weeks in Manhattan. Being raised as a suburban kid on Long Island, my parents' take on NYC was shrill and foreboding. My experience, as a boy, entailed visits to family in Brooklyn and an occasional foray into Manhattan on school "field trips" (the Circle Line, the Museum of Natural History). In 1964 the New York World's Fair in Flushing Meadow was serviced by the Long Island Railroad. I had finished my freshman year in high school and my parents thought it was okay for me to catch the train to the Fair on weekends (they had fond memories of the 1939 Fair in Flushing). I took advantage of their surprising permissiveness and visited the Fair with regularity. As I look back on my life, I realize that I didn't consider living in New Haven as "city life ." The only *City* any New Yorker acknowledges is the Big Apple. I can see now, though, that the move to Boston was my stab at a *practice city* and 1986's summer residency sealed the deal for me. I *had to* move to New York by September 1987.

The summer of '86 was glorious. Once again, I was surrounded by interesting people/teachers from all over the country and Howard Stein, our professor, guide, coach, knew *everyone* in New York theater. We saw 16 productions during our 6 weeks in session, traveled to New London to tour Eugene O'Neill's home, and met with Jerry Zaks, who had just become the Resident Director at Lincoln Center. In our off-hours there was even more to see and do. Hell, it was *New York City!*

Living in the shadow of St. John the Divine on West 111th Street placed me five local #One Train stops away from one of my best friends from Yale, Jay Fasold, which added to the fun of the summer. Excursions to Yankee Stadium, walks around the city, just hanging out in the comfortable environs of the Upper West Side, sold me on my "next stop." One of my Seminar colleagues, Marilyn Elkins, an English teacher from New Orleans, took us downtown to hear the music of Ellis Marsalis (*pater familias* of the prolific musical clan) where we were invited to stay after-hours to listen to Ellis not only play but discuss *teaching* music to generations of New Orleans musicians. (Marilyn has since gone on to become an award-winning professor and renowned author of feminist literary criticism). It was a spectacular summer and I returned to Boston with a three-pronged plan. First, I needed to get a job in Westchester County (so I could afford to live in New York City); second, I wanted to find a place to live on the Upper West Side; and, third, I had to figure out a way to wrangle money from somewhere so I could, essentially, take the summer off. With that in mind I returned to Winchester High School, intent on making 1986-1987 my last year in Boston.

Fall 1986

Basking in my Golden Apple glow, the school year got off to a good start and I was, once again, asked to produce/direct the Fall play. There was definitely a desire (on the part of the school administration) for me to find a play that would employ a far larger cast than *Buried Child*. I thought that could be fun, so I decided we'd do Thornton Wilder's 1943 Pulitzer Prize winner, *The Skin of Our Teeth*. The play requires anywhere from 40 to 60 people as cast members so my challenge was simply to find the students who could best fill the roles of the lead characters and then assign the remaining parts of "conveners" or "drum majorettes" or "chair pushers" to the multitude of auditioners. No one had to be cut.

The Skin of Our Teeth opens, in the original script, with a radio broadcast. Since we were producing the play in 1986, we updated those scenes to a tv anchor man sitting in front of a huge screen with televised images to illustrate his dialogue. Between acts we ran footage from the film *Koyaanisqatsi*, to emphasize the themes of war and the hardships man inflicts upon himself and the natural world. (*Koyaansqatsi* was released in 1983, directed by Godfrey Reggio with Philip Glass music.

It created quite a stir at the time.) Wikipedia describes *Koyaan-sqatsi* thusly:

> *Drawing its title from the Hopi word meaning "life out of balance," this renowned documentary reveals how humanity has grown apart from nature. Featuring extensive footage of natural landscapes and elemental forces, the film gives way to many scenes of modern civilization and technology. Given its lack of narration and dialogue, the production makes its points solely through imagery and music, with many scenes either slowed down or sped up for dramatic effect.*

The video was powerful, and our production was a big success. Once again, Dave Miller and John Fusco (the I.A. teachers) put together an incredible stage crew that built fabulous sets and our *huge* cast had a great time performing for two nights of packed houses.

Spring 1987

My first and foremost concern in the Spring of 1987 was to set my three-pronged plan into action. I applied to the NEH for an *Independent Study Fellowship* (submitting a proposal entitled "Wellspring and Crucible: The Family in Modern American Drama") and scoured the Sunday New York Times *Jobs in Education* offerings looking for my perfect match in Westchester County. In the meantime, I continued to teach my classes and, as Spring rolled around, coached tennis yet again. We didn't have quite as strong a lineup as the previous year, but I knew we'd be competitive and, given a break here or there, could win another League title.

By early April I was getting concerned about my Master Plan, when *there it was:* an ad in the Sunday Times for a Social Studies teaching position in Bronxville, New York. I was familiar with Bronxville from my teaching/coaching days at Blind Brook. What made this ad seem fortuitous, though, was that it said to apply to the school Principal, Judy Codding. I knew Judy since working with Lawrence Kohlberg at Harvard in the summer of 1981 so, before even sending in a resume, I called her *at home* that night. She told me someone was in line for the job (it was a one year maternity leave replacement) *but* if I could get to Bronxville by *tomorrow* (Monday!) for an interview, she could run me by the Superintendent, several Board Members, and the head of the Department — and I'd *have the job.*

It went like clockwork. I flew to LaGuardia and got to Bronxville early Monday morning, where I ran through my paces. As I left, Judy assured me I'd be replacing a woman I had actually *student-taught* with at Greenwich (Connecticut) High School 15 years earlier! She also assured me there would be a new position to fill by the time I was ready for a second year. Phase One of my three-pronged plan was now a reality. As soon as I got back to Boston, I called Jay Fasold and told him to alert everyone he knew to help find an apartment on the Upper West Side. By the second week in April I got confirmation in writing about the Bronxville job and received a letter from the NEH's Council on Basic Education *accepting* my Independent Study proposal. Jay's friend, Rock'n'Roll Lawyer Judy Tint called, informing me *her friend* on West 75th Street was leaving for L.A. at the end of June and needed someone to sublet his studio apartment. Bada-Bing, Bada-Boom! The three-prong plan was complete, and I informed the folks at Winchester I'd be leaving for New York as soon as the school year ended.

They were disappointed I wouldn't be back (I had just been given tenure!) but understood the allure of New York City and wished me well. The tennis team exceeded all expectations, finishing 18-0 with another League title. We lost, once again, in the State Championship Semifinals to Weston (whose coach *cheated* and rigged his line-up to win). Despite that loss, I was named "Spring Coach of the Year" in the local press, leaving on a high note. At the end of June, I packed up my apartment and, with the magnanimous assistance of Steve Jones, drove to New York City, ready to start a new Chapter.

Summer 1987

One of the bonuses of joining the Bronxville teaching staff was the school's participation in Ted Sizer's fledgling *Coalition of Essential Schools* reform initiative. The school was one of the charter members of the group and, as I saw it, on the cutting edge of erasing *Horace's Compromise* in exchange for the New World of Education. I spent the summer in the New York Public Library and out in Riverside Park, reading and researching the works of Thornton Wilder, Eugene O'Neill, Arthur Miller, and Sam Shepard, putting together my ideas about the "Family in Modern American Drama" for the NEH.

At some point in late August I got a call from Bronxville's local newspaper asking for an interview, explaining they wanted to introduce me to the community since they had heard great things about me from Principal Codding. During the interview I waxed poetic about Ted Sizer and how exciting it was going to be to work with Judy and how much I was looking forward to implementing *real* school reform in the coming year. Little did I know that the Bronxville staff was *seriously divided* over school reform issues and the older, (particularly)male members of the faculty, (many of whom I knew from my coaching days at Blind Brook), were *not at all pleased* with their female Principal and what they saw as her top-down strategy for *change.* By the time I set foot in the building, I was already "Judy's Boy" and had alienated a number of faculty.

In August, I finished my NEH Independent Study, submitting a one-act play (in which the characters were Wilder, O'Neill, Miller, Shepard, and a Man(me), who come and go around a kitchen table discussing their dramaturgical views of family embedded in their plays). It was clever by half and I was proud of my work. No one at the NEH ever commented about it, but they *did* send me the second half of my stipend money by September 1st, as promised. At that point I walked into the *Snake Pit* that was the Bronxville Faculty, naively thinking I was entering School Reform Nirvana and quickly discovering I had passed through the *School Reform Hell* portal.

Shifting Focus

The Reagan/Bush years had a stultifying effect on my political consciousness. It resulted in my paying more attention to *cultural* events/affairs. Any political instincts were channeled into school reform. It's not that I didn't hear Ronnie challenge Mr. Gorbachev ("Tear down this wall.") or that I missed any details about the Iran-Contra Scandal. But for me, there were simply *more interesting* things happening on the *cultural* front during the late 1980s and early 1990s.

Miami Vice brought *MTV* into prime time while also setting fashion styles. Michael Jackson, Madonna, Prince, Stevie Ray Vaughn and hip-hop were just a few of the trend-setters in the music world. Despite the Reagan administration's "War on Drugs" and appointment of our first Drug Czar, William Bennett, a crack/cocaine epidemic was sweeping the country. In fact, there was no shortage of disasters vying for peoples' attention: Chernobyl, the Gulf War, the Exxon Valdez oil spill, the Rodney King beating by L.A. police, the candidacy of Democrat Michael Dukakis. Nonetheless, it was a period of significant cultural expansion that I found most appealing.

David Letterman and Arsenio Hall had changed the monochromatic late-night television scene. Bill Clinton's appearance on Arsenio's show, playing the saxophone, undoubtedly helped his appeal with voters, as did his being on *MTV*. Michael Jordan and Mike Tyson were compelling, if not heroic, athletes people couldn't take their eyes off. It was the first popular wave of tattooing and piercing, a new way to announce your rejection of mainstream values and society (I got 2 tattoos by 1993).

And the *school reform* movement was gaining momentum. Ted Sizer's *Coalition of Essential Schools*, the *Paideia Program*, *Project Zero* at Harvard, Columbia's National Center for Restructuring Schools, Education, &Teaching (*NCREST*) were among the leaders in this effort. As the 1990s progressed, the *Annenberg Foundation* became a major donor supporting these causes.

While the political scene was inchoate and chaotic, the *school reform* horizon seemed bright, with those of us involved in it committed, energetic, and determined to *make a difference*.

Chapter 10

School Reform Inferno

In preparing for life in the New World of Coalition of Essential Schools reform, Judy Codding had advised me to go back and re-read *Horace's Compromise*, which I did (as well as re-reading *How to Survive*). As I went through *Horace*, with its proposals that schools restructure, that teachers needed to remember that *students* were the center of the educational process, and that *exhibitions of mastery* were far more important than objective testing, I was reminded of my teacher preparation program in Hamilton, New York, 15 years earlier. I scrambled over to my bookcase and dug out two formative tomes: Carl Rogers's *Freedom to Learn* and Paolo Freire's *The Pedagogy of the Oppressed*. When I first read those books, in the summer of 1972, they were still new (Rogers's work was published in 1969, Freire's in 1970). Like Sizer, they emphasized the importance of liberating students (and teachers) from an oppressive system.

In *Freedom to Learn* Carl Rogers uses several case studies to focus on what he believes are the most *important* principles of teaching/learning. His descriptions of the journey of a sixth-grade teacher and a college professor *still* ring familiar bells for me and, upon re-reading them now (2019)I realize how, like Herndon, they were deeply embedded in my *teaching consciousness*, dovetailing perfectly with Ted Sizer's notions of school reform. In *Freedom to Learn,* Rogers's 6th grade teacher's journal recounts her "experiment" with student-centered learning, group work, contracts (essentially an Independent Education Plan—IEP), and the resultant coaching (Sizer's term) she got to do. As the teacher notes *"I had much more time, so I worked, talked, and spent time with individuals and groups."* (p. 11) Later she says, *"They have learned that they can teach themselves (and each other) and that I am available when a step is not clear or advice is needed."* (p.15) In the professor's case, Rogers's says: *"he has, for years, created an island of opportunity — of freedom to learn — for his students."* (p.29) Most significantly, Rogers points out that the professor clearly discovered that *"A disparity between the academic and rigor need not exist."* (p. 30)

In fact, what *Freedom to Learn* emphasizes is the *teacher's agency* in *creating* vibrant and engaging environments for his/her students. This fits hand-in-glove with Sizer's emphasis on the role of teachers in school reform.

Rogers's professor mentions the mug-jug analogy I referenced earlier, but Freire's *banking* analogy was one that became embedded in my practice as the years as a *Coalition* practitioner proceeded. Freire's focus on liberation of the learner from the systemic oppression the existing structures impose *requires* that teachers *stop* seeing students as receptacles that need deposits, only to be *emptied* at a year-end withdrawal. He also emphasizes the importance of essential *reflection* (p.53), echoing another of Sizer's crucial points. In all, Sizer, Freire, and Rogers became the *formative* texts that guided my years not only at Bronxville from 1987 to 1993 but throughout the remainder of my teaching career.

If you can't stand the heat, don't enter the Inferno's First Circle

The first Tuesday after Labor Day in 1987 I arrived at Bronxville High School to meet the full faculty, expecting to find a staff that was raring to go regarding school reform. Having given my extremely laudatory interview about Judy Codding and Ted Sizer to the local newspaper, many of the staff had a good idea where I was coming from. What I learned, rather quickly, was that Judy's support was from her Assistant Principal, Sherry King, and what could only be described as a small *band* of school reform advocates. The majority of the faculty had an "If it ain't broke, don't fix it" attitude and a solid group of (distinctly male) faculty clearly *loathed* Judy and Sherry. It was neither easy nor pleasant that first year.

I arrived at Bronxville High School as a smoker, having acquired the habit as a bartender starting in 1984 (*never* having smoked before that, not even a *puff*). By Labor Day, 1987, I was smoking two packs of unfiltered Camels a day. (This was in keeping with my lifelong adage: *Everything In Excess, Nothing in Moderation*). In 1987 teachers could still smoke in the Faculty Room/cafeteria at BHS. In fact, there were *two* Faculty Lounges, one for smokers, one for non-smokers. Even though I already knew quite a few of the men who were coaches at BHS (some of whom were smokers) I quickly discovered how rigid the lines were drawn between "Judy's" teachers and the rest of the staff. None of the band of reform advocates were smokers, therefore my time in the Smoker's Faculty Lounge was spent sitting *totally alone* for that first year at the school!

The guys I knew from coaching would hardly talk to me and there was a distinct "us/them" division on the staff.

While Judy and Sherry were implementing changes in school structure and introducing the *9 Common Principles* (see *Endnotes*) of the Coalition of Essential Schools, a significant number of the faculty were digging their heels in against the move. As they saw it, Bronxville was an *Excellent* school, with students accepted at all the elite colleges and the rest of the graduates getting in *somewhere* (many, for some reason, in *something*-Wesleyan colleges). *Why* was there any need to change the place? In my zeal to convert the non-believers I was an abrasive zealot and only furthered the divide. It took time for me to soften my approach and attempt to win people over through thoughtful conversation.

An incident that best typifies just how divided the faculty was at this time involved a workshop we did with Grant Wiggins, the first Director of Research for the *Coalition* and a beacon of thoughtfulness (his *Understanding by Design* text, with Jay McTighe, is a cornerstone of modern progressive education). Grant was a master at facilitating workshops, particularly regarding authentic, performance-based assessment. He visited Bronxville at Judy's request to lead a workshop on the concept of "Less is More" and "Student-as-worker, Teacher-as-Coach." After what seemed like hours of intense opposition (and haranguing) from the Faculty, Grant totally *blew up*, and stormed out, swearing never to work at Bronxville again! It was a disturbing moment.

That's where we were in 1987-1989, my first two years at Bronxville (and Judy's last two, as it turned out. She left after the 1988-89 year to become Principal at Pasadena High School in California). In Dante's *Inferno* two of the circles of hell are *Anger* and *Heresy* and that would be my characterization of this period at BHS. I certainly was an *angry* man who wanted school reform now! Many of my faculty colleagues seemed to believe that changing Bronxville was *heresy* and should be fought to the death. It was not a fun time, except for a brief escape on Columbus Day weekend, 1987.

Dr. Gonzo goes to Caracas

Before everything hit the fan, I did have a moment that harkened back to *Dr. Gonzo and Mr. Bil*, an adventure without the substance abuse (I was regularly attending AA meetings in NYC by now) but was certainly worthy of *Fear and Loathing*. In August 1987, as I was writing my one-act play for the NEH and reading Sizer & Freire & Rogers, I got a phone call from my childhood friend, Bill Harrison. "Johnson, do you have a Passport?" Me: "No." Harrison: "Get one." Me: "Why?" Harrison: "A guy just backed out of a fishing trip I've got planned for Columbus Day weekend, so you are going to take his place. You only have to pay for plane fare." Me: "Where are we going?" Harrison: "Caracas, Venezuela. Flying out Friday night of Columbus Day weekend." Me: "Okay."

As I discovered, the planned weekend was to run from Friday night until Tuesday morning, meaning I would not be able to attend school right after the three-day Columbus Day weekend. I asked Judy and Sherry if that was okay and they said, "No." I also asked if I could leave school early that Friday because my plane out of JFK was leaving at 6:00 p.m. for Caracas and I was going to have to "take the train to the plane," a New York City trek that involved a bus transfer from the subway to the airport. If you ever lived in New York City you know there are several implacable laws. *You can never be too rich; you can never be too thin; you can never leave enough time to get to JFK.* Judy and Sherry also said *"No"* to the *leave early* request.

I left school at 3:00 pm on Friday of Columbus Day weekend, raced home in my leased Plymouth Sundance, grabbed my bag, and jumped on the subway, which dragged its way out to Queens. I then transferred to the JFK bus, frantically looking at my watch as the time sped closer and closer to 6:00 pm. I finally reached Eero Saarinen's gorgeous TWA terminal at about 5:30 pm, ran to the check-in (thank god we hadn't been terrorized yet) where I was told that *everyone* was on board and they were preparing to shut the cabin door. Doing my best O.J. Simpson impression (older folks will remember those Hertz commercials where Simpson dashed through airports, before he became a double-murderer) I sped down the jetway, where Harrison, always the lawyer, was convincing the flight attendant not to close and lock the cabin door yet. I made it.

We got to the *Hotel Macuto-Sheraton* in Caracas around midnight. Lugging two huge plastic tubes (Harrison's deep-sea fishing poles), we reached the front desk and were informed that, in fact, *there were no reservations* for Mr. Harrison. We also discovered, in that moment, that *Columbus Day Weekend* was *the* biggest holiday in Venezuela (and *all* of South America); there were *no* rooms available *anywhere.*

There we were, two bedraggled gringos, holding their huge plastic tubes and not speaking *one word* of Spanish. As luck would have it, the ever-resourceful Harrison called the folks he chartered the fishing trip with and they *just happened to have* recently built several motel-like rooms right on the dock we would be leaving from on Sunday morning. We could catch a cab and stay at their place for the weekend. Right time, right place. And, starting Sunday morning, I would learn how deep-sea fishing works.

Saturday morning broke and our hosts had a lovely breakfast of fresh fruit and juice waiting for us by their pool. It was a glorious day and, after some discussion with the charter captain, Harrison arranged for us to get a local tour, back into the rainforest. By 10 a.m. we were in a jeep, guided by (no kidding) Juan and Juan. Their English was only a little better than our Spanish and we set off for our day's adventure. After visiting a coastal beach, we headed inland, toward the mountains and rainforest. We saw some lovely waterfalls and small rivers and then Juan and Juan decided to drive deeper into the forest. As we drove under an ever-darkening canopy of trees we began crossing a series of small streams, each a bit wider, and deeper, than the last. Bill and I recommended we turn around ("now") but Juan and Juan had a destination in mind. We proceeded to ford a stream/river that lapped over the hood of the vehicle. Not good. We made it to the other side *but,* at that point, the Jeep dropped dead.

I'm now imagining a Monday or Tuesday *New York Times* story (around page A7 or A8) with the headline "*Two New Yorkers Lost in Venezuelan Rainforest Outside Caracas.*" As we contemplated our fate, I told Harrison, "Maybe it's the points. They could be wet. I'll take a look." I asked Juan and Juan if they had a tool kit. They indicated they did not. Using only my Swiss Army Knife (the Phillips-Head screwdriver), I took off the distributor cap and used my bandana to dry off the points and the inside of the cap. I screwed it back in place and told Juan to turn it over, still picturing that *NY Times* headline. *But the Jeep fired up.* Amazing Grace.

We found a safer return crossing, discovered a local village, ate a fabulous lunch of fresh fish, and returned to our dockside abode late in the afternoon, happy to be home safe. We had dinner at a local restaurant and retired to our room where we were able to watch a black and white television broadcast of the Major League Baseball Playoffs (Detroit was playing Minnesota & St. Louis faced off against the Giants). It didn't matter that the narration was in Spanish, baseball is baseball and just a year earlier we had attended the World Series in New York *and* Boston. We were happy campers.

Sunday morning, we set sail on the Caribbean Sea in search of marlin. With a very competent crew, it was fun, if a little scary, to sail beyond the sight of land. Flying fish and dolphin entertained us until we reached a spot the Captain thought would provide a chance to catch marlin.

I had never been this far out in any Ocean, much less deep-sea fishing, but I *had* seen footage of people catching swordfish and marlins, with fish leaping high out of the water and fisherman reeling them in. What I *didn't* know was that, as the fisherman was reeling the airborne fish in, *the boat* was moving (in reverse) toward the fish, shortening the distance between the predator and prey, and *decreasing* the time one is engaged in an aerial, aquatic ballet. I learned about that on Sunday, when the pole I was sitting next to started swaying, the reel singing and its line bolting out into the Caribbean! Before I realized what was going on, a crew member had me standing and was sliding a leather vest over my shoulders, so I could put the butt of the fishing pole in its waistline holster, *waiting* for the fish to leap. Harrison was instructing me as all this went on and, before I knew it, we had a 125-pound White Marlin on the deck, where I was kneeling next to it, getting my picture snapped. It was an exciting moment, and, while a 125-pound fish is *substantial,* the crew was nonchalant about it (they'd seen plenty of 125-pound White Marlins before, apparently). It was the only fish we caught that day.

After another evening of watching baseball on our snowy screen, we left the dock around 9 a.m. on Columbus Day morning and chugged back out into the Caribbean. More flying fish, more dolphins, and, around 10 a.m., as I was writing in my journal, "Looks like we might have a beautiful slow day sailing . . . . " my reel began singing again! Unlike Sunday, I knew what to do this time and quickly stood up, put my arms out, and the vest slid on. As I began to grab my rod and place it in the waistband holster, a crew member on the bridge began shouting and pointing: "*Grande Azul! Grande Azul!*" Unlike Sunday, I had apparently landed a *Blue* Marlin this time and a big ("Grande") one. And that is where this story takes an interesting turn.

The first time the Grande Azul leapt, I began reeling in (as I had been instructed) and heard the engines below me fire up, accelerating in reverse toward the big fish. Then, BLAM! a minor explosion. The boat came to a sputtering halt. The fish was back in the water, I was holding the taut line and, within a few minutes I was told that one of the engines had blown a gasket. The boat *would not be able* to move in reverse while it was being repaired. As a result, it was *me against the fish* until we were up and running again. I asked Harrison how long that might be. "Twenty minutes," he said. Okay....I'll hang on and reel in when he leaps.

There was a 250-pound Blue Marlin on the other end of my line. He was, quite literally, fighting for his life. In October of 1987 I probably weighed 175 pounds soaking wet and, while wiry, needed all the help I could get if I was going to reel this guy in. I hung on, variously standing and sitting in the bolted deck chair, with my thumb on the line. I kept asking, "How much longer?" and kept being told "Twenty minutes." By the end of the first hour the fish was still *at least* one hundred yards from the boat and the engine wasn't fixed. He was still fighting. My thumb could now feel his vibration as he accelerated underwater and I was beginning to be able to anticipate his leap, preparing to reel in. The battle lasted well over two hours. By the time the engine was finally working the Big Blue was right next to the boat, exhausted. He had swallowed the hook. If he hadn't (he was going to die of internal bleeding) I would have let him go. A crew member conked him on the skull with a mallet (it sounded like one of David Letterman's rooftop watermelon drops) and he was dead when they lifted him onto the deck.

There was a strange mix of emotions in that moment: exhilaration from winning the battle and intense sadness, as if I had lost a friend. I've always described the fishing line connection as *umbilical* and, even as I posed for a classic Hemingway dockside pose with the fish, I felt badly. The crew was more than happy to butcher the marlin and have him for dinner but I couldn't eat. It would have felt cannibalistic.

When I returned to New York (having missed school on Tuesday) I pulled *The Old Man and the Sea* off my bookshelf and tore through it. I also got a copy of the Gregory Peck version of *Moby Dick* and watched it. The Caracas trip was a signal moment, a memorable one, and I immediately connected it to *literature*, to texts, upon returning to the *Real World*, where my school reform crusading would continue.

Chapter 11

The Second Circle
(Limbo)

1.One Door Closes

The 1987-88 school year at Bronxville High School was
characterized by chaotic energy. Typical of any school reform
effort, there were fits and starts. "Judy's" teachers were aligned
in interdisciplinary teams (English/Social Studies/Art) and
scheduled with back-to-back classes, allowing for "blocks" of
teaching time. We also had planning periods scheduled at
the same time, to better organize our interdisciplinary units.
This was all well and good, but it essentially meant we were
operating as a *school-within-a-school*, hoping that our *model*
of collegiality and curriculum/assessment development would
encourage others to jump on the Coalition bandwagon. Few
did. I became interested in the fledgling Student-Faculty
Legislature (the student government) and pitched Judy and
Sherry an idea about developing Advisories tied to the SFL.
They liked the concept and told me to come back with a

fleshed-out plan. Before that plan was finalized, we were all hit with shocking news: Judy was leaving Bronxville to take a job at Pasadena High School in California. Needless to say, there was a mixed reaction to this from the staff. The Coalition advocates were concerned, and Judy's opponents were ecstatic. The reform group hoped that Sherry King would be promoted to Principal, but she was too closely associated with Judy's *sturm und drang.* The Board of Ed looked for a candidate who was not in-house. The 1987-1988 school year concluded with an "up in the air" feeling as well as a sense of "when's that other shoe going to drop."

I distracted myself from all of that by getting Bronxville to pay for a summer course in creative writing at NYU, focusing on playwriting. I was, by far, the oldest student in my class. It was energizing and insightful to work with people who were *older* than my students but younger than I. It offered perspective on *who* my students might become in a few years. The critiquing of my writing was excellent: focused, constructive, apropos. I spent the summer reading plays and books about playwriting, only focusing on teaching/learning as August dwindled, not knowing what the coming academic year might bring.

2. Another Door Opens

The School Board, in its infinite wisdom, consciously picked a Principal they clearly believed *would not* make waves. To my mind the new (male) Principal was *Casper Milquetoast* incarnate and I worried about our staggering school reform efforts. Sherry, trouper that she was, remained as Assistant Principal (hoping, I'm sure, to protect and advance our Coalition goals) but it was clear that she'd be gone by the end of the 1988-1989 year. We started the Academic Year in *transition*.

My proposal to develop an Advisory system was moving through the bureaucracy and looked as if it would see the light of day by Fall. My idea was that Advisories, facilitated by classroom teachers, would replace Homerooms (which only served an attendance-taking purpose) and not only meet with their teachers *every* morning *and* afternoon (for 5 to 10 minutes) but also have one or two *full periods* per week, where they would be used as: a) *plenary groups* for the Student-Faculty Legislature (each Advisory would send a Representative to the weekly SFL meetings) and b) be a place where students discuss *Common Principle* issues like "tone of decency," "student-as-worker/teacher-as-coach," "less-is-more," and "exhibitions of mastery." The idea was to make the students *integral* to the school's operation *and* philosophical tenets. The faculty generally supported the concept, with *one* condition: they wanted to be *given a curriculum* to implement. No one wanted to teach an additional class, requiring lesson plans and so on. I was more than happy to oblige and, with the staff behind it and the administration re-designing our schedules, it was a *Go* for 1989-1990.

Our 9th and 10th grade Interdisciplinary teams were intact throughout 1988-89 and we were starting to develop some very effective "student-as-worker" projects, as well as pretty cool (we thought) performance assessments. Sherry King was instrumental in all of that work. I can't give her enough credit for accelerating my personal growth not only as a classroom practitioner but also as a *thinker*, regarding reform issues. Even though Judy's departure had staggered us, we seemed to be up off the canvas for the next round. We were even regaining a little spring in our step.

3. Out in the Hallway (between those doors!)

The 1989-1990 school year proved pivotal in my development as a school reformer. My Advisory Program was initiated in close coordination with the Student-Faculty Legislature and looked as if it might actually work. I had gone to some professional development workshops facilitated by Grant Wiggins and was learning how to implement project-based learning and per-formance-based assessment more effectively. Despite having only tacit Administrative support (Judy *and* Sherry were now both gone) the bright side of that coin was that I was allowed to do and try whatever I wanted. There was still a solid core of teachers (from our original cohort, plus some new recruits) who were excited about working on progressive ideas.

In early November 1989 I drove to Newport, Rhode Island, for the second Coalition of Essential Schools *Fall Forum* — a gathering of like-minded education professionals from around the country interested in implementing thoughtful, systemic school reform. Once again, I got to work with Grant Wiggins on curriculum and assessment. The real highlight of that *Fall Forum*, for me, was meeting Ted and Nancy Sizer. I had gotten on an elevator with Judy Codding at the Viking Hotel (we were catching up on her year in Pasadena) when Ted and Nancy stepped on. Judy introduced me and Ted indicated that my "reputation preceded" me. I assumed that was a good thing and I had a chance, later in the weekend, to talk with Ted and Nancy (you can't mention one *without* the other) about what was going on in Bronxville. I got some thoughtful advice about how I might proceed to be a more effective change agent. Ted also told me to keep my eyes open for professional opportunities that may be emerging in the Coalition in the coming months.

4. Right Place, Right Time & Opportunity Knocks!

An important element in my professional growth during this period was the *Coalition's* newsletter *Horace* (link: http://essentialschools.org/volume/vol23-issue3/). It published about every two months and was generally a 4-to-8 page broadside that focused on *one* aspect of *Essential School* philosophy (*Essential Questions, Assessment, Scheduling, etc.*). In the early years of the Coalition, Grant Wiggins was the Editor-in-Chief but, after his departure (his need for a *Solo* career reminded me of the classic rock'n'roll band breakups of the late Sixties), that task fell into the more than capable hands of Kathleen Cushman, a longtime Sizer comrade and a brilliant writer (who would later play a crucial role in my school reform career). At this point, I was *consuming* everything I could read about alternative/authentic assessment, block scheduling, project-based learning and so on. What *Horace* did, that proved invaluable, was provide examples of *practitioners* from around the country who were actively working at implementing *Coalition Principles* in their schools.

As Spring 1990 unfolded, we received word of an exciting opportunity. *Citibank*, the giant financial services company, was giving Ted Sizer $3 million dollars for the *Coalition of Essential Schools* (part of a larger $20 million, 10-year grant to improve schools around the nation). As the *New York Times* reported (May 16, 1990):

> *One such effort, to which Citibank will devote $3 million over three years, is based on the ideas of Theodore Sizer, chairman of the department of education at Brown University. The Sizer philosophy envisions students not as vessels into which teachers pour*

information but as active participants in deciding what and how they are to learn. It recasts teachers from authority figures to coaches. . . . The coalition's budget is about $3 million this year, coming mostly from private sources, Dr. Sizer said. The Citibank grant, which will increase that sum by $1 million a year over the next three years, is to be used for training large groups of teachers at a summer school at Brown.

This was the opportunity Ted had told me to look for at the *Fall Forum*! Before the *NY Times* article even appeared, *Coalition Schools* across the country (there were between 50 to 100 at this point) had received a *"Request for Applications"* in late April, announcing the plan to develop a cohort of 15 *Citibank Teachers* starting in the summer of 1990, increasing the numbers over the following two years.

No one else at Bronxville seemed interested in applying (it required a 6-week summer commitment and most of my colleagues had families). I leapt at the opportunity and gleefully received my *acceptance* into the program by early June 1990. It was still unclear as to what, exactly, this *Citibank Teacher* Program would entail, but I was definitely *ready* for whatever it was — and it meant a summer (with pay!) in Providence, Rhode Island — a city I had only been to once, as a freshman football player at Yale (Our first game of the season and I had *three* interceptions. This was a place where I had a fond memory). I started packing my bags right away, eager to become a willing pioneer in a new school reform effort.

Chapter 12

Purgatorio Leads to Paradiso

Throughout my first tenure as an NYC resident, I lived on the Upper West Side, the neighborhood I had fallen in love with during the summer of 1986. It was, for me, a *perfect* match, with easy access to the rest of the city by way of the 1,2,3 trains. Rife with *diners,* as well as music and theater venues (The Beacon, The Promenade, Symphony Space), great markets (the first *Fairway, Citarella's Seafood*) — who could want more? In the middle of all of it, for me, was *Big Nick's Burger Joint* on the west side of Broadway between 76th and 77th streets. *Big Nick's* became my touchstone, home-away-from-home and, during my second tenure on the UWS (2009-2014) I actually wrote an essay for a workshop (facilitated by *New Yorker* writer Ian "Sandy" Frazier) about it. Here's an excerpt:

> *When talking to a New Yorker (NOTE: when I use the term "New York" or "New Yorker" I'm talking about Manhattan. Brooklyn, Queens, and Bronx residents refer to themselves based on their boroughs...and*

Staten Island, well, is really part of New Jersey, despite the longest suspension bridge in the world) so, when talking to a New Yorker, two of the easiest and most common topics of conversation are living space and food. For example, "He got a two-bedroom with 900 square feet for only $2500 a month!!" and "Waddaya wanna eat tonight? Italian? Chinese? Thai? Japanese?" And this is why, to me, Big Nick's epitomizes the New York I know.

Standing on Broadway facing Big Nick's storefront, the green awning clearly announces "Big Nick's Burger Joint" while sporting a gay pride flag on top ("Some of the staff are gay...I support them"). The front of the place foreshadows what is to come. The glass door alone has six different signs on it, announcing "Booths and Tables in the Rear" as well as "No Transfats" (great, if unlikely, consolation for a Burger Joint?). A red neon sign in the window announces, "Charcoal Prime Steaks and Ribs" and a placard informs you "Breakfast Special 6 am - 12 noon/ Breakfast 24 hours a day/Daily Specials - Pick Up Our Menu". There are no fewer than 11 more signs festooning the 15-foot wide brick face and window.

The menus sport a caricature of Mr. Nick himself (drawn by his wife ... "she's very talented"), flexing a dumbbell comprised of two large burgers, resulting in an impressive bicep bulge. The cartoon does not particularly resemble Mr. Nick – not even the Mr. Nick I first met in the late 80›s, when his hair was still dark and his height and weight made the appellation «Big» Nick understandable. In those days, as now, he was always a presence overseeing the day-to-day operations of «the Joint.» Mr. Nick started the Burger Joint in 1962, with some friends, when the Upper West Side was still "West Side Story" territory and the neighborhood was dominated by Guiseppe Verdi ("Needle") Park. But the Promenade Theatre was across the street and the actors and theatre goers loved the burgers at "The Big Nick's." As more "Burger Joints" sprung up around town, Mr. Nick created the quarter pound "Big Nick" burger and the name for the "Joint" changed. When McDonald's created their Quarter Pounder, the "Big Nick" went up to a half pound .....and an Upper West Side legend was born.

Sadly, *Big Nick's* has gone the way of Upper West Side gentrification, priced out of the neighborhood. It was the place I *always* took my NYC visitor/tourist/out-of-town friends to, so they would get the real feel of The City. *Big Nick's* represented *everything* I loved about living in New York City. It was *bustling* at all hours, it had numerous characters from Central Casting sitting at the counter, its walls were adorned with autographed photos of the (very) young David Letterman and Mike Tyson, as well as other "stars" from the neighborhood: actors and athletes who were in plays and commercials, singers and record producers. You name it, the Upper West Side had it. The energy of living in New York City in those years was exhilarating and primed me for my first summer in Providence in 1990.

The First Terrace

Where the *Inferno* is a series of Circles where sinners reside, the *Purgatorio* is composed of Terraces, which Dante and Virgil ascend (each Terrace represents one of the *Seven Deadly Sins*). What distinguishes the residents of the *Purgatorio* from those in the *Inferno* is that those in the Circles are *damned*, while those on the *Terraces* have hope for redemption. While they may be guilty of *pride, envy, wrath,* or *sloth,* for instance, they *can be saved!* That analogy certainly worked for how I saw *School Reform* in 1990. There were the Non-Believers (who actively worked *against* reform efforts) whom I believed were *damned*. But there was also a vast mass of teachers and administrators who exhibited an aspect of those *Deadly Sins* (particularly *pride* or *sloth*) but might well be capable of coming around and achieving School Reform *redemption*. Whatever the case, I headed to Providence, Rhode Island *eager* to meet the *Virgils* who would guide me, providing instruction on how to save those souls wandering in the *Purgatorio*; those who, with the proper intervention, might see the light of the *Paradiso*. (We *won't* discuss how the Sin of Pride may well have infected *me* at this time).

Providence

If you have visited Providence in the 21st century you undoubtedly have a positive view of the place. It is, indeed, a picturesque city with great hotels, prestigious institutions of Higher Education (Brown University, Rhode Island School of Design, Johnson & Wales) *fabulous* restaurants, the *Trinity Repertory Company*, a newly renovated *Performing Arts Center,* a great local sports scene (top-notch college basketball & hockey squads, as well as *Boston's* top Minor League franchises in both hockey and baseball), and, in summer, access to fabulous *beaches* (Rhode Island is, after all, *The Ocean State*). That was *not* the case in 1990. When we arrived in late June of 1990, I was shocked that I was in a State Capitol. As I told Paula Evans, the Director of the Citibank Teacher Program, "There's no downtown *downtown!*" There were few decent places to eat, *nothing scenic* to look at, and only *two* hotels in the whole city! Luckily, our cohort of teachers spent almost all our time on College Hill, where Brown University is located.

The First Cohort

Under the outstanding leadership of Paula Evans, ably assisted by the equally fabulous Gene Thompson and Faith Dunne, the first cohort of 15 Citibank Teachers was in great hands. It was an outstanding group, assembled from all over the country. All the loose ends were held together by the incomparable Program Administrator, Kitty Pucci. There were teachers from Arkansas(2), Tennessee, Maryland, Pennsylvania, California, Iowa, Texas (2), Rhode Island, Massachusetts, Missouri, and New York (3). Paula and Gene quickly created a team from this disparate group of like-minded teachers. We were all living in a student dormitory north of the Main Campus, a building whose architecture can best be described as neo-penal, but even that helped create an energetic rapport among the troops.

Our days were packed with activity. There were two segments to the daily routine. In the mornings we were teaching at Brown Summer High School (BSHS), a laboratory school created *every* summer on the Brown campus to give aspiring teachers in the Brown University Education Department's *Teacher Preparation Program* an initial real-world teaching experience. 400 students from the Providence City school system enrolled in BSHS, which met from 8:00 a.m. until 12 noon each day in July, with two Class blocks (8:00 to

9:50 a.m. & 10:10 until noon). It was not a credit-bearing Summer School (although some students, who needed credits in certain subjects could negotiate with their school's Guidance Counselors and receive credit from BSHS. They were the rare exception, not the rule). The student teachers worked in teams of 2,3, or 4 and the courses were built around *Essential Questions,* rather than *content to be covered.* As experienced teachers, Citibank Fellows taught one class solo, designing the curriculum around the same *Essential Question* the student-teachers in our discipline were using. We each taught in one of the blocks and observed our colleagues, or the student-teachers, in the other block. In all, a wonderful, eye-opening experience.

In the afternoon we met as a large group first, to work through the 9 Common Principles and clarify our understanding about them. We then broke into smaller working groups, wrestling with how we would consult with teacher practitioners. The goal for the Citibank cohort was to create a cadre of Classroom Teachers who were not only working on implementing Coalition Principles and reform in their own classrooms and schools, but could also visit Coalition schools, serving as consultants/coaches for teachers. This perfectly fit into the basic philosophy of the Coalition where *teachers* were the fulcrum to lever change in schools.

Our group was exceptional, intelligent, thoughtful, and professional on every level. The summer was a formative experience and, by early August, we were ready to leave Providence and not only return to our schools, *re-charged* and ready to go, but also prepared to work with other practitioners. Returning to school in September, I believe I felt like Dante facing the terrace of the *Purgatorio.*

As noted by Jonathan Jones in *The Guardian:*

> *It is a spiritual journey towards light through darkness, marked by meetings with the damned, who confess their sins and remember their lives with pain, pride, regret and longing.*

Remembering how Herndon and Sizer both likened the Public School to a *secular church,* the parallel to *The Divine Comedy* seemed a perfect comparison.

Chapter 13

Purgatorio: Part Two

Returning to New York in August I was looking forward to the 1990-1991 school year. As a newly-minted *Citibank Teacher*, I was primed to start consulting with *Coalition* and Coalition-curious schools in the New York Metropolitan area. Regarding Bronxville itself, I would continue working on the 9th grade Interdisciplinary team (implementing our Western Civilization/ Humanities curriculum) and would now add two 11th grade American Studies classes, team-teaching with Anthony Angotta, an English teacher I *loved* working with. Added to that, my new Advisory system was starting (I was the Coordinator) in close conjunction with the Student-Faculty Legislature (which I was now Faculty Advisor of). The *Fall Forum* was going to be held in St. Louis in November and I was presenting a workshop. The drama teacher was on maternity leave: would I like to direct the Fall Play? (Sure!) I was also coaching the boys Varsity Basketball team *and* the boys Junior Varsity tennis squad.

Early in the school year our Superintendent announced that he would be retiring in June, allowing a substantial amount of time for the School Board to find his successor. My first consulting job in Westchester County was at John Jay High School, in Katonah-Cross River-Lewisboro, where John Chambers was the Principal. John was a deep-thinker and an excellent administrator. The more I worked there, the more I envisioned John serving as Bronxville's next Superintendent, an appointment that could bring back serious support of *Coalition* reforms. When the *Fall Forum* rolled around in St. Louis in early November, I spent quite a few hours buttonholing and badgering John to apply for the Superintendency of Bronxville. He was reluctant, particularly because he did not hold a Doctorate (he had a Harvard Master's Degree) but I insisted he was perfect for the job: "You're a soft-spoken, highly intelligent W.A.S.P. What could be more perfect for Bronxville?" Plus, I said, "What have you got to lose? Send in an application and, I'm betting if you get an interview, you'll get the job." John was not as confident as I, but he did apply and, yes, *he got the job.*

Knowing John would be taking the School District helm starting in July 1991 was energizing. The resignation of our Milquetoast principal that Spring allowed John to hire his former Assistant Principal to take over as our High School Principal, so I was more than optimistic about the coming year.

Two highlights of the 1990-1991 school year involved some "authentic" work with students: directing the Fall Play and advising the Harvard Model Congress contingent in Boston/Cambridge. In both cases, the students (in keeping with my growing commitment to *performance assessment*) were out in public, "showing what they know" in a setting where they were presenting their work to an audience of adults and peers. I was incredibly proud of what the students did.

When I lived in Boston, I had gone to the American Repertory Theater (ART) in Cambridge to see the first dramatic production of Don DeLillo's *The Day Room*. I was a huge DeLillo fan, having read all his novels, and was eager to see how his writing transferred to the stage. As noted in Wikipedia:

> *The play concerns characters in a psychiatric hospital in which the distinctions between patients and staff gradually blur. The play is written in an absurdist style reminiscent of Beckett and Ionesco, and eschews linear plot in favor of a non-traditional exploration of such themes as empathy, personal identity, fear of death, and the seeming impossibility of meaningful communication. In line with the transformation of identities, the eponymous room of the first act becomes a vaguely defined motel room in the second. As a single memorable example of the absurdist tone of the piece, one of the asylum patients of the first act appears in the second act as Figure in Straitjacket, performing as a television set for the bulk of the remaining action.*

I was blown away by the A.R.T. production and, when asked to direct the Bronxville High School Fall Play, I decided *we* would produce it! As luck would have it, shortly after I announced what play we were doing, my Assistant Director (a junior who did not want to act but *did* want to be part of the show) informed me that her mother was a local Real Estate Agent and had just sold a house to Don DeLillo in Bronxville. Really?!? I told Katie to mention to her mother, *if she happened to talk to Mr. DeLillo* any time in the near future, that we'd appreciate it if he knew we were producing his play and I would *love to* talk to him about it. We then got back to work on the production.

A week or two later I was in my New York City apartment when the phone rang. Me: "Hello." Voice: "Bil Johnson?" Me: "Yes." Voice: "This is Don DeLillo." Me: (stammering, like Ralph Kramden) "Hum-n-ah, Hum-n-ah . . . Oh, hi, Don...." (gasping) DeLillo: "I hear you're producing *The Day Room* over at the high school." Me: "Yes, yes we are." DeLillo: "Would you like to meet and talk about it?" Me: (shocked!) "Sure! Yes!" DeLillo: "You know *Pete's* in the middle of the village?" Me: "Yes." DeLillo: "How about lunch there on Thursday at one?" Me: "Yeah, great." DeLillo: "Okay. I'll see you then." Me: "Yes, yes, of course, Thanks." DeLillo: "Okay. Bye." Me: (flabbergasted) "Bye." I hung up the phone and, once again, couldn't believe my luck. Talk about *right time, right place*!

I got class coverage in case the *lunch with Don* ran long . The meeting lasted almost *two hours*! During that time, we discussed the A.R.T. and Manhattan Theater Club productions of his play. Don was curious as to how I was thinking about staging certain scenes and offered his own perspective on what he liked and disliked about the professional productions. As we wrapped up, I pulled out my hardcover copy of the play (I belonged to the *Drama Book Club*) and sheepishly asked if he would sign it for me. Graciously, he agreed. I didn't read the inscription until I got back to school. Remembering the "*play is written in an absurdist style reminiscent of Beckett and Ionesco*" (and I would add Pirandello), DeLillo had written: "*To the man behind the man behind The Day Room. Don DeLillo.*"

The Day Room was a big hit at Bronxville. Despite being high school actors, the cast delivered a high-level performance, led by Joanna Lara, Jessica Rodwick, and Cathy Becket (who played the television set in the second act!). My old high school classmate (and rock'n'roll bandmate) Robert Dancik, an out-standing Art Teacher at nearby White Plains High School, created a brilliant lighting design. We were told that the noto-riously reclusive Don DeLillo had sneaked in during a perfor-mance. He let Katie's Mom know that he thoroughly enjoyed our show. Who could ask for more?

I'm not sure where I stumbled upon the notice for *Harvard Model Congress*, but I do know that I was fascinated by the prospect. Run by Harvard undergraduates:

> *Harvard Model Congress (HMC) is the largest congressional simulation conference in the world, pro-viding high school students from across the United States and abroad with an opportunity to experience American government firsthand. Although HMC is run entirely by Harvard undergraduates, it is a 501(c)(3) non-profit organization that is operated independently of the university.* (www.harvardmodelcongress.org)

Talk about an opportunity for authentic assessment! I shared the notice with my Department and got Administrative go-ahead, *if* I was willing to organize, supervise, and chaperone (as well as recruit other chaperones). It sounded like it could be a wonderful experience for our students, so I ran with it.

The basic design of *Harvard Model Congress* is that high school students (primarily Juniors because they are, overwhelmingly, the group taking a course in United States History) are given the identity of a member of the Senate or House of Representatives. They are informed as to what issues (usually one domestic or one foreign policy) will be on their three-day agenda, as well as what Committees they will serve on. It is a well-planned, authentic recreation of the United

States Congress. The students then have three days, in committees and full sessions, to craft bills to vote on. It is an incredible experience for the students, and they come away with a genuine understanding of the workings of the U.S. government. I had no problem recruiting a Bronxville delegation and, typical of our community, the PTA and General Fund provided enough money for us to *fly* to Boston and stay at the hotel where the conference was taking place. I recruited Mandy Gersten, a fabulous math teacher/Coalition advocate/musician, to chaperone the girls on the trip.

Harvard Model Congress was a great learning experience for our students. It was also fun to do some Boston-history sightseeing during the rare (and short) breaks we had. In all, it solidified my belief in *performance-based assessment* and got me thinking about writing a piece focused on that topic. As we wrapped up the 1990-1991 school year, I was looking forward to returning to Providence for the summer, where Paula Evans and Gene (now)Thompson-Grove had invited me to work as a Facilitator for workshops with the new Citibank Group, as well as some visiting schools who were exploring joining the Coalition. As I prepared to head off for the summer, I reviewed the year with satisfaction, while looking forward to coming back with a new Administration steering the District into the mid-1990's.

The 1992-93 year at Bronxville went well, as far as our reform efforts were concerned, but I was, once again, getting restless. Heidi Hayes Jacobs, Bronxville's consultant for Interdisciplinary teaching (her book was a Classic in the field), told me, "If you don't get your doctorate now, you never will." I had taken a course with her at Teachers College and Heidi thought the school was a "good fit" for me. I applied and got in, so I took a Leave of Absence from Bronxville for the 1993-1994 academic year to start working toward an Ed.D. at Columbia.

Consulting

The *Citibank* Program had opened up a whole new world for me. What made it both educational and *fun* was the people I got to work with from 1990 on. By the time I took my Leave of Absence from Bronxville in 1993, I had already been criss-crossing the country, doing consulting, and working with like-minded reformers from every corner of the U.S. One of the brightest of all my colleagues, Steve Cantrell, and I began taking jobs together, later adding the wonderfully thoughtful Joel Kammer to our team. The three of us worked extremely well together (we became "Trust the Process" Consultants) and they are still two of my best friends, as well as two of the most impressive educators I've ever worked with. Sometime early in 1993 Steve called and asked if I'd like to do a *weeklong* gig at the American School in London. All I could say was, "When do we leave?"

We caught a 7:00 p.m. flight out of Newark, arriving at Gatwick at around 7:00 a.m., London time. As we proceeded to Victoria Station and on to our B & B, we devised a strategy to beat jet-lag. We were going to stay up for 12 consecutive hours, going to bed sometime after 7:00 p.m. London time and, we reasoned, waking up bright and early, and fully re-freshed the next day (a Sunday morning). Of course, that didn't work at all but we did manage to not suffer too much from jet-lag and Monday morning we were ready to work with the American School of London faculty.

As fate would have it, the interim Headmaster at the London School was my former Superintendent in Bronxville, Bill Greenham. Small world, indeed. I had a good relationship with Bill at Bronxville and he graciously introduced us in glowing terms to the American School staff. It was a great week of work but the real bonus was we were done by 5:00 p.m. each day, free to explore London, particularly its theater district. Because we both had Student I.D. cards (Steve was working on a doctorate at USC and I was enrolled at Columbia Teachers College) we were able to get great seats for dirt cheap prices. As a result, we saw Mamet's *Oleanna,*, Turgenev's *A Month in the Country* (with a luminous Helen Mirren), and Stoppard's *Travesties* on successive evenings with fabulous seats!. We also found time to go the National Portrait Gallery, Winchester Cathedral, Buckingham Palace, and Trafalgar Square. It was an ideal working vacation.

As the years went on, Steve and Joel and I worked together in places like Seattle, Cleveland, Boyne City, Michigan, Los Angeles, and the Bay Area, always having fun but always *focused* on message: school reform and school change is very hard work. You need *to trust the process.*

I'm still in touch with Steve and Joel. We've all moved on, after our years as National Faculty and school reformers, but the flame has not been extinguished. We all still believe schools can work better for more students. I know both Steve and Joel had a huge effect on their students *and* colleagues over the years. The work we did, ideally, was that rock in the pool that is still sending ripples toward shore. At least, that's our hope.

Chapter 14

Halftime!

Life without Teaching

By September 1993 I had spent *20 years* teaching in three public high schools. I had given two graduation speeches, had one yearbook dedicated to me, won the "Golden Apple," and had been named "Coach of the Year." Within the last year I published my first article and was becoming a "name" on the education consulting circuit, getting calls and offers to travel around the country, facilitating workshops and presenting at conferences. My commitment to school change and reform was absolute. I had started a doctoral program at Columbia Teachers College and, several days a week, I was up on 120th Street taking classes and getting advice from my advisor, the incomparable Linda Darling-Hammond. Having gotten involved in Columbia's *Four Seasons Project*, a related reform effort, I was also spending time working with Ann Lieberman. Both Linda and Ann were icons in the school reform movement, having published and spoken extensively. I was incredibly lucky to work with them.

Something I discovered while attending TC was that not all students there are created equal. If you were a Doctoral candidate, all doors opened for you, all professors were accessible, and you were treated like royalty. Taking a few classes with Masters' degree candidates (not necessarily people in Teacher Preparation) I could see how Teachers College used its Ivy League brand to make M.A. programs a huge cash cow, which allowed the Doctoral students to live a privileged existence on campus. Teachers College was, after all, trying to compete with Harvard's and Stanford's Graduate Schools of Education and *only* those students who would become *publishing professors* were going to improve the name recognition and prestige of Columbia. Whatever the case, I was impressed with my Ed.D. cohort and more than happy to take advantage of being granted not only time with Linda and Ann, but also with Maxine Green, a giant in the field of Education. It was a new whirlwind for me, living the academic and consulting life, and I enjoyed every minute of it.

Life took a new turn at the *Coalition's Fall Forum* in Louisville that November. Early on, I ran into Kathleen Cushman, the editor and primary writer of *Horace*. I had contributed some material to the publication over the past couple of years (about *advisories* and *portfolios*) and was curious as to whether there were any new topics on the *Horace* horizon I might be able to send in material for. What Kathleen was most interested in talking about, though, was the *Massachusetts Education Reform Act of 1993* that had recently passed (Kathleen and the Sizers lived in Harvard, Massachusetts, a small town 35 miles northwest of Boston). She said Ted was *very interested* in establishing one of the first 25 Charter Schools the act proposed for the fall of 1995. That would mean writing a proposal *right away*, as there was a March 1,

1994 deadline. Might I be interested in writing/designing a curriculum for a new school, a genuine *Horace's School*? "Be careful what you wish for " was the thought that ran through my head immediately.

How many times, over the years, had I mused: *"If I could only start my own school. . . ."*

It was a thrilling idea and, as I continued to talk to Ted and Nancy Sizer, and Kathleen, over that weekend I enthusiastically said, "Yes." I wanted in. From that point on, the genesis of *The Francis W. Parker Charter Essential School* took on a life of its own.

Parker – Phase One

Technically, the *Founders* of the Parker School were Kathleen Cushman, Laura Rogers, John Stadler, and I. Almost everyone, to this day, refers to Parker as "Ted's and Nancy's" school. Indeed, if we were the Founders they were not only the Godparents but also the Midwives. Regarding the *Founders*: Kathleen was a keen observer and writer about education (and a mother of 3); Laura Rogers was an educational psychologist as well as a parent (and Lawrence Kohlberg's niece); and John Stadler was a venture capitalist/Harvard resident (and parent) who, knowing Ted lived in the town, sought Dr. Sizer out to pitch the notion of a local charter school, shortly after Massachusetts passed the "Reform Act." As a team, we had all the elements to write the charter: John was facile with the economics, Laura with the student services and community outreach, me with curriculum and assessment, and Kathleen with the *Coalition Principles* and parent input, as well as the ultimate editor/writer of our document. The *Parent* factor was an important component, as the MA Reform law *explicitly stated* Charters must be parent/teacher collaboratives. I was the *Teacher* element.

Everything we wrote was run past Ted and Nancy for feedback, comments, etc. The Massachusetts DOE wanted to give *Charters* at least a year to plan and prepare (buildings had to be acquired, students/parents recruited). The first grants were scheduled to be announced in the late Spring of 1994. We believed our application, filled with innovative ideas about curriculum, instruction, community involvement, assessment, and school governance was a strong one, but who knew what they were looking for? We also believed having Ted Sizer's imprimatur *had to* give us a leg up. Ted, after all, had been the *wunderkind Dean* of the Harvard Graduate School of Education *at age 29*. His books and reputation as an educator (at Harvard, Phillips Andover, and Brown) were well known in Massachusetts. How could they not give us the charter?

Of course, they did.

Parker – Phase Two

"Be careful what you wish for." Indeed. We now had to *deliver* a viable working public school by September 1995. I was still living in New York City, periodically commuting to Harvard, MA, to work on the charter while also corresponding on-line(the *Coalition* had actually established an email network in the early '90s & by '93-'94 AOL was connecting people). Once we won the right to start our school, Ted asked if I'd like to be a "more active" member of the start-up. "Yes, of course," I told him, "but I live in New York City." With a sly smile, Dr. Sizer informed me that the Clinical Professor of Social Studies/History in Brown's Education Department (David Kobrin) was taking a *Sabbatical* for the 1994-1995 academic year and needed someone to "substitute" for him. Would I be interested in that? The answer was obvious. There would be a number of loose ends to attend to in New York (including my work at Columbia Teachers College) *but* how many times does one get a chance to actually *start a new school from scratch?* And one based on your own ideas *about what might make a school really good?*

This was really going to happen!

We were really going to start our own school!

Once again, *right time, right place!*

Chapter 15

Crazy-Busy!

1994-1995 was *the busiest* year of my life. So many things happened in such quick succession I don't think I noticed it at the time. Looking back, it can only be described as *crazy-busy*! Broadly, life was divided into *two* segments: Brown University and the Parker School. There were also *subsets* of those segments: Teachers College and writing a book. The number of balls-in-the-air is staggering in hindsight. At the time, it was all exciting and felt so "important" that I don't think I realized just *how much* was going on simultaneously.

Brown – Phase One

My tenure as the "Visiting Clinical Professor in Social Studies/History" began shortly after my interview with the Education Department Chair, Tom James, in late April 1994. With Ted Sizer's blessing and Tom's okay, I was appointed and, in short order, met my new colleagues, Eileen Landay (the English Clinical) and Larry Wakeford (the Science Clinical) as well as

Yvette Nachmias, the Program Administrator. We were *Clinical* professors because Ted, when Department Chair, had established a Medical School teaching model in the schools where Brown placed its student-teachers. Just as practicing doctors teach interns entering their profession, Eileen, Larry, and I, experienced classroom teachers, were charged with mediating the entry into our profession through observation and feedback, as well as teaching courses in Methods and Analysis to our charges. Eileen, Larry, and Yvette (one of those indispensable people who invisibly/magically holds an organization together) quickly initiated me into the Brown Teacher Preparation Program. Our students were undergraduates (U.T.E.P.s — Undergraduate Teacher Education Program) and M.A.T.s (Master of Arts in Teaching candidates). The program heavily emphasized *practice*, starting in June, with one-week of instruction followed by a 4-week practicum at Brown Summer High School, the 400-student laboratory summer program that Brown had been running for almost 20 years. A follow-up week of instruction, with de-briefing followed BSHS and, once September arrived, half our students would be taking courses in their "content" area and the other half were student-teaching in local schools. They would flip-flop assignments in the second semester. Like my students, I felt as though I had been tossed into the deep end of the pool!

Parker – Phase Three

While riding along on my Brown training wheels, the Parker School *Founders* were now meeting regularly in Harvard, MA, at times with Ted and Nancy, to put flesh on the bones of our original Charter School proposal. (The name for the school was the result of my work at Columbia, where I had learned about Colonel Francis W. Parker, a pioneering educator whose reputation was forged as the Superintendent of the Quincy, Massachusetts, schools in the late 1870s. John Dewey referred to Colonel Parker as the "father of Progressive Education" and I thought, given Parker's Massachusetts pedigree, it was a *perfect* name for our school. Because we would be a *Coalition* school, the full name became *The Francis W. Parker Charter Essential School).*

John was working out our economic balance sheet, calculating *how exactly*, we would use the monies granted us from the state (based on a formula that entailed school enrollment numbers in particular) to: #1) rent a facility; #2) hire a staff (how many could we afford?); and #3) buy essentials (like furniture, whiteboards, supplies, and so on). Laura and Kathleen were working on how Parker would offer services to students with Special Needs, how we would conduct community outreach, how we would recruit parents, students, and teachers — as well as how we might tap into Harvard's Education School for resources. I was articulating our curriculum and assessment designs, in broad terms regarding Math/Science/Technology and *very specifically* in Arts/Humanities, our major curricular areas. We all worked on ideas about scheduling and agreed that we needed to hire a Math/Science person ASAP. That was accomplished quickly as Gene Thompson-Grove's husband, Keith, a fabulous math teacher, was *more than interested* in joining the Parker team. So, while I was yo-yo-ing between Providence (RI) and Harvard (MA), there was significant progress toward making the Parker School a reality.

Brown – Phase Two

As June 1994 arrived, so did our new cohort of student-teachers. I learned that about a half-dozen of my charges were recruited from an organization called The Multicultural Alliance. These were students of color, given scholarship money from the Alliance on the condition they student-teach at *private schools* (and consider a future as private school educators). Brown's Teacher Education program was aimed at improving *public* schools, particularly in urban areas, and I was happy to discover most of my Multicultural Alliance students were simply using the organization to help finance their Brown degree while fully planning on working in public schools. Even though I had never taught courses in Methods or Analysis (the seminars the student-teachers took while teaching), I had worked with student-teachers during my days as a classroom teacher at both Blind Brook and Bronxville. I believed I had a pretty good idea of what went into developing effective (*change-agent*) classroom teachers. My summer was spent observing the student-teachers at Brown Summer High School and facilitating a seminar on *Methods of Teaching* one afternoon a week. Office Hours were used to help students plan their course of study and/or student-teaching assignment for the Fall semester.

Once September arrived, I had half my student-teachers in schools (meeting with them Wednesday afternoons for the Analysis of Teaching seminar)while the other half took their Content courses. On Mondays, I was catching the early morning Amtrak to New York, heading into the City to take *three courses* (two classroom and one independent study meeting) at Teachers College. I would catch the Amtrak *Night Owl* from Penn Station at *3:40 a.m.* to get back to Providence by 7:30 a.m. on Tuesday, where I would often drive *directly* to a school to observe a student-teacher. *Crazy-busy!*

As if all that weren't enough, Joe McDonald, now my colleague in the Education Department (as well as a senior researcher at the *Coalition*), told me that he had been offered an opportunity to write a book on *performance-assessment* but was already working on another book. He gave the publisher my number and told me to expect a call. Within the week, Bob Sickles, the owner of Eye-on-Education publishers called and, after a conversation about what he was looking for, proposed we meet at the Oyster Bar in Grand Central Terminal, NYC. We did and, by the end of lunch, had a handshake agreement that I would submit a proposal for a book on *performance-based assessment* as soon as I could. Soon after, I sent Bob a proposal and received a contract. I had a book deal!

Parker – Phase Four

As autumn proceeded, we had less than a year to get Parker up and running. Ted and John continued to scour Central Massachusetts (the area just northwest of Boston, defined by the Route 495 Interstate) for a building and Laura, Kathleen, Keith, and I worked on curriculum, scheduling, and figuring out how we would recruit parents and their students, as well as a teaching staff. We figured we needed 12 to 15 teachers, so John gave us a ballpark budget for staffing. One of my/our design concepts was "*no Principal!*" We would operate with Lead Teachers (LT): me as the Arts/Humanities LT and Keith as the Math/Science/Technology LT. We would share the duties of overseeing the staff and completing the other *administrivia* a Principal was charged with in regular schools. It was an idealistic plan (borne out of *my* prejudice against administrators) and, once the school was up and running, quite a flawed idea. Nonetheless, we made significant progress in the Fall of 1994 and, by Thanksgiving, felt ready to begin taking our show on the road, recruiting parents, students, and teachers.

Chapter 16

Parker

"In the Beginning"

> *The ideal school is an ideal community. An ideal community is a democracy, in the purest sense of that pregnant word. Character, constantly realizing itself in citizenship, in community life, in complete living, is the immediate, everlasting, and only purpose of the school. A day filled with refreshing life mirrors the new ideal.*
>
> *Francis W. Parker, 1900*

What if . . . ?

The recruiting brochure for Parker's second year began with this sentence: *Parker began with parents and teachers getting together in living rooms to talk about how a school could look. What if . . . ?* That was the phrase that drove us throughout the planning and execution of our plan. We even had tee-shirts printed with that phrase emblazoned across the chest. *What if . . . ?* Indeed, Parker was unlike any school we had ever seen. It proposed a structure *totally different* from *any* secondary school we knew. That first year was crazy, chaotic, creative, careening, soul-crushing, educational, exhilarating, and exhausting, all at once.

The Place & the People

That the Parker School was a true collaboration between parents and teachers cannot be overstated. Once we had our (almost-windowless) building, there was a genuine community effort in finding furniture and supplies. We managed to get a quite a bit of office furniture from the U.S. Army, who were all but leaving our site, Fort Devens (they still maintain a small Army Reserve component at the far end of the base) but it was the work of the parents that really put the place together, particularly *the sweat equity* they invested in moving desks, chairs, file cabinets, and so on. It was a magical time, as we watched classrooms and offices take shape before our eyes; our collective vision becoming brick and mortar reality.

The original Parker staff was an exceptional group. It had to be to get the place off on the right foot. There was a combination of veterans and *very young*, new teachers that came together, very quickly, as a team, if not exactly a "well-oiled machine." With no Principal, I was the Lead Teacher in Arts/Humanities and Keith Grove was the Lead Teacher for the Math/Science/Technology group. We both oversaw the Spanish and Health-and-Wellness Domains. I spirited two exceptional young Brown UTEP graduates, Elisabeth Fieldstone and Jed Lippard, to join the staff (they were both A/H teachers) and we had the experienced Mary Wren vander-Wilden serving part-time in both of the major domains. Clare

Ringwall, an experienced English teacher from nearby Brookline High School, threw in with us, as did a brilliant young math/science teacher, Francesca Frommer, who had taught at Masconomet High School, north of Boston. Co-founder John Stadler recruited Roger Capallo, an M.I.T. Ph.D. astronomer who had taught at M.I.T.'s Young Scholars Program, and Roger's son, Trevor, would be among our first Parker students. We also had Suzy Becker as our part-time Art teacher. Suzy had already published several best-selling cartoon/satire books (*All I Need to Know I Learned from My Cat, The All Better Book, My Dog's the World's Best Dog*) and was a natural with the kids — an energetic, brilliant presence. *All* of the teachers I've mentioned were *well-versed* and completely committed to the *Nine Common Principles* of the *Coalition.* Aside from Elisabeth and Jed, Clare and Suzy were also Brown graduates; Mary Wren had worked in a Coalition School in California (where my Bronxville Principal, Judy Codding, was her boss) and Francesca had worked extensively with Keith, who was married to Gene Thompson-Grove, the co-director of the *Coalition's National Re:Learning Faculty.* The staff, then, was all *on the same page.*

One aspect of our original Charter proposed that Parker become a Regional Center for Professional Development of teachers. Along those lines (and thanks to Ted and Nancy) we engaged in conversations with Harvard's Graduate School of Education, hoping to secure the services of some of their Masters candidates to serve as full-time *teaching interns* at Parker. With Nancy volunteering to be their Mentor teacher and Seminar Leader, Harvard agreed to provide *four* interns — for a *two-year* commitment. Surprisingly, we had about ten Harvard students interview for our four positions. We struck gold! Dave Berkley (Spanish), Deb Merriam (A/H), Heather

Douglas (MST), and Matt Smith (A/H) were *stunningly good* novice teachers. All four had excellent academic pedigrees (B.A.s from Dartmouth, Williams, Harvard, Brown, respectively). Dave and Heather had some teaching experience. As the first year progressed, the four newbies proved more than up to the challenges Parker posed. They distinguished themselves from the very start (and Deb and Matt *still teach* at Parker!).

In all, the *adults* (parents and teachers) proved to be the *right* people, in the *right* place, at the *right* time. Fifteen charter schools were opened in Massachusetts in 1995. Some did not survive. *Parker thrives.*

The Plan

The curricular, assessment, and scheduling designs for the *Parker School* epitomized the *Coalition* aphorism, "less is more." Our curriculum was pared down, featuring only four Domains: Arts/Humanities, Math/Science/Technology, Spanish, Health and Wellness. The A/H and M/S/T domains would be taught by *teams of two*, each with 20 to 24 students. Likewise, Spanish classes (all taught by a solo David Berkley) would have 20 to 24, and Health/Wellness, essentially *physical education* and *health* classes might have 30 to 40 students at a time. The A/H and M/S/T sections would meet for two-hour blocks (with a ten-minute break offered when the teachers decided) while Spanish and H/W were one-hour blocks. There was a 45-minute lunch period and teaching teams had a built-in one-hour meeting block each day. Early on, we created an "X" block, a 45 minute to one-hour elective period during which students/teachers/parents could offer a course of their own creation once a week. In the first few months, maybe up until the December holiday break, the Daily Schedule changed weekly, as we tried, as

Mary Wren stated, "to change the tires on the bus while it was moving." Luckily, the students, parents, and teachers were all totally committed to making the place work.

The unifying factor for the curricular areas was our *Essential Question: "What is Community?"* All projects, lesson plans, essential sub-questions, would derive from that one. Another guiding principle was that the school would be aggressively *democratic*, ensuring *all* voices be heard. That principle led to a very early school-wide project: a *Constitutional Convention*. As noted on the *current* webpage for the Parker School:

> *During the first month of the operation of Parker, the students met together to create a school constitution. Their task was to create a document that would describe how the students, teachers, and parents would work together to make a fair, democratic, and safe school. The students were divided into four committees: the executive, legislative, judicial, and preamble committees. Each group spent two to three days writing the document that would bring the students together as a community. (www.theparkerschool.org):*

That Constitution has been amended since 1995-1996, but its core remains intact and the *Preamble* sums up what our 7th and 8th grade aged students created.

> *We, the members of the Parker community, in order to form an outstanding learning environment, hereby write this Constitution to establish equality, to encourage educational and verbal freedom, and make this school a safe place where the members feel respected. As a whole, we maintain a balance between*

order and freedom and grant each individual their own
respect, rights, and responsibilities, in order to attain
this exceptional environment, we call the Francis W.
Parker Charter Essential School.

Pretty good work for 11/12/13 year-olds. In action, the
Constitution created a *Community Congress*, which drew representatives from each Advisory (another integral component of
the Parker structure), as well as "at-large" reps. There was also
a Justice Committee, to ensure fairness in conducting business
(discipline) at the school. The Congress had more student than
teacher representatives, which illustrated to the students it was
their school. Having had a positive experience at Bronxville
High School, creating and advising the *Student-Faculty Legis-*
lature, I saw *Parker* as the logical next-step in creating a *truly*
empowered student voice in a school.

The *Advisories* were a key component of *Parker*. While
Laura Rogers oversaw *Student Services* and counseling for Special Needs, *every Parker* adult was in charge of an Advisory,
which met at the beginning *and end* of each school day. More
than a simple homeroom or check-in period, Advisories were
used so that each adult could work with his/her charges to
develop another feature unique to *Parker*– the *PLP*.

PLPs were *Personal Learning Plans.* When designing the
school we had decided that, in the same way Special Education students each have an Individual Learning Plan (IEP) in
regular schools, we would incorporate a *Personal Learning Plan*
into *Parker's warp and woof*, thereby guaranteeing that *each*,
in consultation with his/her parents, would *set goals* for the
academic year in the Fall, meet for a *progress check* at midyear,
and do an end-of-year assessment/review regarding *progress* in
the Spring. It was all very collaborative.

One other unique feature of *Parker* was that we *didn't have grade levels* (like 7th grade, 8th grade) and we *didn't have number or letter GRADES*. Students were organized by Divisions (with Division One being, roughly, 7th/8th grade age students, Division Two 9th/10th, and Division Three 11th/12th). Students would move from one Division to the next by way of *Gateway Portfolio* presentations: challenging *public presentations* (before a panel of outside experts, teachers, students, and parents) of a year or two's worth of work, based on *written standards and criteria* (that were *public*), *showing* what student's *knew and could do*. This system allowed for multi-age classes *and*, more importantly, for students to operate at their own pace with support (thanks to the PLP), so they would never publicly *present* their work until they were *sure* they could Gateway to the next level.

Anticipating parent concern about our students eventually reaching *college admissions* age, Kathleen devised a brilliant package that we could send to admissions offices providing not only *narrative* assessments of students but *samples* of their work, with a full explanation of Parker's unique assessment system. Thanks to Ted, Nancy, Laura, and Kathleen, we started inviting admissions officers from colleges, near and far, to *visit* Parker, *from Year One,* so they could see for themselves how capable our students were. This not only helped future admissions but also allayed the concerns parents had about the whole "college thing."

Chapter 17

Parker

And then the kids showed up!

According to the *Valley Dispatch* from September 13, 1995: "*Parker opened with 120 seventh and eighth grade students from 19 communities. . . .. It will continue to add students and grades each year until it reaches a maximum of 400 students with the class of 2000 being the first to graduate.*" It described how the teachers and school trustees (an awesome group led by Ted, Nancy, Bob Moran, Paula Evans, and the co-Founders) watched the students, *en masse*, cross the front lawn and gather on the front steps of the former Army Intelligence building. We had just completed a three-day, two-night retreat (sleeping in Army barracks!) and the students, escorted by their parents, were eager to start attending *the Parker School*. Each student had written his/her hopes/dreams for his/her time at Parker on a piece of paper that was rolled up and, collectively, assembled to form a "Dream Line." As reported in the *Dispatch:*

Opening ceremonies ended as Parker School trustee Kathleen Cushman held up a "Dream Line" created by the students. But rather than cut the line, she brought it together in a circle "to symbolize the gathering of all of our communities." Then the students moved forward, up the steps into the building to begin the adventure.

Just prior to that, I had addressed the students and their families, saying, "*This is history and you are part of making history. You are pioneers and to be a pioneer is tough because there is no path, but it is also great because you get to make the path. This is not just a school, it's an adventure!*" (There was an Army recruiting video on television at the time that wrapped up saying, "It's not a job, it's an adventure!" Since we were at Fort Devens, it seemed an appropriate phrase) Little did we know how much of an adventure it would be!

Aside from "What is Community?" and our Constitutional Convention, the staff knew we had to establish some *school traditions.* I had been through this before, working at Blind Brook in the early Seventies. We let the students there choose their school colors and mascot. The Blind Brook kids came up with *red, white, and blue* as school colors and a *Trojan* as a mascot (*not* because it was the University of Southern California's mascot). During one of our first Halloween dances at BBHS, a student arrived in costume, wearing a Glad bag with a hula-hoop attached at the ankles and a sign reading "Blind Brook Trojan" emblazoned across it. BBHS remains *The Trojans* to this day, illustrating the power of traditions.

As noted in my opening speech, *I thought* a great mascot would be a *Pioneer*. I loved the alliterative *Parker Pioneers*. Despite my lobbying, the students voted overwhelmingly to be the *Panthers* (the 8th most popular mascot nationally). As for

139

colors, they wrangled a bit before coming up with green, black, and white. (What?) Democracy is democracy and the Voice of the People ruled. We became (and remain) the Parker Panthers, sporting green, black, and white uniforms.

Another tradition started early on was the notion of *The Parker Way*. Starting in Advisories, we discussed how most schools conducted their business but we, here at Devens, had *The Parker Way*. It was already the name of our *newsletter* (written and published with regularity by Kathleen) and it seemed appropriate. The kids quickly came up with their own catchphrase: "*If it was easy, it wouldn't be Parker.*" They got the message that *challenges and hard work* were inherent in the bones of the *Parker School*, and they took pride in it.

As I mentioned, we started the school with a three-day, two-night retreat (What *were we thinking*?). Those days were filled with *experiential* learning (e.g. *Ropes courses*) and team-building exercises — with students, parents, and teachers *all* participating. Students and teachers bunked together in former Army barracks made available to us. The teachers and parents rode herd in the evenings, sleeping in bunk beds, with about 12 to 14 in a room.

Once the school was rolling, the Constitution written, and new schedules being introduced on a regular basis (the kids were incredibly adaptable), we got down to the process of teaching/learning, and it was great fun! Outside of regular classes, the students wrote and published a *Parker School Handbook*, a six-page document that enumerated school policies established by the Community Congress (CC), including guidelines on *vandalism, outdoor rules, being on time, lunch, harassment,* and *restroom upkeep*. The last policy was created because of a *particular* challenge we faced in our first months of existence. Early on, the toilets in the Boys Room were being stuffed with *full rolls* of toilet paper. If flushed, the toilets over-flowed — mini-Niagaras! At one point, this became a *daily* problem (very middle school) and it brought back a flood of Herndon memories for me. In *How to Survive*, the author returns again and again to his idea of "the permanent hall pass" and that is, essentially, what we had given *all* the students at *Parker*. This *stuffing-the-toilet* incident created our first major Community Crisis.

The adults decided the way to deal with the issue was to *lock* the Boys Room and have an adult (with a *key*) *escort* students to the room, unlock it, and then — after checking to insure nothing was stuffed down the toilet, lock it up, escorting the student back to class. Needless to say, this was more than inconvenient for *everyone* and, the students quickly pointed out, *undemocratic*. As a result, the Community Congress and the Justice Committee came up with a policy. The students composed this:

> *Anything found in the toilets or sinks of both bathrooms that should not be there will result in that bathroom being locked for the remainder of the day, or if it happens at the end of the day, the bathroom will be locked the next day. If the incident happens again, then the bathroom will be locked for a week. Bathrooms that are locked can only be accessed by getting a key that will be in the office. (Parker School Handbook - 1995-96)*

The incidents ceased almost immediately and, as we had hoped, *the students* took charge, proving our heavy-handed reaction was, in fact, an *over-reaction*. Allowing *them* to develop the rule/policy is what made it work; an invaluable lesson for the staff/teachers.

Other traditions we started during 1995-1996) were: a student-faculty basketball game (still around), *La Copa Parker*, and a *Spam-eating Contest*. After a great deal of trash talk, the (co-ed) Faculty basketball team soundly defeated the 7th/8th grade team. *La Copa Parker* was a soccer tournament in which Advisories played against each other *and could only speak Spanish* during the game. This was Dave Berkley's brilliant idea and it generated a huge swell of student enthusiasm. I created a trophy out of a Boston Baked Bean ceramic pot and an old recreation league softball trophy I had. It was a crazy-looking symbol for our tournament but *absolutely Parker perfect!* As for the tournament itself, it was noted in the school's first Yearbook, "Remember . . .*when Bil's Advisory won La Copa Parker and Dave's advisory stole the cup?"* It was great, great fun and some students improved their Spanish to boot. As a unifying event for the school, *priceless.*

The Spam-eating Contest was held in the Gym/Field House and was between me and Matt Davidson, one of my favorite "bad boy" (but not really) kids. The Contest was simple: who could eat a white bread, Spam -and-American cheese sandwich *fastest?* The whole school was in the bleachers, cheering for Matt (including the teachers). He beat me easily and it was a loss I heard about regularly for the rest of the year. It was a goofy, silly event, to be sure, and it was wonderful.

Two "cultural" events that also swept the school were *The Macarena* and the O.J. Simpson trial. According to *Wikipedia: "The Macarena: One of the most iconic examples of 1990s dance music, it was ranked the '#1 Greatest One-Hit Wonder of All Time› by VH1 in 2002."* It seemed to be playing somewhere, *all the time* during the *entire* school year, with students dancing to it with reckless abandon. The O.J. trial, of course, had dominated the news (particularly fledgling cable-news networks like *Court TV*) for over a year. The verdict was reached on October 3, 1995 at 10:07 a.m. Pacific Daylight Savings Time (1:07 p.m. at *Parker*). We somehow set up a television on our "Front Porch" (where our opening ceremonies had occurred, and the *entire* school could fit) and watched the verdict come. I recall a certain stunned silence when O.J. was found innocent on both counts of murder. It seemed so *obvious* to all of us he had killed Ron Goldman and Nicole Brown Simpson. But it certainly provided rich fodder for afternoon discussions about racism and the legal/justice system in the larger United States. It was quickly forgotten, however, as we returned to the business of conducting our experiment in school reform.

It should be noted that, aside from creating the first *Parker School Handbook*, the students also created the *first Parker School Yearbook*, noting on the cover: "First Class Ever 1995-'96." It contained pictures of each Advisory (each group designed their own page), three pages of Student Survey results (about items such as "Favorite Animals," "Favorite Magazines," "Favorite – Actors, Actresses, Bands, Radio Stations, Sports, etc." It also had, as noted earlier, a "Remember . . . " page (which listed: "the retreat? The DJ with 8-track tapes? Spanish dinners? Project exhibitions?") and pages and pages of candid pictures (some posed, of course). At the book's end the only color photo in the book, a shot of the *entire school* on those front steps, was a fitting conclusion to our first year.

As that year wore on, it became obvious to the Board of Trustees and the Faculty that we *needed a Principal*. Keith and I were spread too thin, trying to teach *and* administer the school . By springtime, we began looking for someone to take the helm in 1996-1997. I had made it clear I was only going to stay at Parker for its first year, fulling expecting to return to New York City for '96-'97. Living in Cambridge, on Arlington Street, right across from my old pal, Craig Lambert, I missed NYC and really only wanted to *get Parker off the ground* in that first year. In looking for a new Principal I got the idea that a guy named Jim Nehring, who ran an alternative school near Albany, New York, might be a great candidate. I had particularly liked Jim's book, *Why We Gotta Do This Stuff, Mr. Nehring?*, an account of a "Teacher's Day in School," so I gave him a call, to make sure he knew that Parker was looking for a Principal and discovered Jim was a huge Ted Sizer fan Long story short: Jim interviewed and got the job. He began as Chief Academic Leader in July 1996. At the same time, Teri Schrader, a brilliant teacher at the *Coalition's* Watkinson School in Hartford, and a member of the *National School Reform Faculty* of the Annenberg Institute (an ancillary program Ted started at Brown), came on board as the Lead Teacher in Arts/Humanities. Parker certainly seemed to be in capable hands as I anticipated leaving — when the phone rang.

Larry Wakeford, the Science Clinical from Brown, called to let me know that David Kobrin (whom I had substituted for in 1994-95) was *leaving Brown permanently* and the Clinical Social Studies/History position was open, full-time. Might I be interested? I hadn't given Brown much thought, even though I *loved* the year I spent there (particularly working with Eileen, Larry, and Yvette). This opportunity seemed *too good* to pass up. I made the appropriate calls, got letters of recommendation and my C.V. in order, interviewed with the new Department Chair, Cynthia Garcia-Coll, and, before I knew it, I had the job! Instead of moving back to New York I was headed to Providence, Rhode Island, with no idea of what the future might hold.

Postscript: During Parker's first year, the Coalition's Fall Forum was held in New York City in November 1995. Bob Sickles, my publisher, arranged for boxes full of my books to be delivered to the event, so I could have a "book release party" and (sell, as well as) autograph copies. This, of course, was a great marketing opportunity for Bob and it created positive "buzz" about my two-volumes on performance assessment. The book was "officially" published in January 1996 — and helped secure the job at Brown, as it made me a "published author" (even if I didn't have a doctoral degree).

Those Clinton Years

I remember the *palpable excitement* at a Coalition Fall Forum in 1992, as we all purchased *Clinton for President* sweatshirts, even as our colleagues from Arkansas explained he was called "Slick Willy" in his home state for a reason. That didn't discourage us. We were swept away by the notion that one of "us," a Baby Boomer, might get elected. The election was generational: the Baby Boomer v. the WWII war hero. For me, it reflected the gulf between myself and my Dad, a WWII Navy veteran, like Bush, Sr. Clinton's election appeared to be a significant historical page turning.

Quickly running into obstacles (the Health Care plan defeat and Newt Gingrich's *Contract with America*), Clinton moved the Democratic Party closer and closer to the center-right, adopting policies (economic and social) that seemed more Republican than Democratic doctrine. Foreign policy wasn't much better, although he helped resolve the conflict in the Balkans. Clinton's best moments were probably during the Oklahoma City bombings. I was in Allentown, PA, on a consulting job, and remember returning to my hotel room to view the devastation being broadcast on every channel. Clinton, always good as *Healer-in-Chief,* provided the right words and expressions of outrage and grief.

Most of that is forgotten, though, as the *Baby Boomer* became the *Boomer Busted*, facing impeachment because of his dalliance with a White House intern. The entire affair tainted his second term and, despite a surging economy and the dot-com boom, Clinton will be remembered for his failure to keep *his* business *in* his trousers.

Because Clinton had led a national Governor's Commission on education reform before becoming President, we believed we might have an advocate in the White House. His appointment of former South Carolina governor Richard Riley as Secretary of Education did little to excite the *school reform* world and our lack of enthusiasm proved well-founded, as the Clinton/Riley years provided little by way of federal leadership or support. Nonetheless, school reform, particularly in assessment and charter public school creation, *was* progressively moving forward, even without help from D.C.

Chapter 18

Brown
(Round Two)

My original plans to leave Parker after one year and return to New York City were detoured by the Brown Teacher Preparation Program. The Education Department was caught off-guard by David Korbin's abrupt move to Washington, D.C. in the Spring of 1996 — *but* they had an *experienced* Teacher Educator just up the road in Massachusetts. When they called to ask if I might be available to do another "interim" year (and *then* apply for the *permanent* position) I didn't have to give it much thought. Having thoroughly *loved* working at Brown in 1994-1995, I looked forward to the possibility of settling into the position for a longer term. Living in Providence would allow me to remain on the Parker Board of Trustees and commute to monthly meetings, while occasionally visiting the school to observe its progress. It was an opportunity I thought I should take advantage of and, by mid-June 1996, I was headed back to Rhode Island.

Luckily for me, one of my old pals in New York City, Ahvi Spindell, grew up in Providence and his dad, a dentist, had an apartment available right above his office on Humboldt Street. It made for an easy transition, eliminating the anxiety of apartment hunting and its attendant hand-wringing My ties with NYC would always be strong, but life in Providence decreased any urgency to escape to New York City. I had all but completed my doctoral coursework at Columbia but my *Dissertation Committee* (which consisted of Linda Darling-Hammond and Ann Lieberman) had, literally, *left* Columbia Teachers College to work at Stanford, a continent away. Having published my book, I saw no urgent need to write a dissertation and, in hindsight, should have simply proposed that *The Performance Assessment Handbook* be my dissertation. I had loved the course work at TC and truly enjoyed the camaraderie with my Ed.D. cohort, but preparing teachers at Brown was a far more enticing prospect than getting a degree and joining the academic rat-race.

As it stood, when I returned to the Teacher Education Program, I had the title Clinical Professor of Social Studies/ History Education, so I *was* a professor. Years later, doctors at the Brown Medical School made a fuss about *who*, in fact, could be deemed a Clinical and we had to change our titles to "*Director of (subject area) Teacher Education.*" Technically we had the rank of Lecturer, with the possibility of becoming a Senior Lecturer after five years. Never one for titles, I really didn't care what I was called, as long as I could work at preparing aspiring students to become educators.

The Team

My substitute year at Brown, joining the Teacher Prep Team of Eileen Landay, Larry Wakeford, and Yvette Nachmias, had been a rollicking roller-coaster of nonstop work, team-meetings, observations of student teachers, interviews for the next year's cohort, Education Department meetings, and learning about how "the University" operated. There was also some consulting as well as the creation of the *Parker School*, while writing a (two-volume) book. What I most remember about that year was the incredible chemistry our Team had, starting with our preparation for Brown Summer High School, and carrying throughout the summer and the academic year. We worked very well together (maybe because three of us — Larry, Yvette, and I — are all *left-handed?*). Using a workshop tool called *Compass Points*, which I had learned from Faith Dunne, we developed a shorthand for working together. *Compass Points* is a team-building exercise that's great to use with high school faculties (or content-area Departments) to get people to better understand how they each have a *particular teaching/learning* style which *may not be* like that of their colleagues (or their students). When I used it in workshops I would point out, during the de-briefing, that *Compass Points* was about as scientific as *astrology*, but it did give us some useful information as to *why* we might butt heads with someone we were otherwise friendly with.

One reason for using the *Compass Points* exercise was that most faculties confused *congeniality* for *collegiality* (I learned this from Rob Evans, an education psychologist *and* Paula Evans's husband). Most people, not just teachers, don't like conflict and, rather than make waves, will get along — *congenially* — with their colleagues. The *Coalition*, as the result of research by Joe McDonald, was developing the concept of *Critical Friends*: that is, colleagues who would *honestly* assess each other's work *without* making it a *personal* attack or negative criticism. In keeping with that notion, Faith's *Compass Points* was a good jumping-off exercise to prepare people to become *Critical Friends*. Simply put, the *Compass Points* focus on *four* work-styles people exhibit. A *North* is a "need it now, do it now" personality who, once some facts are collected, wants to plow ahead, picking up pieces and revising *after* a project is underway. An *East* is a thoughtful, philosophical, reflective person; one who wants to consider *how* what we're doing will not only work *now*, but what might its effects be in the future. What might the unintended consequences be? A *South* is a person who is oriented toward making sure everyone in the team/group is okay. They are natural caregivers and mediators. The *West* is a nuts-and-bolts, "Let's get all our ducks-in-a-row" individual, focused on outcomes and the *logical next steps*.

No person, of course, is *only one of these* worker/personality types, and most of us apply *all* the *Compass Points* at some time or another. But, as I would explain in my workshops: we all have a *default* mode, and that's the one you choose. There's no *equivocat*ing — you *cannot* be a "Northwest" or "Southeast." When we applied this exercise to our *team* —Eileen, Yvette, Larry, and me — we were a *perfect* amalgam.

I was clearly a *NORTH*, bursting with half-baked ideas but ready to try them, right away (The *Parker School* was a prime example). Eileen (and Yvette) were our thoughtful, philosophical *EAST*: "Let's consider the long run," and "But, wait....what if?" Our conscience and soul. Larry, the Science Guy, was our *WEST*: "What are the details? *How*, exactly, are we going to do that?" Yvette, as our Program Administrator (and Jill-of-All-Trades) proved adept at filling the (very necessary) role of the *South*, taking incredibly good care of the Clinicals throughout our time together. As it turned out, our complementary styles meshed perfectly, and the Teacher Preparation Program had the energy and excitement I had experienced starting *Parker*. It was yet another growth experience and another case of *right time, right place*.

An element that also accelerated my growth was starting *Brown Summer High School* with an outstanding group of *Mentor Teaches*. Elma Shannon, Orah Bilmes, and Ed Abbott all taught at Central High School, the red-headed step-child of the Providence secondary schools. Sharing a broad concrete "courtyard" with *Classical* High School, Providence's "exam" school (for the "smart" and *privileged*), Central was seen as the lesser high school. What I could see, pretty quickly, was that Central had a much stronger teaching staff and those teachers were doing a great job with their kids. Elma, Orah, and Ed were all well-versed in *Coalition* principles and not only applied them in their practice but were *wonderful* mentors to our student-teachers.

Brown Summer High School, from the moment it started, was a *beehive*. I was surprised to see how much *energy* the high school students brought to my student-teachers' classes. (Wasn't this *Summer School?*) The experienced Mentors did a great job coaching our aspiring teachers, who were working in teams of 2/3/4, teaching about 25 students in a one-hour fifty-minute block. It was intense, for sure, but a great way to give these rookies a *trial by fire*, as well as a safe place to experiment with the various Methods the Mentors and I were sharing during our two-and-a-half-hour Wednesday afternoon Seminars.

Regarding texts, my predecessor, David Kobrin, had written a very serviceable book, *In There With the Kids* (1992), and I used it as my basic Methods text. As Publishers Weekly noted in their 1992 review: *A professor of education at Brown University offers a valuable and entertaining course in pedagogy following two fictional teachers in realistic classroom scenarios.* I, of course, added Freire's *Pedagogy of the Oppressed* as well as the recently published *Lies My Teacher Told Me* by James Loewen, which *Wikipedia* describes as follows:

> *It critically examines twelve popular American high school history textbooks and concludes that the textbook authors propagate false, Eurocentric and mythologized views of American history. In addition to his critique of the dominant historical themes presented in high school textbooks, Loewen presents themes that he says are ignored by traditional history textbooks.*

Armed with those books, as well as the input from the Mentors, journal articles, and myself, the summer proceeded in fine fashion and, after our charges departed in August, I was informed that not only were my responsibilities the same as when I had served as David's interim replacement *but* I would now *also* have to teach an undergraduate course: *Education 101: The Craft of Teaching*.

And that's when the *real* fun began.

Chapter 19

Education 101

In an ideal situation, a teacher is always a *learner*. Indeed, an adult, no matter what your profession, should always be a *learner*. Too often, schools do not teach this, students are simply *objects, receptacles, cogs, numbers*. As a result, too many adults have lost the spark, the curiosity *to know*. I bring this up because once I began teaching *Education 101: The Craft of Teaching*, my personal *learning curve* accelerated exponentially.

Ed 101 was designed as an undergraduate gateway course for the Education Department. Intended for freshman and sophomores, in particular, the course should excite, ignite, and invite students to become members of the Ed Department, as *Majors* or teacher prep candidates. There were people on campus (including *professors*) who did not even *know* there *was* an Education Department at Brown! My challenge, then, was not only to create my *own* version of *The Craft of Teaching*, but to do so in a fashion that would *attract* as many undergraduates as possible, promoting the Education Department in the process.

At most universities, there are courses *associated* with particular professors that become legendary. When I was at Yale in the late Sixties Vincent Scully's *Introduction to Art History* and Charles Reich's *The Individual in America* were two such courses. At Brown, Gordon Wood's *American Revolution* was a similar such course. The atmosphere at Brown, among the undergraduate population, was exciting. Like Yale, Brown had made progressive revisions to its curriculum in the late Sixties (it was still called "the new curriculum" in 1996) that granted students freedom regarding requirements and established a liberal attitude for creating *Independent Study* or *Group Independent Study (GISP)* projects. I had only been on campus during my one-year *sabbatical leave replacement* position and *did not* teach undergrads, so 1996-1997 was revelatory. Brown *felt like* the *Sixties* Yale campus I had loved being part of. I was looking forward to teaching *Ed 101* during the Spring term.

There were no strict guidelines defining the *Ed 101* curriculum. I was told I could make it whatever *my vision* of *The Craft of Teaching* might be. There were about 60 students signed up for the course, starting in mid/late January, and I'd have a medium-sized lecture room in Manning Chapel. Brown, like most universities, had a two-week *shopping period*, where students checked out classes they *might* want to take, so a course's final enrollment (regarding size/numbers) wouldn't be complete until early February. Nonetheless, one *did* have to start *teaching the class*, whether students were *shoppers* or not. So, what was *my* vision for *Education 101: The Craft of Teaching?*

Over the course of two or three years, Ed 101 emerged as a natural, organic, evolving creation. The bones of it were there from the start. Even if I had 50 or 60 students, I *would not* lecture. The class met *once a week* for *two and a half hours*!

The course would use *Coalition* and *Parker School* principles: student-as-worker/learner, *no grades* (Brown allowed courses to be "S/NC" — satisfactory/no credit — and students could request a written *narrative* evaluation for their transcript). It would be *democratic*, students would have a voice. The course would *have to* confront two key issues: #1) *Why do we do what we do the way we do it?* and #2) RACISM. Brown is a place of privilege and, while it strives to be liberal and affirmative, most of its (white) students have *not* seriously confronted the sticky and uncomfortable questions of *Racism in America*. Since *everyone* gives lip service to the importance of education as a stepping-stone toward success in America, it seemed only natural to embed questions about racism, white privilege, and educational opportunity into *The Craft of Teaching*.

Luckily for me, there were some wonderful texts available, and I would make sure my students not only read them but delved deeply into the work. Even today (and maybe *especially* today) if one has not read Lisa Delpit's *Other People's Children* or Beverly Tatum's *Why Are All the Black Kids Sitting Together in the Cafeteria?* you should go out, get copies, and *read them now*. As noted in the *Harvard Review*:

> In *Other People's Children: Cultural Conflict in the Classroom*, Lisa Delpit . . . *provides an important yet typically avoided discussion of how power imbalances in the larger U.S. society reverberate in classrooms. Through telling excerpts of conversations with teachers, students, and parents from varied cultural backgrounds, Delpit shows how everyday interactions are loaded with assumptions made by educators and mainstream society about the capabilities, motivations, and integrity of low-income children and children of color.*

The book is eye-opening on a number of levels and does a great job of methodically presenting how the educational system is *anything but* a level playing field.

Tatum's book:

> *has become a modern classic in college and high school classrooms, used to educate and prompt healthy discussions among young people about race. The premise of this book is that adults both White and of color, often hesitate to speak to children about racism for fear they will create problems where perhaps none exist, afraid that they will make "colorblind" children unnecessarily color-conscious. Through her research and educational background she attempts to respond to these questions and others that creates useful clarity in the daily discourse about race.*
> (*Goodreads*)

The issues of *racial identity* and social/political power are convincingly argued in Tatum's work and, like Delpit's, are *revelatory* to most white readers.

To begin a discussion about *white privilege* I would have the students read Peggy McIntosh's classic: *White Privilege: Unpacking the Invisible Backpack.* The author relates, through her study of *male* privilege, how, as a *white* person (even though *female*), she had *advantages* that were built into the culture, *privileging* her over people of color. Nothing is more striking than her list "identifying some of the daily effects of white privilege on my life." Here is a sample from that list, many of which my students had never thought about:

1. I can, if I wish, arrange to be in the company of people of my race most of the time.

2. If I should need to move, I can be pretty sure of renting or purchasing housing in an area, which I can afford and in which I would want to live.

4. I can go shopping alone most of the time, pretty well assured that I will not be followed or harassed.

5. I can turn on the television or open to the front page of the paper and see people of my race widely represented.

10. Whether I use checks, credit cards or cash, I can count on my skin color not to work against the appearance of my financial reliability.

21. I can go home from most meetings of organizations I belong to feeling somewhat tied in, rather than isolated, out-of-place, outnumbered, unheard, held at a distance, or feared.

22. I can take a job with an affirmative action employer without having coworkers on the job suspect that I got it because of race.

26. I can choose blemish cover or bandages in "flesh" color and have them more or less match my skin

The two *most formative texts* that emerged as I developed *The Craft of Teaching* were *Teaching to Transgress* by bell hooks (Gloria Watkins) and Henry Giroux's *Teachers as Intellectuals: Toward a Critical Pedagogy of Learning*. These two books, for me, are direct descendants of Carl Rogers (*Freedom to Learn*) and Paolo Freire (*Pedagogy of the Oppressed*). Freire, in fact, wrote the *Introduction* to Giroux's book (and, years later, *Giroux* would write the Introduction to *my second book*). Simply put, bell hooks's book is about:

> *Teaching students to "transgress" against racial,*
> *sexual, and class boundaries in order to achieve the gift*
> *of freedom . . . is the teacher›s most important goal. Full*
> *of passion and politics, Teaching to Transgress combines*
> *a practical knowledge of the classroom with a deeply*
> *felt connection to the world of emotions and feelings.*
> *This is the rare book about teachers and students that*
> *dares to raise questions about eros and rage, grief and*
> *reconciliation, and the future of teaching itself. "To ed-*
> *ucate is the practice of freedom," writes bell hooks, "is*
> *a way of teaching anyone can learn."* (Buffalo & Erie
> County Public Library summary)

Teaching to Transgress struck the chord for *what Ed 101* was going to attempt to be about. Added to that were Giroux's ideas about *critical pedagogy.* In *Teachers as Intellectuals,* Giroux clearly shows how teaching is a *political act* and, taking a direct cue from Freire, about *freeing people* to not only become *active learners* (agents) but, as important, *engaged citizens.* As I had often noted in my own teaching, students cannot learn to become engaged, democratic citizens if they are constantly being told to "sit down and be quiet." Giroux's insistence that teachers (and administrators!) become *"transformative intellectuals"* (p.xxxiii) is a powerful call and re-orders our thinking about teaching and learning. Laying bare what teachers know (but *don't confront*) about curriculum, that it *is not "neutral and objective,"* fits hand-in-hand with Jim Loewen's *Lies My Teacher Told Me* and insists that teachers (as *intellectuals*) take on the task of presenting *the truth* to students, in order to "liberate" them. Here was the *key* to what I wanted *Education 101: The Craft of Teaching* to epitomize. And, over two or three years, that's how it emerged.

Chapter 20

Education 101
Bil's World & Welcome to it!

Teaching *Education 101: The Craft of Teaching* was the *only* time, in all 42 years of my career, that I had *total freedom and control* over what I was doing in the classroom. There were no state mandates, no university guidelines, no Departmental strictures. Because Universities operate as fast-and-loose partnerships between professors and administrators, there is *little oversight* about what *anyone* does in his/her classroom space. As a result, Ed 101 was my *Frankenstein*, created from tools in my education warehouse. In 20 weeks, I was going to offer a *distillation* of what *I believed* were the *best* ideas about teaching/learning and, *not only* present that material to my students but, as important, *model it*.

This meant I could *apply* everything I thought I knew about teaching/learning based on Herndon, Rogers, Freire, Sizer, Delpit, Tatum, hooks, Giroux, and all the others. The class would have to be *personalized* (and students would have to be *known*) and *democratic*. It would have high standards but not be driven by *getting-a-grade*. It would confront the uncomfortable questions about Racism and Privilege. And I would be *evangelical* in promoting the idea that students become *change agents* for school reform. A tall order, but, given *carte blanche* and *tabula rasa*, Ed. 101 had the *possibility* of becoming the *ideal* undergraduate Education class.

The first year, in Manning Chapel, went well. The space was not great for doing the activities I was committed to: short periods of large group instruction followed by intensive small-group seminar work. I had three undergraduate Teaching Assistants who were well-versed in *Coalition* philosophy and were *Stars* in the Education Department. They had been involved in the course planning and were well-prepared to facilitate the small group work. One facet of the class that began from that first year and became a mainstay of the course were *one-page* writing assignments. Generally, students were required to read one-book-per-week. They would then have to write a *one-page* critique (*not* a book report or summary *but* a critical review) about an idea/concept in the book they found revelatory or challenging. In the same way, students were given a weekly *journal prompt* ("*Write an 'autobiography' of yourself as a student*" "*Write a personal 'literacy autobiography.'*") which often were one-page assignments, too (though the "autobiographical" works could run to 3-pages, maximum). One thing I knew about college undergraduates: they could *bullshit* a five-page paper in their sleep, fulfilling an assignment and saying *nothing*. I told them exactly that on Day One, along with announcing the course was *S/NC* (Satisfactory/No Credit) *required* (at which point flocks of *Shoppers* walked out. You can't afford S/NC when you're looking to pad your GPA). *All* writing was to be saved and used in an end of term *portfolio*, with *reflective* assessments of what students saw (or didn't see) regarding their growth during the semester.

I did my best to learn the names of all my (60 to 70) students as quickly as possible, particularly because I wanted to match names/faces with the *autobiographical* writing I would receive in the first few weeks. Starting in Year Two (1997-98) I took Polaroid pictures (still a pre-digital world) of *all* the students in the class in the first two meetings and, by week three, knew everyone's name. A parlor trick on its surface, using the Polaroids as *Flash Cards* provided a quick way to learn everybody's name.

The *Coalition* stresses that each student needs to be *known*, and I believed that should be true in *Ed 101*, no matter how many students were in the class (one year there were 120). As two of my former students (who became Undergraduate TA's after taking the class), Leigh Fitzgerald and Julie Schumacher (Class of 2000) noted:

> *Many students are shocked that he learns everyone's names. . . It humanizes students and creates a learning community to which everyone contributes.*

That was the goal, and *Ed 101* developed a momentum from its early weeks because I would, without hesitation, call on students *by name* (they could, of course "pass") and, more often than not, they had things to say (my questions were usually asking for their *critical* opinion about what we were reading or discussing). Even at liberal Brown, students were not used to being *known, particularly* in a large, lecture course.

The class, at its best, was a fluid environment, moving from large group activities to small group discussions/de-briefings, particularly when we were looking at *Racism* and

Privilege. By the second year of the course, we were meeting on the Pembroke campus (before the co-education of Brown in 1971, Pembroke College was the *Sister* school in Providence), in Alumnae Hall's auditorium, a very large space equipped with folding chairs, providing a wide-open unencumbered area, if we desired.

That space allowed us to implement the *Privilege Walk* exercise early in the year, a stark, physical way to confront Racism/Privilege, leading to intense small group analysis and discussion. If you are not familiar with the *Privilege Walk,* here's a brief sample of the exercise (you can *Google* "Privilege Walk Exercise" to get the full list):

The Privilege walk:

The typical classroom version of this activity involves between 10-40 participants. Throughout the privilege walk, the following statements are read by the facilitator and the participants are asked to take a step forward or backward based on their responses. This activity forces participants to confront the ways in which society privileges some individuals over others.

- *If your ancestors were forced to come to the USA not by choice, take one step back.*
- *If you were ever called names because of your race, class, ethnicity, gender, or sexual orientation, take one step back.*
- *If there were people who worked for your family as servants, gardeners, nannies, etc. take one step forward.*
- *If one or both of your parents were "white collar" professionals: doctors, lawyers, etc. take one step forward.*
- *If you studied the culture of your ancestors in elementary school, take one step forward.*

- *If you went to school speaking a language other than English, take one step back.*
- *If there were more than 50 books in your house when you grew up, take one step forward.*
- *If one of your parents was unemployed or laid off, not by choice, take one step back.*
- *If you attended private school or summer camp, take one step forward.*
- *If you were ever discouraged from academics or jobs because of race, class, ethnicity, gender or sexual orientation, take one step back.*
- *If your family owned the house where you grew up, take one step forward.*
- *If you saw members of your race, ethnic group, gender or sexual orientation portrayed on television in degrading roles, take one step back.*
- *If you were ever accused of cheating or lying because of your race, ethnicity, gender, or sexual orientation, take one step back.*
- *If you had to rely primarily on public transportation, take one step back.*
- *If you attended private school at any point in your life take one step forward.*

After the entire 44-statement list was read, it was not a shock to me or the TAs, that the white students were lined up on one side of the room while the students of color were all gathered on the other side. For many of the *white* students, however, the *physical* representation of their *privilege* was a shock. The small group seminars were *abuzz* with discussion after the *Privilege Walk. This* was exactly where I wanted *Ed 101* to go. The *Privilege Walk* created a safe space for white students and students of color to discuss the *realities* of Racism and Privilege, at Brown and in the wider world.

Another Exercise we did examined high school curriculum by critically analyzing *textbooks*. The TA's and I arrived early with milk crates (literally) *filled* with high school textbooks, particularly social studies/history and science (bio and chem). Having already done the *Privilege Walk*, (as well as having read hooks, Delpit, and Tatum), students were well-attuned to looking for examples of *privilege* and *racism* in the assembled texts. Part of the fun of this exercise was the invariable "Hey, that's the book we used at *my* high school" we would hear as the discussion groups assembled around the books. More important, the longer they examined the texts and shared what they were finding, the more they detected the *cultural biases* in these books. Reflecting on how many of their secondary schools used the text *as the course curriculum*, the students rightly concluded the textbook industry was actually promoting a biased curriculum that *privileged* the dominant culture while handicapping everyone else.

Ed 101 concluded each semester with an *Annual Ed 101 Curriculum and Pedagogy Conference*. As the end of the course approached, students were polled (in our Large Group) as to what topics *they* were most interested in studying *in greater depth*. The TAs and I recorded the suggestions (Curriculum, Media, Assessment, Special Education, and so on) and, by the following week, distributed a sheet with five/six/seven *possible* Research Topic choices. Students would rank order what they most wanted to research and we guaranteed they would get one of their first *three* choices. After some tabulating and sorting, we organized our Research Teams and they had two weeks to #1) do their research, #2) organize a presentation, and #3) teach a two-hour class based on their Topic. We would then publish a Conference Schedule (which took place during the final two weeks of the semester) and students would be responsible for *presenting* one week and *attending* a presentation the other week. *All* this work was included in a Final Portfolio.

Ed 101 became one of those *legendary* courses among the Brown undergraduates and resulted in my winning the *The William G. McLoughlin Award for Excellence in Teaching in the Social Sciences* for the 2000-2001 academic year. Winning the award entailed receiving a small stipend and a medal (to be worn during graduation ceremonies in the Spring).

The Award Ceremony occurred during the Fall *Convocation,* the September opening event at the University. I was informed I *must* attend *and* (much to my chagrin) had to wear the ceremonial *academic gown* (something I did during *graduation* ceremonies, but *always* wearing a black Brown *baseball cap* with a tassel hanging from it). I went to the Convocation, wearing the academic robe (but hatless) and waited as our interim University President made an opening address (way too long), a few other administrators greeted the assembled freshman, and then the Provost read off Faculty Award-Winners. I sat with my colleagues from the Education Department and waited to hear my name called for the McLoughlin Award. The John Rowe Workman Award for Excellence in Teaching in the Humanities was called. The Elizabeth LeDuc Award for Excellence in Teaching in the Life Sciences was called. The Philip J. Bray Award for Excellence in Teaching in the Physical Sciences was called. The Provost congratulated the Award winners, thanked everyone for attending the Convocation, and wished everyone a great year.

At the luncheon held after the Convocation, the *interim* University President and Provost (the wife of an Ed Dept.

colleague) turned all the colors of the rainbow when they saw me and realized they had, somehow, forgotten to announce the *McLoughlin* Award. At least I didn't have to wear that academic robe at the luncheon. I eventually got my medal but never attended another Convocation. *Ed 101* remained *legendary*, even if the University didn't want to publicly acknowledge it.

9/11

It was a crystal clear, cloudless morning when I left my Humboldt Street apartment around 8:40 a.m. on September 11, 2001. Listening to *Imus in the Morning*, as I often did, Warner Wolf, the sportscaster, was reporting from his apartment in Lower Manhattan. One of the Twin Towers had been struck by an airliner. It was 8:46 a.m. I turned around and went back to my apartment, flipping on the tv to see the destruction. Glued to the screen, the next images were horrific. As I watched the first Tower billow black smoke I could see, coming in from screen right, another airliner. It was clearly banking, readying for a turn and, within seconds, crashed into the *second* Tower. The sense of horror and helplessness only heightened as the morning wore on. Watching the Towers burn, as innocent people threw themselves off the building to certain death, was excruciating. The collapse of one Tower, then the other, was soul-crushing. In the Rick Burns documentary *New York*, which chronicles the history of the City, Pete Hamill talks about how the Towers, initially derided, had become beloved by the residents of Manhattan. Hamill describes how Phillippe Petit's illegal tightrope walk from one Tower to the other in 1974 *humanized* the monstrosities. And now, in a few short hours, they were gone, along with almost 3,000 lives.

9/11 was a Tuesday. Wednesday afternoon, Larry, Eileen, and I knew we had to have a *joint* Analysis of Teaching seminar, so our students could process the tragedy. Like us, they would have to deal with their students, trying to help them understand this horrendous event. Unlike our student-teachers who were working in Providence, *we* actually had students *from* New York, some of whom had relatives in the City, in Lower Manhattan. One of Eileen's sons was a filmmaker who lived in Manhattan and would produce a brilliant documentary about 9/11. Some of our students broke into tears during class. Emotions ran high. Making sense of the senseless is never easy. Yet you knew this was a *generational* tragedy, like JFK had been for us, or the *Challenger* was for my Winchester students. Even knowing that it will someday be "just" *another* event in a history book does not alleviate the *immediate* weight of the tragedy. As teachers, our job, always, is to mediate the pain for our students and help find the path beyond the tragedy.

In mid-October 2001, I had to be in Queens. Looking over at Manhattan it struck me that I was looking at the skyline I remembered as a boy. The Twin Towers had been built when I was in college, living in New Haven. While my Dad had taken pictures as they were being constructed, my awareness of them was as a completed structure, creating a new skyline for the City. They became my touchstone whenever I was returning from trips to Pennsylvania, my beacons of "home." And now they were gone. The Empire State Building defined the horizon again, as it had when I was a boy, taking the Long Island Railroad into the city to ride the Circle Line or visit the Museum of Natural History. It seemed wrong, regressive. As Pete Hamill noted, the buildings had been *humanized* and this felt like losing two friends, not two buildings. It created that heartache you feel when a loved one dies.

Chapter 21

My Bifurcated Brown Career

Looking back, I can see that my career at Brown, a place I worked at longer than any other, was divided into two distinct segments. There were the *pre-Alaska* years (1996-2004) and the *post-Alaska* years (2005-2007). The 2004-2005 academic year was spent on sabbatical in Alaska and then back in New England developing a new course under the auspices of a University Fellowship. I didn't have to leave Brown at the end of the 2007 Spring term, but I chose to, for a variety of reasons, but that's getting ahead of the story.

Pre-Alaska Brown: 1996-2004

My time at Brown was very productive, and not just because of *Ed 101*. My primary job, of course, was to *prepare* teachers (note: I *ABHOR* the term "teacher-training." As I would often tell my students: "I *trained* my dog, I *prepare* teachers." Words are important and the distinction between *training* and *preparing* is *significant*). An important goal for me, working with the Teacher Prep Program, was to *diversify* our teaching pool. Since we worked in an urban school system, we needed to recruit and prepare teachers-of-color as much as possible. This became a personal goal for me and, with great support from my department chair, Cynthia Garcia-Coll, the number of teachers of color in the Social Studies/History cohort steadily increased over the years.

Selling young people on the idea of becoming a teacher is not easy (and not just young people of color). Improving the teacher candidate pool, regarding educational preparation as well as temperamental fitness, is a challenge. At Brown, we usually received an above-average candidate pool (Harvard was our main competition). Because we were a small program, our acceptance numbers were low (particularly compared to Harvard's *Education School*) and we had to work at making sure people even *knew* we had a program. Nonetheless, we maintained steady numbers and provided an extremely high-quality program. We were given more than ample support from departmental colleagues — Luther Spoehr, Jin Li, Carl Kaestle, John Modell, to name a few— who, though not *directly* associated with the Teacher Prep Program, did yeoman work *promoting* our *brand* and supporting our students.

One thing I learned working at a University is that even though your classroom hours (teaching time) is far less than that of a public-school teacher, your *meeting time* is astronomical. There are committees and sub-committees up the wazoo. Aside from the expected *Education Department* and *Teacher Prep Program* meetings, there are a wide variety of activities conducted by the University which required our Department to send representatives. Given that we were a small department, we often served on multiple committees and sub-committees, all of which met *far too often* and accomplished *far too little*.

There was always a *Search Committee* (or two) being conducted *within* our department as well (people *constantly* come and go at Universities). Beyond that, we had to serve on the Graduate Council *or* the Curriculum Council *or* the Academic Standing Committee *or* the Diversity Advisory Board (there are no fewer than *27* councils, committees, and boards that require faculty participation). A personal problem for me was that if a meeting wasn't scintillating I would, with regularity, *fall asleep* (If one of my Ed Dept. colleagues also happened to be on that committee, I could count on getting a "wake-up" nudge). Then, and now, I believe far too many *person-hours* at the University are wasted in meetings, hours upon hours you'll never get back.

Two organizations I actually *enjoyed* working with at Brown were the *Sheridan Teaching Center* and the *Royce Fellowship Committee*. The Sheridan Center was created as a professional development resource for anyone teaching at Brown (significantly, it was *voluntary* for the professoriate). As they note on their website: *The Center advances effective liberal learning, encourages ongoing professional development, and fosters reflective teaching and learning.* Aside from attending (sparsely populated) meetings with professors to discuss issues of teaching/learning, my central interaction with the Sheridan Center was facilitating workshops every fall (my colleague, Larry Wakeford, also did this) during the Center's "orientation for new instructors." This was usually 50 to 60 Graduate Teaching Assistants who were sent by their (full/assistant/associate) Professors to prepare to facilitate discussion sections of the Professor's *lecture course*. I found it telling that few professors attended the teaching/learning seminars the Sheridan Center conducted, and *never* attended any workshops on *how to* develop *more effective* teaching practices. They were perfectly happy continuing to work in their medieval model: *"professor reads Latin, owns the books, and relays knowledge to the (empty vessel) students."* Given that we were living in a more and more digital environment I, of course, believed it was time for the University, like the public schools, to *reform itself*. As I spent more time at Brown, and working with the Sheridan Center, I came to the conclusion that there should be a *Teaching* faculty and a *Research* faculty at the University (with professors opting to serve on one or the other each year). What led me to that notion was that there were, in fact, some professors who did far more than profess, they were great *teachers*! Others, however, barely hid their disdain for teaching and working with students (particularly undergraduates) and were *only* interested in publishing their research for other professors. Nonetheless, working with the Sheridan Center was a highlight each year, and I always found it an excellent *professional* organization.

Royce Fellowships arrived in 1996, when I came back for my second interim year. Overseen by the Swearer Center, the community service arm of Brown, I happened to have worked with some of the Swearer Center staff during my first interim year and they thought I'd be a good faculty person to help get *The Royce* off the ground. Simply put:

> *Established in 1996 through the generosity of Charles Royce, '61, the Royce Fellowship supports Brown undergraduates as they carry out independent engaged research projects of their own design in locations across the United States and around the world. Fellows conduct their research under the supervision of a faculty member and as part of an interdisciplinary cohort of students from across the university.* (Students receive a $4000 stipend to carry out their research

and must present their work in the Spring of the year after they receive their Fellowship) (source: Brown University website)

I became part of the Faculty Committee on admissions for the Royce program and have to say that some of the most fun I had at Brown, aside from ED 101 and working with the Teacher Prep Program, was wrangling with colleagues from other departments over *who* should win a *Royce* . Because we agreed there had to be *consensus approval,* the discussions/debates over worthy applicants were rip-roaring affairs. Since some of us had encouraged specific candidates to apply, there were times when a faculty advocate had to be challenged. Great fun. What was particularly impressive were the independent study proposals the students submitted. Here's a quick sample of projects that are currently being pursued (not unlike some of the projects we approved over the years I was on the Royce Faculty Committee):

- *Investigating the Beneficial Use of Plant-Based Medicines Through Combining Traditional African Medicine and Western Technology*
- *Predictors of Eating Disorders and Disordered Eating Including Previous Injuries in Collegiate Women*
- *Healing Through A Feminist Latinx Arts Education: Developing Curriculum with the RISD Museum and the Los Angeles County Museum of Art*
- *Botanical Imperialism and Ecological Resistance in Southeast Brazil*
- *Towards an Anti-Nationalist Pedagogy: A Comparative Exploration of Cuban and U.S. Teachers' Relation to the State*

- *Examining the Impact of Primary Care Providers' Perspectives on HIV Prevention in the U.S.-Mexico Borderland: Focus on El Paso, Texas*

The list goes on but suffice it to say that the students did incredible work as *Royce Fellows* and I was pleased and proud to be part it.

The Band

During the 1997-1998 year, one of my M.A.T.s, Liz Newton, a Rhode Island local, kept telling me I *had to meet* Carolyn Sheehan and her husband, Billy Legenza, Liz believed we were *simpatico.* Carolyn ran the very successful *Spirit Educational Program* in Pawtucket, a summer and after-school enterprise that focused on 7th, 8th, & 9th graders with the objective of enhancing their academic future. Bill was a retired police officer and naturalist (he became the local Audubon Center supervisor) who loved to play blues guitar (also a personal passion of mine). At Liz's graduation in the Spring of 1998, I finally met Carolyn and Billy and Liz was right, we hit it off like old friends. In short order, I was traveling up to their house in Smithfield where they had an out-building on their property and we quickly established a band. A Providence police officer, Billy Baldessari, played drums; Billy Legenza was on lead guitar; Bil Johnson played bass,; and Carolyn Sheehan did the singing, often joined on vocals by a friend (and another Pawtucket community leader) Diane Dufresne. I quickly dubbed us "*The Overdue Bills Blues Band*," and our garage (blues) band was born. I can't even begin to describe the countless hours spent playing (sometimes very good) music. It was great fun. More significantly, Rhode Island had passed Charter School legislation and Carolyn, well-aware

175

of the *Parker School* and my role in it, was talking about *morphing* the *Spirit Program* into a full-blown Charter High School. Long story short: Carolyn assembled a group to start planning the application for *Blackstone Academy*, a Charter High School in Pawtucket, Rhode Island.

Using the *Parker School* curriculum design as a model, Carolyn and her assembled crew began to put together their plan for *Blackstone*. I served in an *advisory* capacity and now our band rehearsals included discussions about the new school. As plans materialized, I agreed to serve as the Founding President of *Blackstone's* Board of Directors. A *Coalition* school from the outset, *Blackstone* adheres to the *Coalition's 10 Common Principles* (see *Endnotes*) and articulates the *Habits of Mind* their students aim for. It is a Rhode Island Department of Education (RIDE) *Commended School* and has proven the *Parker* model adapts to an urban environment. While not a *carbon copy* of Parker, they are certainly kissing-cousins and prove that you do not have to adhere to that 100-plus years-old factory model that has been so stultifying for so long.

A most important *Pre-Alaska* facet of my time at Brown began with my birthday in 2000. Kathleen Cushman knew I had been talking about getting a dog for several years. I hadn't had one since I left New York City in 1994. As a birthday gift she gave me the most incredible present: a Black Labrador Retriever puppy. He was the last in his litter and, as we approached the house (with me incessantly asking Kathleen, "Is it going to be a dog?") the owner swung the front door open. A small black mass of energy came bounding out. I squatted down, like a baseball catcher, and, without missing a stride, he leapt into my arms and started licking my face! Within minutes, he was named *Jack* and soon became a *legend* in the Education Department and on the Brown Campus.

Chapter 22

Pre-Alaska, Part Two

Northern Exposure

In November of 2000, while Jack was still a puppy, I flew to Seattle (my brother, god bless him, took care of the dog) to present a workshop at a conference. I had been to Seattle a number of times before, so it was a fun trip, seeing old friends and touring the city. The conference was a good one, focused on school reform with an emphasis on curriculum and assessment. After my presentation on *performance-based assessment*, a tall gentleman hung around to further discuss what I had presented. Greg Sandstrom was the principal of *Howard Luke Academy*, an alternative pubic high school in Fairbanks, Alaska. He thought the material I presented was *perfect* for his school and staff: would I be interested in doing some consulting with them? (*Note: This was still a time when State and Federal funds were accessible, if not plentiful, for schools to tap into*) Without hesitating, I said, "Sure," and gave Greg my contact information. *Consulting in Alaska*. All I thought, in that moment, was, *"What an adventure!"* It wasn't until I got back to Providence and actually looked at a map that I saw where Fairbanks was — and began thinking this whole idea might be a *big mistake*. But I had already said "Yes" to Greg and I was still intrigued by the possibility of *adventure*.

For those not familiar with Alaska, here are a few fun facts.

- *Alaska is the largest state in the United States by total area at 663,268 square miles, over twice the size of Texas, the next largest state. Alaska is larger than all but 18 sovereign countries. (Wikipedia) (It's 20% the size of the entire Lower 48!)*
- *Alaska has more coastline than the rest of the United States combined, roughly 34,000 miles.*
- *Alaska has the lowest population density in the nation at one person per square mile.*
- *If New York City had the same population density as Alaska, only 16 people would be living in Manhattan.*
- *Most of America's salmon, crab, halibut, and herring come from Alaska.*

I didn't know *any* of those things when I told Greg "Yes" and, when I finally did look at a map, I saw that Fairbanks was *in the middle, northern part of the state* — only 100 miles from the Arctic Circle! It wasn't until I booked my first flight I learned that after you flew 6 hours, coast-to-coast, then changed planes in Seattle *and flew another three hours* to get to *Anchorage*. Once there, you *changed planes yet again and flew north for another hour* (Fairbanks is *360 miles* north of Anchorage).

My first trip to Fairbanks was in January 2001. It was well below freezing when I arrived at the Fairbanks airport that evening. I located my rented Ford *Escape* and, as I pulled onto the highway outside Fairbanks International, the moon was sitting right above the tree line and looked HUGE. It was a clear, cold night and a shot of adrenaline coursed through me: *I was in f-ing Alaska!* I stayed for a week, met the staff, had some productive workshops, and set up a schedule for returning every few months, for a week at a time. Given Brown's schedule, I'd be able to go to Fairbanks, in January, late May, and late August. This worked well with the *Howard Luke Academy's* opening & closing of school, as well as mid-terms. From 2001 until the Spring of 2004, I became a regular visitor to Fairbanks, Alaska, until I was eligible for a sabbatical at Brown in the Fall of 2004. Greg and I worked out a way for me to spend that semester in Fairbanks.

Back at Brown

There was a lot going on at Brown between 1996 and 2004. An *Elementary Teacher Preparation Program* had started under the excellent guidance of Romi (Romina) Carrillo, a fabulous educator who easily meshed with the *Secondary* team. When Romi left after the program was off the ground, Polly Ulichny seamlessly moved into the role of *Director of Elementary Ed*, and she, too, proved to be an outstanding teammate. It was also during these years that Yvette got married (to the debonair & brilliant Dieter Baeu) and left us for a woodworking/furniture making mill in South County. This initially created genuine concern because Yvette, for all intents and purposes, kept *everything* running smoothly in the *Teacher Prep Program*. Luckily for us, Carin Algava, a recent graduate of the *Elementary Prep Program*, slid into Yvette's role with surprising ease, keeping us running like the well-oiled machine we believed ourselves to be.

It was also during this period that I decided I needed a definitive *Methods* book for preparing my future teachers. I had been working on an idea for a while, and I contractually owed Bob Sickles another book. Slowly but surely, I began to piece together a new book, one that would satisfy Bob and, more importantly, provide my students with *the* Methods book that fit perfectly with my course. *The Student-Centered Handbook* is only 115 pages but its 5 Chapters covered all the bases my students needed. Using specific classroom-tested exemplars and models, the book proved to be very effective, and an excellent companion piece to my two-volume *Performance-Assessment Handbook*.

Jack

Jack was my constant companion from the time I got him in May 2000 until he shuffled off this mortal coil in March 2012. I had already owned a number of dogs: *Maxwell,* the stray I picked up on the streets of New Haven in 1969 (predictably short-circuited on the Hutchinson River Parkway five years later), *Beau,* the 120-pound Golden Retriever who lived with me in Port Chester and Boston for 12 years. There also were my parents' dogs, *Coffee* and *Radar,* who became *my* dogs when Mom & Dad sold our family home in the late 70s. Both were mutts and each lived to be 17. By 2000, I had gone about a half-dozen years without a dog and then along came *Jack.*

In several words: *Jack* was huge (about 115 lbs.), brilliant, and the sweetest dog I (or anyone) ever met. He became a beloved fixture in the Education Department, with students often coming in to visit *him,* particularly those who had dogs back home. *Jack,* from early on, learned to take his leash in his mouth and, obedient to a fault (via voice commands), would walk with me, when he wasn't on the lawn next to the Ed Dept., spinning and spinning his leash like a lariat. The only time *Jack* would break into a run was when he saw a squirrel, at which point he would *bolt*!! Nonetheless, if I called out his name or simply shouted "NO!" he would put on the brakes like Wily Coyote. *Jack* always accompanied me to *Ed 101*, greeting students and then laying down as I gave the agenda and instructions for the day. When the students broke into discussion groups, *Jack* would wander around, checking in with everybody and, when we re-assembled as a large group, he'd lay down quietly. He went to conferences with me (often wearing his own Name Tag), he drove from Providence to New York or Stroudsburg, PA, without a whine. He adapted to every situation and had what can only be described as "human" eyes (my brother called them "Mighty Joe Young" eyes, after the giant movie Ape we grew up watching on *Million Dollar Movie*, Channel 9). He was unique in every way and anyone who set foot in the Ed Department in those years can tell you about *Jack*. He was *legendary*.

Urge for Going

As 2004 approached, I was informed that I'd be eligible for a sabbatical, a *semester* off with full pay and benefits. That was fine, but I wanted to take the whole year off. At that point I learned there was a Fellowship (the Henry Merritt Wriston Fellowship) *specifically* for Junior Faculty Members (The Wriston was a competitive Fellowship: you submitted a proposal to design an undergraduate course you'd like to teach and, if the Wriston Committee liked your proposal, you got the Fellowship. This meant a semester off with full pay and benefits, as well as several thousand dollars to support your research). Here's what was published in *the George Street Journal* (a campus-wide weekly newspaper) in April 2004:

Bil Johnson

Education Faculty Member
Receives Wriston Fellowship

Wilbur Johnson, lecturer and clinical professor of Social Studies and history in the Department of Education, has been awarded a Henry Merritt Wriston Fellowship for the 2004-2005 academic year. He will use the award to design a new undergraduate teaching seminar on the subject of "white privilege" — the idea that Caucasians receive unearned advantages because of their skin color.

The Wriston Fellowship is one of the highest awards Brown bestows upon its teaching faculty. It is awarded annually to a junior member of the faculty to recognize significant accomplishments in teaching and to allow for scholarly research and preparation of new contributions to the undergraduate curriculum.

Johnson will use the Wriston Fellowship to do research, conduct interviews and observations, and organize an undergraduate seminar that examines more deeply the fundamentals of teaching, issues of white privilege, and critical pedagogy. Johnson plans to structure the course to look at how and why (or why not) educators teach about "whiteness" in the United States.

Having consulted extensively with Greg Sandstrom, the 2004-2005 year would see me working in Fairbanks, Alaska as a School Coach during the Fall Semester and then spending the second semester researching and writing my *White Privilege and Critical Pedagogy* course for the Spring 2006 semester. The die was cast. I would be off for Fairbanks in August and a voyage into the unknown.

Chapter 23

Alaska

In the spring of 2004 I traded in my ten-year-old, black Toyota Celica for a brand-new, five-speed, black *RAV-4,* in preparation for the trip to Fairbanks. Because of costs, I didn't spring for 4-wheel drive, hoping for the best, as Alaska's winter would set in by late September. The plan was to visit my mother and brother in Stroudsburg, PA and then head West/Northwest, leaving on Saturday, August 7th. The itinerary was: Stroudsburg to Toledo (OH), Toledo to Wisconsin Dells (WI), Wisconsin Dells to Winnipeg (Manitoba), Winnipeg to Saskatoon (Saskatchewan), Saskatoon to Dawson Creek (B.C.), Dawson Creek to Watson Lake (Yukon Terr.), Watson Lake to Whitehorse (Yukon), Whitehorse to Beaver Creek (Yukon), Beaver Creek to Fairbanks, Alaska. 4,168.5 miles (according to AAA) in 9 days. Back in August of 1970, Gil Schaeffer and I (with several other folks) drove from San Francisco to Bay Shore, New York in *four days,* with somebody at the wheel almost 24 hours a day. Needless to say, we didn't see much scenery and my only indelible memory of that trip is wending through *Independence Pass* in Colorado, seeing *far too many cars*, wrecked, and riddling the un-guard-railed mountainside. The trip to Fairbanks was more scenic and *extremely* educational.

The first couple of days were pretty routine, cruising through familiar farmlands in Pennsylvania, Ohio, and Indiana. Day Two, from Toledo to Wisconsin Dells, skirted around Chicago before arriving at "*The Waterpark Capital of the World,*" Wisconsin Dells, a big summer resort/gambling destination. On Day Three, the education began. Heading into Northern Wisconsin, more and more farms — corn and soybeans. What was *most* striking was *the soil*. It was *black* and *rich*, you could *smell* its fertility. The drive through northern Wisconsin, across Minnesota (around Minneapolis/St. Paul), and up along North Dakota's eastern border toward Canada (passing through Fargo and Grand Forks) was astounding for the sheer *amount of food* that was rising out of the earth. After passing into Canada, the drive from Winnipeg to Saskatoon was as fertile as the U.S. Great Plains, but this time the fields were covered, horizon-to-horizon, with plants bearing bright yellow flowers: *canola* (Canada is the world's largest exporter of canola, producing 20% of the *world* supply). Saskatoon to Dawson Creek (the only stop in British Columbia *and* the start of the *AlCan Highway*) meant moving into the Canadian Rockies and, approaching Edmonton (about 2200 feet above sea level) *the* darkest *storm clouds I had ever seen* came rolling directly over the mountaintops, right above the *AlCan*. It was genuinely frightening and, luckily, blew over with a brief but severe pelting of rain. Dawson Creek to Watson Lake led not only to the Yukon Territory but also to the *SignPost Forest*. As described on the *explorenorth.com* website:

One of the most famous of the landmarks along the Alaska Highway was started by a homesick GI in 1942 and is now one of the attractions which make Watson Lake, at Kilometer 980 of the highway (Historic Mile 635), a must-stop. And you can even add your own sign to the over 72,000 already there!

Having no prior knowledge about the *SignPost Forest*, it was quite something to stumble upon while rumbling along the AlCan Highway.

After Watson Lake came *Whitehorse*, set right along the Yukon River. The town is named for the River's surging rapids, which early gold-rush settlers thought resembled "the manes of charging white horses"(*www.yukoninfo.com*). My concern, looking at the Yukon River, was to not let Jack get anywhere close to it. Those surging rapids made me think if Jack somehow went into that river, his next stop would be the Bering Sea. The town itself had seen better days and marked the first of many, from the Canadian Yukon Territory all the way to Fairbanks, which were clearly struggling. The last stop in Canada was a tiny place called Beaver Creek, the westernmost town in the Yukon Territory (population 93), only 17.8 miles from the U.S. border. Early on the morning of August 15th (my mother's birthday!) the sun was up (it's a "Land of the Midnight Sun" scene at that point in summer) and Fairbanks was "only" 317 miles of highway (5 & a half hours) away. Arriving in the early afternoon, I headed for Ester — a village of 2400 in the Fairbanks North Star Borough — where one of the teachers at the *Howard Luke Academy*, Cindy Caserta, and her husband, "Cajun" Bob Thoms (a highly decorated Vietnam vet), lived. They would kindly be putting me up until I found my own place. And that's when my *Alaska Education* began in earnest.

Chapter 24

Fairbanks

Fairbanks is a city in the *Fairbanks North Star Borough*, a district comprised of 7,444 square miles. That's larger than Connecticut and Rhode Island combined. I bring this up because high school students who live in the *Fairbanks North Star Borough*, no matter *how far* from the *city*, have to attend high school there, which means there are dormitories for students from those villages in the far reaches of the Borough, creating an odd teaching/learning dynamic for anyone used to working in a community-based system.

Even though Fairbanks is a city, the population in 2004 was only 82,000. There was *one* eleven story building. That was the skyline. There are also *two* army bases in the Borough, Fort Wainwright and Fort Greely, as well as Eielson Air Force base. This explained why I saw a surprising number of African Americans within my first few days living in Fairbanks (I hadn't expected to see *any* Black people in Alaska). Within those first few days, before any work for school began, temperatures were in the low to mid 70's, with a soothing warm breeze. Fairbanks sits north of the Alaska Range and south of the Brooks Range, in the Tanana Valley. As the *Alaska Mapbook* 2003 said about the city:

> *Fairbanks is situated in the heart of the Tanana Valley with the Alaska Range to the south and the gold-bearing hills to the north. It is still, in spirit, a frontier town.*

There was also about 20 hours of *daylight* during the third week of August, which was disorienting, to say the least. I had to wait until later in the fall to see the Northern Lights (they can be seen 243 days a year in Fairbanks). *Everything* was *new* in this environment. Like the afternoon I was driving back to Cindy's and Cajun Bob's from school and, just after the paved road became a dusty dirt street, I looked up to see a *moose* standing in the road. His front legs were in what would have been the oncoming lane of traffic and his rear legs were in my lane. And he wasn't going anywhere. Wisely, as it turned out, I stopped dead, about 50 yards away and waited until he decided to clop off into the woods. When I got back to Cindy's and Bob's, "Cajun" told me it was a good thing I stopped — moose were known to charge an oncoming auto — and the moose seldom lost those encounters. *Welcome to Fairbanks!*

Fairbanks is, as the *Mapbook* noted, a *frontier* town. Even in 2004, you had people not only living "off the grid" regarding *electricity*, you had citizens of *Fairbanks* who were off any *water* grid. If you go to *https://www.myfairbankshome.com* you'll find a blog post entitled: *How is the water supply different in Fairbanks, Alaska?* It starts by saying, "*A large portion of homes in Fairbanks and North Pole, AK are not connected to city water, sewer, natural gas, or anything else for that matter."* The author, Brian Stoltz, explains that folks in the area get water from:

> *City Water (a delivered public utility), Private Well (expensive!), Water Delivery (500-4000 gallon tanks/ cisterns filled by the Water Wagon Company), Haul Your Own Water (this requires you have a huge tank on your truck & 'there are several bulk water fill stations around town' where you can 'fill up.'); and Water? Not Here ("Surprisingly enough there are a number of homes in Fairbanks and North Pole that do not have water - more affectionately referred to as Dry Cabins. Most people who live in dry cabins use outhouses, shower at work or school, and drink water from 5-gallon camping containers. Definitely a different lifestyle, but one that is fully embraced up here in the Far North!").*

If you watch any of those Alaska reality shows (*Life Below Zero, Alaska State Troopers, Buying Alaska, Ax Men, Ice Road Truckers*) I can vouch for their authenticity. I quickly realized I was living in a *different world*. My previous weeklong consulting visits, where I stayed in nice hotels and basically only went to *Howard Luke Academy*, Cindy's & Bob's, and Greg & Jane Sandstrom's houses, did not *at all* prepare me for *real life* in a frontier town. Having been there in January (where the *average temperature* is *minus-4* degrees!) and experienced a couple of minus-33-degree days, I thought I was ready for the *Full Monty*. I wasn't.

When I finally got my own place, after about 10 days of living at Cindy's and Bob's, I also became more aware of the *frontier town* gun culture, too. As Bob dropped me off, after driving me around town in his pickup truck to buy

RIGHT TIME, RIGHT PLACES

furniture for my new apartment (from second-hand stores). he told me to open the glove compartment. I did, and there was a 45-caliber automatic pistol. "You can take that if you want," Bob said, "Everybody's got one, you might need it" (or something to that affect!). We had already ATV'ed into the back woods to do some target shooting with Bob's impressive 50 caliber Smith & Wesson revolver (a gift from his Vietnam platoon), so he knew I wasn't much of a shot. Nonetheless, Cajun generously offered me the pistol, "just to have" on hand. I declined but surely knew I now lived in the *wild west*.

It took a little over a week to find my own place. There was a unit available in a home, a downstairs apartment. It had one-bedroom, a kitchen, a living area, a full bath and its own side-door entrance. An added benefit was that it had an entrance through the two-car garage which sat below the main living quarters. I had already wired my engine block with a heater (you see cars all over Fairbanks with electrical cords sticking out of their front grills, attached to hitching post/electrical outlets, to prevent the blocks from freezing.) but having a *garage* was a huge luxury. There was also a fenced in back yard (with its requisite *two* cars up on blocks: an old Camaro and a rusting Buick) for Jack, another bonus. The neighborhood was close to the *Howard Luke Academy* (I could come home for lunch and take Jack for a walk) and was composed of the usual patchwork of Fairbanks architecture, running from new, *lower-48* stylish homes, to classic White Trash shacks and doublewides. Every other yard seemed to have an abandoned car or two up on cinder blocks and there certainly wasn't any landscaping— (there's snow on the ground from September through early April, followed by two months of mud season). By late September there was two feet of snow, much to Jack's delight! Our walks in the knee-deep snow made me feel like a *real* Alaskan.

To give you some idea of what it was like, living in Fairbanks in August, September, and October of 2004, here are headlines, sub-heads, and paragraphs from the *Fairbanks Daily News-Miner (The Voice of Interior Alaska since 1903)*. The Friday, August 27, 2004 "Outdoors" section featured:

> *Essential Alaska Skills – Seven Things every Alaskan who ventures into the outdoors should know how to do. The seven items were: How to Fillet a Fish; How to Build a Fire; How to Build a Shelter; How to Read a River; How to Deal with a Bear; How to Perform First Aid; and How to Use an Ice Ax.*

While I had *no intention* of spending *any* time in the Great Outdoors, this article was very educational, increasing my appreciation for those Alaskans who were masters of these skills.

The September 2nd *Daily News-Miner* featured a front-page headline that shouted: *Woman Loses Nose in Shootout with Troopers*. The opening paragraphs from staff writer Amanda Bohman read as follows:

> *Alaska State Troopers and a suicidal woman exchanged gunfire Tuesday night after a 6 ½ -hour standoff in Goldstream Valley, according to a statement from troopers. The woman, Margaret Mary Patrisso, 40, had her nose severed in the gunfight, said trooper spokesman Greg Wilkinson. No troopers were hit. Fairbanks Memorial Hospital declined to release information on Patrisso's condition at the woman's request.*

Even a jaded New Yorker was taken aback by that one.

The September 23rd front page featured a photo to accompany this curious headline: *Exotic critter eludes capture.* The sub-head stated: *Fairbanks woman working on a plan to rescue free-roaming llama cousin.* The picture showed a cute, white *alpaca* walking across the top of Chena Dome, "about 60 miles east of town." No one knew how the *alpaca* had gotten there, but it was first spotted on Labor Day weekend. This proved to be an ongoing story.

The front page of the Sunday, September 26th edition of the *Daily News-Miner* ran an Associated Press story from Anchorage: Battling bull moose die with antlers interlocked.

> *The carcasses of two bull moose that died with their antlers locked in battle have been discovered near the University of Alaska Anchorage. They were found Friday in a stand of black spruce 50 feet from the parking lot of the university's arts building, two bulls in rut among the skinny trees with their antlers fused in a fatal tangle.*

It went on to graphically describe how the moose looked ("its tongue hanging out") as well as how strong moose antlers are. All quite educational for a city boy and, again, a headline you're unlikely to see in the *Lower 48*.

In the Local section of the September 26th edition there was a story about *Unsightly parasites in moose perplex hunters. But officials insistent meat still OK to eat.* To appreciate that headline/sub-head one needs to know that the 15-day moose hunting season was a *crucially important* part of Fairbanks culture. One moose can feed a family for a year. So, when Tim Mowry wrote:

> *Worried hunters have been showing up at the state Department of Fish and Game in Fairbanks with hunks of meat or organs infected with one of the three tapeworms that are typically found in moose and caribou around Alaska. And while they might not be appealing to the eye, according to officials they shouldn't offend the palate.*

The story was accompanied by a *color photo* of a "piece of moose lung with a cut open hydatid cyst" that was genuinely stomach-turning. Classic Alaska, classic Fairbanks.

Monday, September 27th featured a tragic headline: Wandering Alpaca found dead. Amanda Bohman's story told us that the alpaca was found by a "would-be" rescuer. "It's unknown how the alpaca was killed but the best guess is a bear." Remembering the photo of the adorable *alpaca* from September 23rd made this a particularly disturbing story.

The Sunday, October 3rd *Daily News-Miner* "Local" section led with this headline:

Wandering Alpaca was shot, officials say. Amanda Bohman quoted Jeanne Olson, the manager of the *Fairbanks North Star Borough* Animal Shelter saying: "*We found the entrance and exit holes. The bullet went completely through. I am sorry to report this because it certainly reveals the dark side of humanity.*"

Indeed. What made it worse, as you read the story, was that "*It's not illegal* (Olson said) *but that animal is not feral, and I know it was not attacking anybody.*" The story further revealed how the animal got there in the first place. Apparently, its owner was hiking around the Chena Dome, using the *alpaca* as a pack animal. When the animal "became stubborn and refused to continue down the trail" the owner simply left it! Welcome to Fairbanks.

Finally, the October 17th front page featured a bizarre photograph with this headline & sub-head: Wired Moose – Utility workers find bull suspended on power line near Pogo gold mine. As reported by the intrepid Tim Mowry:

> *In one of those only-in-Alaska stories that will shock even the sourest of sourdoughs, a trophy size bull moose was accidentally strung up in a power line under construction to the Teck Pogo gold mine southeast of Fairbanks. The moose apparently got its antlers tangled in the electrical wires before workers farther down the line pulled the line tight about two weeks ago.*
>
> *The moose was suspended 50 feet in the air when workers, recognizing something was wrong, backtracked and found it.*
>
> *The moose was alive when it was lowered to the ground but was later killed when official from the Department of Fish and Game decided against tranquilizing it to remove the wires because they were worried the moose, already stressed, would die and the meat would not be salvageable as a result of the drugs.*

There's a lot to unpack there but my question was: if that poor moose was "already stressed" why did they have to kill it? The answer, of course, is that a moose provides enough meat to *feed a family for a year*. The story went on explain that people thought the picture was Photoshopped, even though "Most Alaskans have seen pictures of bull moose with swing sets, tire swings, lawn chairs and Christmas lights tangled in their antlers this time of year" (mating season). Even having seen all that, folks were more than impressed with this latest bull moose photo and story. I was learning more and more by the day living in Fairbanks.

Chapter 25

More Fairbanks

Looking back on my time in Fairbanks I can see three distinct "Acts" to life there. Act One was the work at *Howard Luke Academy* with Greg and Cindy and the rest of the staff, as well as interaction with the *Fairbanks North Star Borough Department of Education*. Act Two was *weekends*, that time away from the school where steam was released. Finally, there was Act Three, the *process* of planning and executing my return to the *Lower 48*.

Howard Luke Academy

Howard Luke Academy was a small (100 to 120 students) 9 through 12 alternative high school. The *Fairbanks North Star School District* had about 14,000 students, K-12, with approximately 2500 in high school in 2004. Most went to *Lathrop* or *West Valley*, large comprehensive high schools with over 1,000 students each. Another chunk of students went to the vo-tech *Hutchison High School* and the remainder, the true *square pegs*, attended *Howard Luke Academy*. The school was named for an Athabascan Native elder, a champion *musher* (the state sport, dog-sled racing), and a genuine leader in advocating programs for the youth of Fairbanks. The staff at *HLA* was a dedicated group and, as I noted, were willing to consider new strategies to use with their students.

Initially, I was going to be the School Coach, observing classes, planning and team-teaching with staff members, as well as supporting Greg implementing changes in curriculum and assessment practices. As we started meeting and planning in mid-August, the Central Office (*every district* has one of these and they seldom seem to work *in the interest* of the schools) issued an edict about *budget cuts*. Greg suddenly had to decide between cutting (what he *and I* saw as)a key staff member *or* using my consulting fee to pay me as an *on-staff* Social Studies/ History teacher. Bye-bye School Coach, *hello* classroom-teaching-for-Bil. This was the first of a series of speed bumps and roadblocks we encountered in getting *HLA* off the ground in the fall of 2004.

There were a number of challenges at *Howard Luke Academy*. Despite being only 100 miles or so from the Arctic Circle, our school population had very similar characteristics to any *Lower 48* inner-city cohort. By that I mean: minority-majority (most of our students were Native Alaskan), poor preparation (re: literacy/numeracy), serious attendance problems, and widespread legal/domestic issues. Many came from the outer Villages which, once they were described to me, seemed to closely-resemble something we had in NYC: *the Projects*: that is, low-income, high-crime & violence, high substance abuse neighborhoods. Many of our students had *witnessed* incidents of violence and drug/substance abuse up-close and personally. Our problems as educators were compounded, as I saw it, by the fact that, as Autumn progressed, daylight became scarcer and, by mid-October, we weren't getting sunrise until 10 a.m., despite school starting at 8:00 a.m.. Students were straggling in late (if they showed up at all) and those who were on time were sleep-deprived. *Despite all that*, it was actually fun for me to be back in the classroom and, early in the semester, a *galvanizing* issue arose, creating a bond between me and the students.

For some reason, the *Fairbanks North Star School District* had decided that the Fall of 2004 was going to be the year it would *BAN smoking* on public school campuses. This would apply to students *and* teachers. As a highly addicted smoker, *I* would be affected by this ruling. My students, about 90% of whom were smokers, were up in arms about it. It was a perfect issue for me to introduce *democracy* to my Social Studies/History course. In classic rabble-rouser fashion, I pitched an idea to my kids: *Let's petition the School Board and make our case for creating a* Designated Smoking Area *on campus.* I convinced my charges that *if they could present their case* in persuasive fashion, they might get a Special Dispensation from the District Superintendent. They bought into the idea and attacked it full bore. We spent two weeks crafting our argument, writing our petition, practicing speeches (with a slideshow/Power Point) and arranging a meeting with the Superintendent at *HLA.* When the Big Day arrived and the Superintendent visited the school, my students were *spectacular.* They calmly and rationally explained how having a Designated Smoking Area at *HLA* would actually *improve the Learning Environment* ("We'll be more relaxed and open to learn.")! They presented statistics and "witness testimony," laying out pros and cons while lobbying for their cause. By the end of the meeting, the Superintendent, clearly impressed, told them she would seriously consider their proposal and let them know by the end of the week. She did — and we won! The students (and a number of teachers!) at *HLA* were given a Designated Smoking Area on the edge of our property, out by the trail that led to the Coffee Shop on Geist Road. The students (and I) were ecstatic, and they probably learned more about *citizenship* than I could have taught in any didactic lesson.

Here's what else I learned at *Howard Luke Academy*: I learned about salmon roe and I learned about Moose Season. Regarding the salmon roe: there was a yearly fall project at *HLA* involving local Native women setting up a Smoking Tent in the school's parking lot, bringing in about a half-dozen *huge* empty, topless oil drums and, literally, *hundreds of pounds* of Alaska Salmon. After setting up *butchering tables*, our students got to watch: #1) *how to* fillet a salmon; #2) *how to* prepare it for smoking; and #3) *how to* smoke it in those empty oil drums, preserving it as food for the winter. What *I learned* was that the salmon roe, *piled in huge red pyramids at the end of the butchering tables*, was as delicious as *caviar* — and was being given away *for free*. Bring on the Tupperware!

Moose Season is 15 days long and is, essentially, a *religious* holiday in the *Fairbanks North Star Borough*. Our school population (students *and* teachers) was reduced by 50% during the two weeks of Moose Season. As I've noted, the meat from a moose can *last a year* for a family. Therefore, for many of our students, it was *crucial* that their family bag a moose. Any moose killing outside the designated season was *illegal* and incurred *severe penalties* (which could include *jail* time). So, the school emptied out for almost two weeks. Being a naïve *Lower-48-er*, I thought it would be easy to bag a moose, as they seemed more than plentiful. Whenever I was at Cindy's and Cajun Bob's, *Minnie Moose*, a huge cow, would amble into their yard to graze. Even our noisy presence on their balcony porch didn't scare her away. One morning, driving to *HLA* along Geist Road in my RAV-4, I heard a distinct *clip-clop-clip-clop*. Looking in my sideview mirror, there was a huge bull moose trotting along the highway *right next to my vehicle!* He pulled even with me (his neck and head were easily as high as my window seat in the car) and, as I turned right on to Loftus Road, toward *HLA*, he clip-clopped left, heading toward the University of Alaska, Fairbanks, just up the hill across the street, as if he were late for a class. Based on *Minnie* and my Geist Road encounter, as well as the earlier experience on the dirt road in Ester, I figured moose were *everywhere* and would be easy to hunt. Apparently, the moose know when they are "in season" and make themselves scarce because, as I discovered, *almost no one* actually gets a moose during the season.

There was one other thing I learned when I was teaching at *Howard Luke Academy* and that was about gender inequality. Alaska is the only state in the Union, I believe, in which *men outnumber women.* The state statistic is about 52% to 48% but *everyone* in Fairbanks assured me that the numbers in the *Fairbanks North Star Borough* was more like 10 to 1, male/female. It sure looked that way in my classrooms. Our staff was a bit closer to the 52%/48% stat, but our female assistant principal wore a tee-shirt that summed it all up. Emblazoned on the front of her shirt was this: *The Odds are Good, But the Goods are Odd.* Indeed, the women on the staff vouched for the fact that, while the numbers were good *statistically*, the *quality* of the "product" was straight from an *Odd Lots* catalogue!

Chapter 26

True North

Weekends

There are things about living in Fairbanks that you could tell people but, ultimately, it boils down to one of those "you have to be there to appreciate it" experiences. For example, Fairbanks is *FOUR* time zones away from the East Coast of the *Lower 48*. On the surface, that may not seem like a big deal, but it is. If all your friends and family live on the East Coast, you have to *always* remember the time difference. No impulsive calls at 7 or 8 p.m., Fairbanks-time. More significantly, the time difference really effects *watching sports*, and that's where this story begins.

When I stayed at Cindy's and Cajun Bob's in August the three of us realized we had a number of commonalities, and a great friendship evolved as a result. On the surface, you probably couldn't have put three more different people together. Cindy grew up in Columbus, Ohio, a neighbor of New York Yankees outfielder Paul O'Neill, and wended her way through other professions before becoming a (very good) secondary English teacher. Cajun Bob was a Silver Star recipient (*the United States Armed Forces' third-highest personal decoration for valor in combat. The Silver Star Medal is awarded primarily to members of the United States Armed Forces for gallantry in action against an enemy of the United States. Wikipedia*), a guy with *multiple* Purple Hearts, a genuine Vietnam War *hero* from Baton Rouge, Louisiana, with a gravelly voice that makes Sam Elliott's pale. And here I was, the New York City/suburban guy from the East Coast. But there were several things we all loved, leading to a strong bond. #1 -*Dogs*. Cindy and Cajun had a house full of dogs (and cats). Jack immediately became part of their pack. #2 - *Food*. We loved to cook and eat! #3 - *The Blues*. All three of us were *huge* fans of the blues and could spend hours listening to, and talking about, the music. #4 - *Football*. Both Cindy and Cajun Bob were big college *and* pro football fans (Cindy, coming from Columbus, was a HUGE Ohio State rooter), as was I, at that time. And finally, #5, Cajun and I were particularly fond of Grey Goose vodka, and there was always some in their freezer. Bob taught me to creatively mix it with Diet Coke, a bizarre but oddly satisfying treat.

If you combine the dogs, food, blues, football, and vodka, what do you get? Great weekends! Adding to the fun, we were often joined by Jane and Greg Sandstrom, and sometimes went to their place, where Jack had two other big dog buddies. I'm not sure who started to call us "The Group W Bench," but we all thought it was appropriate. If you're not familiar with Arlo Guthrie's classic song, *Alice's Restaurant*, the singer/songwriter explains how, during his U.S. Army Induction physical, he admitted being convicted of a crime and, as such, he "was sent to the '*Group W*' bench to file for a moral waiver." The other convicts ("mother-rapers... father-stabbers... father-rapers") were initially put off that his conviction had been for *littering* but accepted him when he added "and creating a nuisance." (Wikipedia) Looking at each other, we believed we were an equally motley collection of *less-than* felons and, like Guthrie, were *Group W Bench* material, needing moral waivers. We even had tee shirts made and snapped a "team" photo before I left Fairbanks.

Because college football games began at noon, East Coast time, it meant I was at Cindy's and Bob's house at 7:30 a.m. (Fairbanks time) Saturday mornings. We would start cooking and drinking, listening to the blues & smoking cigarettes, while the *pre-game* shows rolled out. Before the snow hit, the dogs would be out in the yard/woods, running around and playing. One day, we heard ferocious barking from Jack, which was unusual. His deep, loud bass of a bark penetrated the music in the kitchen and we ran out on to the second-floor porch to see what was going on. With our clear view of the driveway, which sloped down to the house and parking lot, we could see a *very large* bull moose standing at the top of the hill, looking down. Jack was about halfway up the driveway, clearly trying to let the moose know this was *his* territory. Unfazed, the moose, in a very measured, steady stride, headed down the driveway. In what can only be described as a cartoon leap, Jack sprang up and pivoted, in one motion, hightailing it into the garage until the moose reached the bottom of the driveway and turned left, into the woods. Cautiously, the big black lab came out of the garage and looked around, as if asking, "Did anybody else see that *huge dog* that chased me?"

While the weather was still warm, and before football season started, Cindy and Cajun Bob taught me how to drive an ATV (all-terrain vehicle) and we would head off on narrow trails into the woods to target shoot. Bob had been given a beautiful, long-barreled .50 caliber Smith and Wesson revolver at a recent reunion of his platoon. The gun had significant kick for a pistol and I was determined to learn how to shoot it accurately (I never succeeded). Once the snows came, my ATV training easily translated into Snowmobile driving and it was great fun careening around the roads and trails of Ester, trying to outrun the cold. But most of our time was spent indoors, watching lots of football, eating and drinking and listening to the blues.

One week, Cindy came up to me at *Howard Luke Academy* and said, "Bob needs you to head over to our place right after school, he needs your help." Without asking any questions, I picked up Jack after school and headed out to their place. When I arrived, I learned what the "something" was. Our television viewing was dependent on the two *huge* satellite dishes in the front yard of Cindy's and Bob's house. You can't get cable in Alaska because the ground is frozen and the distances are too great to run overhead lines (which would also be susceptible to wind, snow, and ice damage). Everyone has a Dish. It seems that the previous evening one of the local moose, maybe it was Minnie, needed to scratch his/her back and used Cindy's and Bob's satellite dish as the scratching post, knocking it out of alignment and ruining our reception! In what probably could have been developed as a comedy sketch, Bob and I re-aligned the dish thusly: he went out in the yard, with pliers and a wrench, and began to re-position the dish while I stood in the doorway to the porch, staring at the tv screen in the living room, relaying the condition of reception on the television. I gained a genuine appreciation that day for how *finely-tuned* a satellite dish must be to receive a *clear* signal from space and transmit it, *equally clearly*, to a living in room in Ester, Alaska. Happily, we lined it up and were ready for football on Saturday.

One other notable incident from that time was an evening, after the football games were over, when Cajun and I, for whatever reason, decided it would be *fun* to go out on the porch and do some target shooting (in relative darkness) with the big Smith and Wesson pistol. Needless to say, we had consumed a significant amount of Grey Goose by that hour and were not our steadiest. Nonetheless, we thought doing a little target shooting would be a fine way to cap the day off. We were out on the porch and Cajun took a few shots, hitting a tree stump out in the yard. He handed me the pistol. I lined up my aim and fired, totally forgetting to *lock* my elbows to resist the recoil of the gun. Sure enough, the next thing I knew, the hammer of that pistol was stuck in my left cheek, right next to my nose! I pulled the gun away and blood shot out. Cajun Bob, battlefield veteran, looked at me and, in that great gravelly voice, said, "Damn it, Willie, you're gonna need stitches for that." Bouncing up, I said, "Ah, c'mon, Cajun. We can put this back together with some butterfly band-aids. Get the First-Aid kit." Bob was probably right, but there was no way I was heading to a hospital on a cold Alaska night. We eased the bleeding, put on the butterflies, covered them with a larger patch, and I was good to go. I can still feel a bump on my cheek, right where it meets my nose, a fond memory of my time in Fairbanks.

Heading Home

At the end of the First Quarter of school at *Howard Luke Academy*, I was headed back to the East Coast. Easier said than done. There would be no driving back, as the AlCan highway was closed in winter, impassable due to snow. I had to arrange for my car to be *shipped back* to New England. Air travel had to be arranged, which meant I needed to find a crate big enough for Jack and arrange for him to be on the plane, in the cargo hold. I was particularly concerned about that because, when I lived in Providence, I used to regularly meet a couple who walked their Rescue greyhound in my neighborhood. Our dogs would play while we chatted and they related a story about going to Europe (he was German) and bringing the dog with them. They had to change planes in London. When they got to Hamburg, they discovered their dog had been shipped to *Venice*. He was put on the *wrong plane*. That story reverberated in my mind as I brought Jack, in his crate, to the check-in at Fairbanks airport. We were going to have to change planes in Seattle and I wanted assurances he'd be on the Seattle to Boston flight *with me*. I was told not to worry.

When we got to Seattle, there was supposed to be a little paw-print sticker on my tray table indicating *my dog* was in the cargo hold. There was *no* sticker. I marched up to the front of the cabin and informed the flight attendant I would not sit down until I *knew, for sure,* my dog was on the plane. It was about a half-hour before our scheduled departure, so she said she'd personally head down to take a look. Within a few minutes she was back and told me, "Yes, there are several dogs in crates in the cargo hold." "Fine," I said, "but I want to know if *my* dog is one of them. His name is on the crate. Please go back and let me know if he's there." I told her he was a Black Lab. When she returned, she was all smiles. "*Jack* is on the plane," she assured me, and I returned to my seat.

By the time we arrived at Logan Airport, where my old friend Jamie Jacobs was picking us up, we had spent 12 hours on planes. I couldn't imagine how Jack was and I was worried. After picking up my luggage I went to the loading dock where dog crates were delivered. Jack's, of course, was the *last* to come out. I was informed that I couldn't let him out *inside* the terminal (it was after 9/11) because he might distract or engage with the German Shepherds who were *on duty*. We got a palette-cart, loaded the crate onto it, and rolled Jack *outside* the terminal, where I could finally release him. He climbed out of the crate, stretched a bit, walked over to a nearby, short shrub, lifted his leg, and peed a long stream, marking his spot. He then ambled back over to me and Jamie and sat down, as if to say, "Where we headed now?"

We loaded our stuff (bags and crate) into Jamie's truck and headed to his place for the night. The northern lights, the freezing cold, the whole Alaska experience, was now behind us, and our next adventures would be back in Providence, at Brown.

Chapter 27

Is there Life after Alaska?

Returning to Providence in the spring of 2005 I had to find a new abode. There was a 3X5 card on the North Main Street *Whole Foods* Community Bulletin Board, advertising a place on the South Side of Providence, not far from the Roger Williams Park and Zoo. My previous apartment, on Humboldt Street, was on the tony East Side (my next-door neighbor was the then-State Attorney General, now-U.S. Senator, Sheldon Whitehouse) and a stone's throw from the Education Department. After being away for an academic year, I was feeling a need for a change and I checked out the South Side place. It was beautiful! Half of a small house, my new home was the upstairs of a (former) single-family dwelling. With two ample bedrooms, a bathroom (with a tub raised on lion's feet) a *full* kitchen, and a nice sized living room — it was more than I needed and the price was right. There were windows all around, a driveway to park the RAV-4 in and a very big front yard, bordered by 8-foot hedges along the street . The landlord, Mark Fonseca, lived around the corner and was a very nice guy. When I pitched the idea of planting a vege-table garden in the front yard he not only said "yes" but also *loaned me* a roto-tiller to turn the soil. By the time we started Brown Summer High School in late June 2005, Jack and I were living happily on Roger Williams Avenue in South Providence.

Back at Brown

Resumption of duties at Brown were expanded upon my return. Eileen Landay had (kind of) retired (she was still over-seeing the Arts/Literacy Program), so I was now the "Czar" of Brown Summer High School (the Faculty advisor). Two new-ly-minted M.A.T.s were the Co-Principals and ran the day-to-day operations. We also had a new Department Chair, John Tyler, who was not as sympathetic to the Teacher Ed Program as Cynthia Garcia-Coll had been. Larry Wakeford, Laura Snyder (Eileen's replacement), Polly Ulichny, Carin Algava, and I be-came *very sensitive* to the cold shoulder we believed the Teacher Ed Program was receiving, while watching the "Policy" side of the Department become ascendant. Nonetheless, we charged ahead and Brown Summer High School was as successful as ever. I continued to facilitate "Methods of Teaching" on Wednesday afternoons, advise my student-teachers regarding their fall or spring teaching assignments, and observe & de-brief their BSHS classes. Come Fall, I would be teaching *ED 101* while observing student teachers and running the *Analysis of Teaching* seminar. Spring semester would see the first iter-ation of the *White Privilege and Critical Pedagogy* undergrad-uate seminar, as my student-teachers switched places and half entered classrooms as teachers, with the other half resuming their academic studies.

Amid all this, I was wrestling with withdrawal from Alaska, particularly the very heavy drinking habit I had acquired. In December, over *Winter Break*, I admitted myself to Butler Hospital and did an intensive *rehabilitation program*, which continued with regular AA meetings for the rest of my time at Brown. Knowing I have an *addictive personality* has done nothing, throughout my life, to deter me from serious bouts of substance abuse. The time spent at Butler was definitely needed and helpful. I can probably be thankful it led to a much healthier life since 2005. Regarding my teaching that Fall: I don't think my students suffered from my bad habits, but it certainly did *intrude* on my life with my colleagues, which is what led to the Butler stay. While falling short of an *intervention*, it was made clear to me I needed to clean up my act.

Conferences

Beyond my teaching and observing at Brown during this time, there were several *Conferences* that proved very positive, regarding continuing professional growth. One was the annual *Coalition of Essential Schools* Fall Forum in Chicago in 2006, and the other was the annual *Pedagogy and Theater of the Oppressed* Conference in Minneapolis in the Spring of 2006. The third, and most meaningful, was a conference I organized, with Kurt Wooton, who directed the Arts/Literacy Program, a brainchild of Eileen Landay. The *No Teacher Left Behind* conference was held at Brown and its organizing and execution saw some of my best work.

CES FALL FORUM 2006

The Chicago Fall Forum was an energetic, raucous affair that brought together a *host* of my favorite *CES* educators, colleagues, former students, and luminaries I had great respect for. In four short days my time was filled with workshops, spontaneous & intense meetings, as well as some great blues music!. Whenever I visited Chicago during my consulting/Brown years (1993 to 2007) I stayed at the *House of Blues* hotel, a unique setting, centrally located. The rooms were decorated as if by a New Orleans *Madam*, with garish colors, striped wallpaper, and very interesting folk art. The hotel was attached to a *House of Blues* nightclub, so there was often great music available on the club's two stages. Chicago, of course, has countless music venues (particularly blues clubs) and I was lucky enough to find time to stop into *Sweet Home, Chicago, Buddy Guy's,* or *The Checkerboard Lounge* whenever I was in town, guaranteeing I'd get my fill of great, *real* Chicago blues.

That year's Fall Forum was like a Who's-Who of Education stars for me. Ted and Nancy Sizer were there, of course, as was Deborah Meier (the *Grande Dame* of our Reform Movement). Glenn Singleton (whose *Courageous Conversations* is must-read) and Linda Darling-Hammond. I was excited to reconnect with my old Citibank colleague, Steve Cantrell, who now lived in nearby Naperville, IL. Aside from Steve, Jennifer Prileson, another original Citibanker was there, along with an array of my former UTEP/MAT students: Mary Finn, Rachel Bello, Chris Magnuson, Dina Blum, Charlie Plant, the list goes on. The entire event was a cross between *the best professional development* session and a wonderful class reunion. It not only upped my game, regarding thinking about teaching/learning and school change, but it also *energized* me, as only contact with beloved and inspiring people can.

Pedagogy and Theater of the Oppressed Conference

I had already attended a PTO conference in Omaha, Nebraska, *before* my Alaskan journey and found it informative, if not inspiring. Nonetheless, when the 2006 PTO conference announced Augusto Boal was actually going to *attend* and *present his ideas* to the collected throng, I had to go. Boal was a disciple of the late Paolo Freire (1921-1997) and had applied the *pedagogy of the oppressed* principles to *theater*, making an Art out of what began as "guerrilla theater" in the 60s. As explained in *Wikipedia:*

> *Boal's techniques use theatre as means of promoting social and political change in alignment originally with radical left politics and later with center left ideology. In the Theatre of the Oppressed, the audience becomes active, such that as "spect-actors" they explore, show, analyze and transform the reality in which they are living.*

It is a fascinating application of Freire's philosophy, and extremely powerful when seen at work. Boal's presence alone made the trip to Minneapolis worthwhile. A bonus, when I got there, was the opportunity to spend quality time with UMass-Boston professor Donaldo Macedo, one of the foremost experts on critical pedagogical theory and multicultural education in the U.S. He provided excellent insight into, and suggestions for, the *White Privilege & Critical Pedagogy* course. I also got to meet, and spend time with, Jimmy Santiago Baca, a poet whose cultural critiques (within his writing) are searing, lyrical, and revelatory. Already familiar with Baca's work, it was thrilling to hear him discuss his process for writing (something I later incorporated when teaching in NYC) and its *vital* connection to his lived experience. Boal's presentation capped off a great conference and I returned to Providence with a "head full of ideas" (apologies to Bob Dylan/*Maggie's Farm*).

No Teacher Left Behind

It happened that in the Winter of 2007, the Rhode Island Department of Education notified the Teacher Preparation schools in Rhode Island (there were eight) of a Federal "*Teacher Quality Enhancement Partnership Grant*" (known as *RITER* – Rhode Island Teacher Education Renewal). It was a bloc of money that would be divided among the programs *but* each had to *show* how the funds would go toward *improving teacher quality* in the state of Rhode Island. My idea was simple: "Let's have a conference — and call it 'No Teacher Left Behind.'" Classically Johnson-glib (it was a play on W. Bush's "No Child Left Behind" program) but I did have substantial ideas to go with the "clever" title .

Not only did we recruit several of the other programs to throw in with us, but Eileen Landay, who, as I kept telling her, was "retired but not gone," was overseeing the *Arts/Literacy* program she helped create and offered to share sponsorship. Kurt Wooton, the Director of Arts/Lit, and always a fount of ideas, happily joined. Through *Arts/Lit*, more funds were secured from *the Nellie May Foundation* and *The National Endowment for the Arts*. We had the funding, now we had to *create* our conference.

Kurt and I were the co-chairs and stated, in our "Welcome" note in the Program, that this was an unabashedly *progressive* conference focused on school reform/change. We were giving a Lifetime Achievement Award to Ted Sizer and our Keynote Speaker was Deborah Meier, both giants in the field of Progressive Education. Our conference design was simple: a Friday night Opening Reception, Keynote, and Presentation to Ted from 4 p.m. to 7:30. On Saturday, we offered morning workshops (26 from 8:45 to 10:45 a.m.) and afternoon workshops (22 from 1:15 to 3:15 p.m.) with a Panel Discussion about Arts/Literacy for the hour before lunch (11:00 a.m.-12:00). 3:30 to 4:00 p.m. was a closing video (of workshops & roundtables in action) and a celebration. The offerings were all *coded* in the program, to indicate whether they were for elementary or secondary *and* whether they were Roundtables or Workshops. We also coded Arts/Literacy, Content/Subject Areas, Technology, Diversity, and Induction/ Retention, so people could really get the most bang for their buck (not that anyone was paying *anything*, that was part of the conference's appeal). Hundreds of teachers and administrators attended and it proved a wonderfully successful event. Having run NCREST's "Assessment Fairs" back in the 1990s, I was happy to see that I could still organize and execute a decent conference (with a great deal of Kurt's help and the *exhaustive hard work* of Meg Springer — our RITER grant coordinator).

While all this was going well, there were problems emerging in the Education Department at Brown, problems that would ultimately lead to my departure.

Chapter 28

The Dark End of the Street

Life was good at 141 Roger Williams Avenue. My vegetable garden was thriving. Green beans, zucchini, several kinds of lettuce, peppers, corn, parsley, oregano, and tomatoes, and tomatoes, and *more* tomatoes. I had a grill and a smoker for making *real* barbecue. Throughout the summer, until early fall, the food and fun were plentiful. Come spring, the garden was re-tilled and started anew. There is something very satisfying about growing food, aside from the obvious nutritional rewards. Getting up early and watering the garden, coming home in the evening and watering the garden becomes a meditative act. Nurturing the plants so they could, in turn, nurture you. There's a primal quality to it all in a very simple, gratifying sense.

The one drawback of the garden had to do with living in a city. I didn't have to worry about deer or even rabbits getting into my crops. No, the varmints destroying my garden were *rats*! Big, fat *city* rats. My neighbor, Glen, also had a garden and was experiencing the same problem. We'd come out in the morning and find our tomatoes, particularly, were being eaten in shockingly large quantities. Our solution was primitive and simple: spring traps — the kind that snap with ferocity and finality, immediately breaking the neck or spine of the trespasser. It *was* grotesque, seeing each other in the morning, clutching big, black Glad bags, harvesting the night's collection of executed rats and disposing of them in the garbage (surely breaking all kinds of health codes). Word must have spread throughout the rat community, though, because our problem rapidly subsided and, eventually, ceased altogether. Our tomatoes, once again, thrived.

Living near Roger Williams Park was great for Jack. There were acres and acres of open lawns, with man-made ponds and lakes everywhere. Jack chased squirrels to his heart's content, and occasionally took off after various waterfowl, which inevitably led to his failing to brake at the water's edge. I often had to bail him out of the ponds, in particular, because they were bounded by concrete walls which the 120-pound Lab couldn't negotiate on his own. It took a solid grip on his scruff and a big pull from well-planted legs to extricate Jack from the water. And he never learned. About every other week I'd be bailing him out again. Nonetheless, the time in Roger Williams Park was relaxed fun for the dog and me.

Things at the Ed Department were not nearly as much fun. While my classes were going well and my student-teachers were doing fine, I was getting a clear lesson in the *realpolitik* of the University. John Tyler had received a vote of "no confidence" from the Department when it was time to renew his Chairmanship. While I liked John personally, he reduced decision-making to the numbers (he was an economist by training) and seemed to harbor a belief that the Teacher Ed Program was *soft*, whereas *Policy* in education matters was where *real differences* were made. John's ouster as Chair didn't help us, though. In his place, the University appointed a newly acquired Professor (from the University of Chicago), Ken Wong, who was specifically brought in to start an *Urban Education Policy* Master's Degree program.

The University had recently done some Institutional Soul-Searching and produced a report about *Slavery and Justice*, recounting Brown's complicity in America's Original Sin. The Chair of the S&J committee, Jim Campbell, a Professor of American Civilization/Africana Studies/History, was someone I knew and he interviewed me, asking what recommendations I would make to the University regarding how the Education Department might support Brown's attempt to make up for its past. What appeared in the final report were the following recommendations:

- *increase funding to Brown's Masters of Arts in Teaching Program, including full tuition waivers for students who commit themselves to working for at least three years in local public schools;*
- *invest substantial resources, including dedicated faculty positions, in the new Urban Education Policy Program, with an eye to establishing Brown as a national leader in this vital field.*

The first recommendation was never implemented. The second one was. And that tells the story as far as *where* the Education Department was headed. More and more, with Ken Wong as Chair, we saw the Department assertively moving in the direction of *Policy* and *away from* Practice. The *UEP* program was the new darling of the University's Administration and, because Ken had a significant national reputation, they were happy to herald their commitment to Education (even

215

though it was only a commitment to *Policy* and *not* to teaching/ learning *in classrooms).*

This was a familiar enemy for me. Going back to the early 1990s, when *Teach for America* first reared its ugly head, I was wary of *policy makers* proposing solutions for education. The *Coalition's* strength was that it supported bottom-up reform, coming from classroom teachers and moving *up* to administration and district levels. *Policy reform* is *not only* inherently *top-down* but also made by people *who very often have never spent one-minute teaching students in a classroom setting.* It is not unlike the way too many school districts are run by an elected Board of Education, featuring an array of dentists, businesspeople, car salesmen, and other non-educators, who are chosen to *lead* a multi-million-dollar enterprise and are charged with *educating our children.* It is no wonder our secondary schools look like they did in 192o. It's not that I'd don't believe *policy* is important, it is. I just don't believe in conducting educational business when it's being led by people who have *little to no* experience in the day-to-day mechanics of schooling. That's where Brown University was headed, full speed, by 2006-2007. Despite being happy with my students and my classes, despite enjoying living at 141 Roger Williams Avenue with my garden and the nearby park I, once again, sensed it was time to move. And that's when an interesting opportunity appeared on my horizon.

Yale?

It happened that as the Education Department at Brown was moving more and more in the direction of *Policy,* and away from *Practice,* I ran across an advertisement for an opening in the *Yale Urban Education Program.* I had a vague recollection about a *Yale Alumni Magazine* piece announcing the start of the program in 2005. It was a collaboration with the New Haven public schools. Yale graduate students would receive a *tuition-free* two-year Master's degree in exchange for committing to teach for at least three years in the New Haven schools. The program needed a *Field Supervisor*, someone over-seeing the undergraduate student teachers who were working toward public school certification (like Brown's *UTEPs*). It seemed like the perfect opportunity for me to leave Brown but continue my work as a Teacher Educator, this time back in the place where my passion for teaching began.

I told my colleagues I was applying for the job (much to their chagrin) and drove to New Haven for the interview. There I met the Director of the Urban Education Program, Jack Gillette, and the Assistant Director, Linda Cole-Taylor. My interview was conducted by those two, plus several members of their current teaching cohort. It all went swimmingly and, before I left, Jack took me aside to ask if I *really* wanted to do this job. After all, he pointed out, it was *not* a faculty position (like the one I had at Brown) and there would be a significant decrease in salary. I asked if I'd be able to continue consulting while doing the *Field Supervisor* job and Jack said that would not be a problem. "Then, I'm good to go, "I told him. By the time I was back in Providence I had a job at Yale, starting in late August of 2007. I'd be able to bring in my new group of UTEPs/MATs, oversee Brown Summer High School, and then head out for New Haven with Jack, the Dog, at my side.

It was a bittersweet summer at Brown. I loved working with my Mentor teachers, particularly Ed Abbott, Ruth Macaulay, Royce Connor, and Orah Bilmes, my longtime compatriots. Among the students, Darnell Fine, a UTEP who had taken *Ed 101* several years earlier and demonstrated uncanny insight and intelligence, proved to be a Star from the get-go. He remains a committed and talented professional educator all these years later.

After BSHS concluded, I packed up my office (as I had my apartment/house) and prepared to move to New Haven. I found a place on Elm Street, not far from the Yale campus, where the landlord seemed a bit sketchy but the apartment, the bottom floor of a corner-lot house with a beautiful porch and bay windows, was a steal! My Education Department colleagues, organized by the incomparable Ann D'Abrosca, our Department Manager, prepared a wonderful send off on the lawn next to the Ed Dept. building, featuring a huge sheet cake in the image of *Jack*. I was given a Brown University Captain's Chair and a series of lovely valedictory remarks from Larry, Luther Spoehr, Ed Abbott, and others. A number of former UTEPs/MATs were present for the occasion — and the weather was pleasantly accommodating. I got to say my piece and, just like that, another Chapter closed.

November 4, 2008

It was chilly. Brisk. And still dark when I got in line at P.S. 54, The Samuel Barnes School, around the corner in Bedford-Stuyvesant, Brooklyn. There was a good-sized crowd and it was festive. Mostly Black people, with a smattering of white folks, everyone *knew* we were going to be part of history. *Everyone* there was going to vote for Barack Obama and by the time we all got home from work that evening we would begin to hear the network speculation. Results dribbled in at first, but we knew there would be a flood of States called quickly and, by nine or the o'clock, it was inevitable we would have a Black President of the United States.

After work I was headed out to Long Island, to have dinner with two high school classmates, Michael Lynch and Bill Harrison. The three of us had watched the very first Super Bowl (before it was even called the "Super Bowl") together on January 15, 1967. *Tonight* would be an even more historic event.

We were going to meet at the Peter Pan Diner, just off Sunrise Highway in Bay Shore, at 6:00 p.m. or so. When we were high school students, the O-Co-Née Diner on Montauk Highway (Bay Shore's Main Street) was our primary diner. The Peter Pan, in those days, was in "North" Bay Shore, a bit off the beaten path . But the O-Co-Née had changed hands and now had a different name. The Peter Pan seemed fine. Seeing each other was more important than the venue.

Michael and I had grown up playing baseball and football together and remained friends throughout our adult lives. Billy and I became friends when he moved to Bay Shore in the 6th grade. He had open-heart surgery in 7th grade and I went to Southside Hospital to visit him a few times – the only one from our school to do so. We remained friends even as his parents shipped him off to Choate (which he *hated*) and I was there to greet him when he returned to Bay Shore High School after getting himself kicked out of Choate midway through Junior year (Bill very blatantly *plagiarized* a paper, insuring he'd be thrown out, much to his parents' chagrin and his delight). The smartest guy we knew (800 on ALL his SATs & Achievement Tests), he could only get into Michigan State because of the Choate incident. He was my biggest cheerleader, aside from my family, when I got into Yale. Bill finished MSU in three years, got a Master's in his 4th year and then distinguished himself at UVA Law School. We went to baseball games, including the World Series, together and he took me deep sea fishing in Venezuela.

It was a shock, then, when I slid into the booth at the Peter Pan Diner across from Michael and he said, "Bil, I have some bad news. Billy died this morning." I could tell from Michael's demeanor he wasn't kidding. I went into shock and don't really remember anything else from that evening.

Apparently, Bill's heart, the one that was repaired in 7th grade, gave out as he was headed out to Long Island's East End to go fishing. That's all we knew and it's all I know to this day.

We had been through our lives together, the ups and downs, marriages and divorces, his eldest son's suicide, the

Yankees World Series run. You name it, we had fun together, or consoled one another. He was a dear friend. Like family. And, in the midst of the joy of Obama becoming President, I was leveled by the loss of one of my oldest and dearest friends.

Time heals wounds, and loss, but only to an extent. When we lose those people we are closest to, part of our own soul is eroded. In that WORST year of my life at *Essex Street Academy* it seemed only appropriate that I would also lose one of my best friends.

Chapter 29

You CAN'T Go Home Again

Going to Yale University between 1967 and 1971 was *the formative* experience of my life. In ways I can't count, Yale made me who I am. I learned how to read critically, write effectively, and think deeply. The *people* I went to school with, some of whom are still my closest friends, had a huge influence on what I learned and how I came to see the world. We were at Yale at a very volatile time in America's history and that also had a deep impact on my thinking, and how I proceeded. That half my time was spent in an all—Male bastion and the other half in a Co-Educational community was also significant. After my summer working for the Yale Council on Community Affairs (1970), I headed to California for the month of August, where one of my closest high school friends, Gil Schaeffer, had moved after dropping out of Princeton. My parents were concerned that I, like Gil, wouldn't come back and finish my degree. I never thought twice about not returning. Having already placed a deposit for a cottage on Lake Quonnipaug in North Guilford (CT) with Karl Pavlovic, I totally intended on returning, writing my *Intensive Major* "thesis" (on Modern American Literature & Mythology), checking out what Skull & Bones was like, and being the first in my (extended) family to get a college degree. And that's pretty much what happened.

One of the things I had relished working at Brown from 1996 to 2007 was that the undergraduate campus life reminded me of my experience at Yale. Despite it being 25 years later, Brown's campus buzzed with undergraduate energy and a sense of exploration and freedom that harkened back to my time in New Haven. For some reason, I thought that Yale's campus, in 2007, would also crackle with undergraduate zeal. I was dead wrong. What I found when I began working at Yale was a campus where the undergraduates were *heads-down* serious about their studies (not that Brown students weren't, but things seemed far more carefree in Providence) and there was a competitive edge to everything. The Teacher Prep Program's offices were, literally, in the shadow of Morse College, my residential home sophomore and junior year, so the contrast to *my* experience in Sixties New Haven, as well as Nineties Providence felt all the starker.

And then there was the job itself. I had been used to a freewheeling, collaborative environment, working with Larry, Eileen, Yvette, Carin, Romi, and Polly. Things were quite different in New Haven. Jack Gillette *was* the *Director* of the Program and not particularly open to my "fast-and-loose" approach to Teacher Preparation. It was also made clear to me, early on, that my "domain" was *strictly* observing the Undergraduates, and I really had little or nothing to do with the *Urban Education Program* students. That was a curve I hadn't expected. At Brown, we made little distinction between our UTEPs and MATs. Linda Cole-Taylor, the Assistant Director, was in charge of making sure all the students in both programs were on track, academically, and taught some classes, while overseeing the adjuncts who taught content-courses in the Education certification process. What became obvious, the more I was there, was that Jack seemed to enjoy his teaching at the School of Management more than pushing an aggressive *school reform* Teaching Program in New Haven. Needless to say, this led to some friction.

On the home front, I moved into my spacious apartment on Elm Street, a house that bordered the *far edge* of Yale's campus as well as the southern tip of the Dixwell Avenue ghetto. It made for interesting evenings with lots of noise: music, arguments, shouting, singing, and only occasional gunshots. Early on, because the kitchen was so large, I bought a five-burner gas stove. My grill and smoker were set up outside my back door (sadly, I couldn't have a garden) and friends from New York came up for some barbecue cook-outs that fall. As mentioned, the landlords, Tom and Vickie Applegate, were sketchy (they lost the house in foreclosure right after I moved away) and, when their son Bryan was home, Tom had a restraining order to stay away. Since I could take Jack the Dog to my Yale office, the time spent on Elm Street was basically weekday evenings and weekends, so it was livable, if not ideal.

The three fringe benefits living in New Haven were: #1) a regular slate of good, *live* music at Toad's Place (formerly *Hungry Charlie's*, our favorite burger joint in the late Sixties) and Café Nine, down on State Street; #2) *Pepe's Pizza* (the *best* pizza in the world!); and #3) the presence of Vincent Scully, who was teaching his Introduction to Art History course that Fall. Regarding the first item, I got to see the legendary Johnny Winter at Toad's, as well as a number of pretty good blues and rock bands at Café Nine.

Pepe's is legendary and deservedly so. Spending time with Vince and his wife, Tappy Lynn (Catherine Willis Lynn, also an architectural historian), was a pure joy, as was sitting in on Scully's lectures in the Art Gallery Auditorium. As when I was an undergraduate, I *never* attended a Scully lecture without walking away having learned *at least* one new thing I had *never* thought of before. He was a remarkable teacher and a remarkable man — and it was definitely the most "value-added" element of my second tour of duty in New Haven.

On the Teacher Prep front, I was having a fine time observing and de-briefing my student-teachers. The undergraduates were placed all over the city, in an array of subject areas. There were music teachers in a middle school as well as at Wilbur Cross High School. Social Studies and English teachers were at Hillhouse High, New Haven Academy, and *The High School in the Community*, the school I had a hand in creating back in 1970! My connection to the *Urban Education Program* graduate students was mostly as a drop-in" advisor and, while I got to sit in during meetings Jack and Linda held regarding the Program, I did not feel my input was particularly valued. Our work was cordial but not *collegial*.

A further negative turn experienced during my year at Yale came when I submitted a proposal to teach a College Seminar. The Residential College Seminar program started when I was an undergraduate:

The Residential College Seminar program, instituted in 1968, is devoted to the development of innovative courses that fall outside traditional departmental structures. The instructors for the seminar program are drawn from the University community and from the region, including individuals outside academic life, such as writers, artists, journalists, and participants in government and the public sector.

Since I was a *Staff Member* and not part of the Faculty, the only way I could teach an undergraduate course would be through the Residential College Seminar Program. The way it works, an instructor submits a proposal to a student committee, which has representatives from each of the (then) 12 Residential Colleges. The students then request an *interview* with the instructor to see if they want to offer his/her course as a College Seminar. I interviewed with two Colleges (Berkley and Saybrook), talking up my "White Privilege and Critical Pedagogy" proposal. The students reacted positively and *both* Colleges wanted to offer it. They agreed to offer it to the Undergrads as a joint presentation of both Saybrook *and* Berkley. I was excited at the opportunity to work with undergrads who weren't part of the Teacher Ed certification program. The wrench in the works was that the *Masters' Council,* the Heads of the Residential Colleges, had to approve all College Seminars. They rejected my proposal. I was not given a reason and could only conclude they didn't want to touch White Privilege or simply had no idea what Critical Pedagogy was. Either way, it was a huge pin in my balloon and added to my discomfit and discomfort.

I realized I needed to move on from Yale/New Haven when we met to admit the next *Urban Education Program* class. There was money enough to admit *TEN* students each year, not a huge number, but the New Haven school district was only 25,000 students. To my mind, that meant the Yale Program could place *50* teachers in the public high schools over the next five years and, if they were prepared to be *change agents* (as we did at Brown), we could have a *real impact* on the New Haven schools. The first two cohorts of the Program each had only been 7 students and Jack quickly informed me that this year's would also be that size, or maybe smaller. He told me that he preferred the Program "fly under the University's radar." I'm not sure why, but a quote from Jack, after he had become the Dean of the Graduate School of Education at Lesley University in Cambridge, MA, provided deeper insight for me.

> *Transformation is a term for funders. The reality is that this is a very complex organizational field, ill-designed to do any human development of teachers. No neo-liberal market intervention, no well-designed policy alone is going to be effective. What needs to line up is policy space, tied with huge increases in backroom management competency and innovation.*

The buzzwords, for me, are "organizational field" and "backroom management." Looking back and thinking about how Jack enjoyed his work at the School of Management, I realize that, even though I left Brown because of its shift toward *policy*, I had landed at yet another place where *policy* ruled the roost. The combination of the College Seminar rejection and the *Urban Education Program*'s lack of commitment to large-scale school reform proved to be the death knell for my time at Yale.

Through some of the teachers at New Haven Academy, I had a lead on a job in New York City. When I was working in Providence, I often visited the City and, as the years went on, I mused that I was "getting too old" to live in New York again. The pace seemed too fast, the noise incessant. By Spring of 2008, however, I was ready to return to the Big Apple and began considering going back to high school classroom teaching. Having been a Teacher Educator for 12 years, I thought it might be good to get back in the classroom to make sure I had been telling my students *the truth* all these years! Before pulling the trigger on that notion, however, I was given a wonderful opportunity to test drive my High School *Teaching Chops* by way of an ad I found for a San Francisco Video test-prep Company called Big Tree Learning.

> *Our mission at Big Tree Learning is to be the best place to learn in the world. We believe that great learning starts with great teaching. So, we find the best teachers, film them teaching, and build learning solutions around those great teacher videos.*

One of the areas Big Tree wanted to offer instruction in was *Advanced Placement United States History.* I applied via email and was scheduled for an online video interview.

Sitting in my home office on Elm Street, the interview lasted almost 45 minutes and, when it was over, I was pretty sure I had the job. Several days later, I got a call, confirming I would be the *AP U.S. History* instructor for Big Tree Learning. This entailed spending a week in San Francisco, all expenses paid, plus a handsome stipend. We stayed at the *W Hotel*, a posh new upscale place off Market Street. The company had rented a suite of offices on Market Street which were set up as studios. We put in 8 to 12 hours a day, videotaping our presentations. For my APUSH videos, we moved around the city, shooting a number of outdoor scenes. Presentations were 15 to 20 minutes (I did over 20) and I earned the nickname "One-Take Willie," as I *never* had to re-shoot a segment. Our cohort was about 20 teachers across an array of subject areas and specialties, and the week was fabulous! By the time the videos were released in the Fall, the company had changed its name to *Brightstorm*, and my videos are still available there (www.brightstorm.com).

The lead I had gotten for a New York City teaching job from the New Haven teachers led to an interview at *Essex Street Academy*, on the Lower East Side. It was, purportedly, a *Coalition School*, and I interviewed for positions in both English and Social Studies/History. By the end of the interview I was told I had a job. It would be decided at a later point in time whether I'd be teaching Social Studies/History or English. I didn't care. I was happy to have a job and be returning to New York. For some reason, I decided I would live in Brooklyn, the Borough of my birth and, in 2008, the *hippest* place to live in New York City. I'd soon learn that I wasn't all that hip and that things could actually be *worse* than what I was experiencing in New Haven.

Chapter 30

The WORST Year of My Life!

By 2008 I was looking at a pretty successful career. Awards had been won, progressive schools had been started, books had been written. This new Chapter, living in Brooklyn and teaching on the Lower East Side at a *Coalition* school, *should have been* a piece of cake. Nothing could have been further from the reality, as it turned out. The 2008-2009 school year was unquestionably *the WORST year of my life*. A constellation of factors combined to make it so. I failed to do adequate research regarding housing and let the bottom line (rent costs) dictate *where* I ended up living. I also made assumptions (as one *never* should) about the school, based on the fact that it billed itself a *Coalition* school. The Principal was a Brown graduate, and there was a young, energetic staff. Housed in Seward Park High School on the corner of Grand and Essex Streets, it was a building that covered an entire city block and was home to five "small" schools, of which *Essex Street Academy* was one. There were about 350 students in grades 9 through 12, with a faculty of 25, plus Support Staff. In my eagerness to get out of New Haven, and get back to New York, I dropped the ball in every possible way.

My new apartment was on Spencer Street, at the northern edge of Bedford-Stuyvesant (the landlord claimed it was the *Clinton Hill* neighborhood. It wasn't.). It was between Willoughby and DeKalb Avenue, a block away from Bedford Ave. and Myrtle (once called "Murder") Avenues, in an area poorly served by public transportation (the erratic G train is the *only* accessible subway line) and, at that time, was close to being a *food desert* neighborhood. There was *one* grocery store (a *Bravo* supermarket) within walking distance, with several fast-food establishments. You know you're in a sketchy neighborhood, though, when your *KFC* and local liquor store separate the employees from the customers with a *wall of bulletproof glass*! Up Willoughby, as you crossed into the *real* Clinton Hill neighborhood, was Pratt Institute and Fort Greene Park, where I often took Jack for head-clearing, long walks on weekend mornings. My downstairs neighbors were entitled Pratt students, whose parents were footing their bills. I broke up one of their parties by storming downstairs with a billy-club in hand (a memento from my Dad's days on the Babylon Police Force in the early 1950s) and *demanded* the noise cease, it was a weekday night. I must have looked pretty crazy because the place cleared out. My upstairs neighbors were named "Lefty" and Melissa and seldom left the house, although they had lots of "friends" visit for very short periods of time and seemed to derive income from that.

Despite being in Bed-Stuy, gentrification was creeping in, and a new, chi-chi apartment building was going up on the corner of Willoughby and Spencer. One had already been built across the street from my row house, in stark contrast to the small single and two-family dwellings in the neighborhood.

Don't get me wrong, this area was not run-down, but it did have several abandoned buildings and couple of vacant lots. My RAV-4 was broken into one night (the window was smashed) and my GPS holder, along with a bag of Jack's dog food, was stolen (there really wasn't anything else of value in the car). It was my fault for leaving the GPS holder on the windshield. The thief was clearly hoping to find the device in the car. The point of all this is: while Brooklyn, in 2008, was riding a rising tide of "coolest, hippest" Borough praise, *none* of that applied to the area I had moved to. I hadn't done my research.

The apartment was fine: a one-bedroom floor through with a decent size kitchen (My new New Haven stove wouldn't fit through the doorways. It's still "in storage" in my brother's basement in PA) and more than adequate living space for me and Jack. Neighborhood parking wasn't a problem and I spent many Sunday mornings in the laundromat around the corner with Jack at my side. My New York City friends all lived in *Manhattan* and, without an easy public transit ride there, I had to *drive* over a bridge to visit and then try to find *parking* on the Upper West Side (a nightmare). In all, I had isolated myself in a neighborhood that didn't even have a local coffee shop. It was not a good year as far as habitat was concerned.

School did not shape up any better than my neighborhood. The daily commute was an easy 10 to 15-minute ride over the Manhattan Bridge and Alex, our Principal, gave me a parking space in the *very limited* school lot on the premises. Beyond that stroke of good fortune, the rest of the year proved disastrous. Despite having gone to Brown, Alex was only vaguely familiar with what the *Coalition* was really about. We did have two former Brown MAT's on the staff (one member of my final MAT group and one of Larry's Science MATs, who was the *Music* teacher at Essex St.) and one of the "Deans" was a former *ED 101* student of mine. That, however, made little difference regarding *Essex Street Academy*. I decided to keep a journal. The September 10, 2008, 9:50a.m. entry reads: *The beginning of a log I need to keep each day!* While I didn't keep the journal *every day*, I did keep the log on a regular basis right up until *June 26, 2009*. As a result, I can apply my skill as a historian, using the tools of historiography, to provide a detailed, graphic account of *the* WORST *year of my life*.

Here then, in my own words, my (debilitating) 2008-2009 *journey*.

2008

Thursday, September 11: 7:00 p.m.
How to balance the depressing prospect of teaching kids who don't know how to learn & defend themselves by taking a position of not caring.

Friday, September 12: 9:30 a.m.
The overall lack of academic culture is nettlesome, to say the least . . . there's definitely a Social Service orientation here which supersedes academics.

Thursday, September 18th: 9:45 a.m.
So, we've waived the Regents. . . . nice kids but undisciplined, unfocused, and think they have a "free pass," I'm afraid, w/out the Regents.

Explanatory note: As a *Coalition* school, *Essex St. Academy*, along with 28 other NYC schools, was *exempted from* having to take the State Exam — a test I had often railed against but now saw as a valuable way to check literacy/numeracy competence of "borderline" students (who were the *majority* of the *Essex St.* student body). We would offer "Panels" — public presentations of student work that would ensure they were achieving "State standards."

Monday, September 22: 3:00 p.m.
There is no academic culture — no sense of urgency about succeeding academically — it is sad — and depressing.

Wednesday, September 26: 3:30 p.m.
The language from staff — altar-ego, complementary tickets, "are," for our ....whoops!
... It's Sept. 24ᵗʰ & I'm feeling very discouraged about the total tone, the lack of academic focus, the seeming acceptance of mediocrity, etc. . . . The kids can't write, they can't read critically, they don't know how to use an Index . . . They do not care about learning — they do not care about skills — How can you make this work?

Monday, October 6ᵗʰ: 3:00 p.m.
My students think copying is "writing a report." The idea of "putting it in your own words" is not even on their radar screen. . . They throw the "F" and "N" words around as if there's never an adult in the area . . . How how how do I make headway here?

Tuesday, October 14: 9:15 a.m.
Have I given up on these kids? Am I just going through the motions?

Wednesday, October 15ᵗʰ: 12:40 p.m.
My students are barely literate, do not really take the academics seriously (it has neither immediate meaning nor long-term

234

relevance to them, as they see it) . . . and are headed into, at best, cul de sacs if not outright dead-ends. . . . It's farcical to say these kids are really getting an education . . . And it gets back to me feeling as though I truly make no difference — there's certainly no learning of any kind really going on here. . . . There is a total lack of discipline . . . self-discipline.

(At this point I began checking job advertisements, looking for a way out.)

Monday, October 20th: 9:00 a.m.
What can you say about a day that starts with locking yourself out of the house? Luckily, I was able to rouse Lefty and Melissa at 5:30 a.m. and get into the house.

Thursday, October 30th: 3:00 pm.
My borderline feral Advisees (9th Grade) ... Still Middle Schoolers.

Friday, October 31st – Halloween (*not* a journal entry)
We had to secretly release our students early and stand guard on the street and at the corner subway station because there was a rumor circulating that some local Gang had a Halloween initiation that required *slashing the face of a young girl with a razor.*

No incidents occurred, luckily and thankfully.

Monday, November 11th: Veterans' Day
I have a typewritten entry folded into my Composition Book/Journal, written after visiting my family in PA, where my brother taught his classes that day. The entry is about my brother teaching in a school which was, demographically, very similar

to mine (though much larger, regarding numbers). He had brought our Mother in to tell her stories about living through the Depression and World War Two and his students *"were very curious and very respectful and asked great questions."* I noted *"I would not bring my Mother to Essex Street Academy. I would be embarrassed. I would not want her to hear the way people talk to each and act toward each other."* I finished the entry with this:

So, should I continue to work in a place where I am consistently disrespected, unappreciated, and where I receive no satisfaction as a "teacher" (since I don't teach, really — in fact I'm not sure what it is I am doing here, other than "overseeing" some young adolescents. Hmmm, that has some eerie historical overtones, doesn't it?) It is very distressing and I feel extremely powerless, hypocritical, and confused, even, by the situation I find myself in. I like my students . . . but I'm terribly frustrated by what I can see will await them as they leave here, essentially without a decent education. What does one do in a situation like this?

Thursday, November 13th: 9:25 p.m.
I really am at a loss & at a low point. How am I going to feel by March?

Friday, November 21st: 11:30 a.m.
Resigning myself to the notion we will be giving Certificates of Attendance which, as my brother pointed out, are good for dead-end jobs.

Monday, December 1st: 10:45 a.m.
The degraded culture of poverty —which blinds people to possibilities — which is so limiting in how it channels these children into predetermined ruts which lead to dead ends and tragedy — Does this school really think it's changing that?

Friday, December 5th

Lunch w/Alex yesterday which pretty much amounted to, "This is the way ESA is and we're pretty pleased w/it — and it's pretty much going to stay that way . . . " Who am I to ask for real academics? . . . There is so much enabling . . . hand-holding . . . Simple organizational skills, conventions, protocols are TOTALLY lacking.

Tuesday, December 9th: 1:10 p.m.

This is like serving a sentence . . . Enabling Street Academy . . . The whole situation sucks

Friday, December 19th: 9:30 a.m.

I'm honestly starting to think that the staff here is delusional . . . the waxing poetic about the Skating Trip (note: we had taken The Whole School to a rink in Brooklyn, which was accomplished without incident) *Monique's email soliciting funds for the Senior Trip saying these students would be future neurosurgeons or whatever. . .*

Monday, December 22nd: 11:20 a.m.

Quality doesn't exist here. Getting the assignment done is seen — at least by the kids but, I'm afraid, accepted by the adults — as enough — as "good," it seems . . . Many of these kids are subliterate.

2009

January 8th: 2:45 p.m.

I've never counted days before, never felt them pull on my skin, my nerves, my psyche, the way they do here. It's hard to remember being this miserable for this long a period.

January 12th: 3:00 p.m.
I have to say that, today, I hate my job.

Wednesday, January 21st: 1:17 p.m.
Definitely one of my lowest days here — Kind of broke this camel's back today — Right at the end of the First Semester — Perfect.

Thursday, January 29th: 12:30 p.m.
ESA is already "past-tense" in my mind.

Tuesday, February 10th: 9:45 a.m.
Seniors can't focus, read, take notes, produce simple work. I can't overcome the greater ethos of the school which is about "counseling" & social services.

Thursday, February 26th: 12:25 p.m.
It's the inherent lack of respect, of understanding — or accepting – how a classroom is supposed to operate — that is debilitating after a while. It's the "Hugs not Drugs" greeting from Alex every morning which makes the kids love him, and this place, but it's also the lack of focus, of serious academic intent that permeates the culture . . . there is an inmates running the asylum quality to the place . . .

Wednesday, March 4th: 10:40 a.m.
This is really not the place for me. I'm too old, too jaded? Too realistic? Too out of touch?

Friday, March 6th: 7:45 a.m.
The chaperone at a Social Club — that's what my job seems to be here. . . .the adults are here, it seems, to go through the

motions of presenting/providing the illusion of education, but few of the kids actually take that seriously. This is a highly enabling culture (how is K.J. allowed to play on the basketball team when he never goes to class?) This is not the right environment for me . . . 10:27 a.m. There is no sense of urgency or importance about education here — it's secondary — That what ESA means by secondary school — School (Academics) is Secondary. I'm about as discouraged as I've been all year.

Wednesday, April Fool's Day: 10:16 a.m.
Town Meeting — I'd rather stick knitting needles through my ear drums!

Publicizing # of days left (45) is a negative, Think — Doesn't it play into, "We can't wait to get out?" Enabling Street Academy — does it mean anything to be a Coalition school?

(Note: Town Meeting was a weekly all-school gathering in the beautiful art-deco auditorium. Seward Park High School was built in 1928-1929. The Town Meeting was supposed to be a "community building" activity but it was generally a *HUGE* waste of time in which students would perform (off-key musical groups, double-dutch jump rope, and so on) and adults would make "important announcements")

High unanxious expectations? We've got the unanxious part down, that's for sure . . . Tone of Decency — Puh-lease . . .

Monday, April 6th: 9:28 a.m.
Advisory next — That's like Root Canal Waiting to Happen . . .

Monday, April 20th
First day back from Break . . . My morale, to say the least, is as low as it can go. I feel like I've forgotten how to teach . . .

there is such a low bar here for students — if you don't spoon feed everything, they don't "work."

Thursday, April 23rd: 8:36 a.m.
Nothing works! I am now having nightmares about this place.
(NOTE: I had *NEVER* had nightmares about teaching. By April, they became a regular part of my nights)

Tuesday, April 28th: 9:37 a.m.
Is this going on all over the City? God forbid.

Tuesday, May 5th: Cinco De Mayo
This gets more difficult each day.

Friday, May 10th: 10:25 a.m.
I cannot wait to get out of here. This is like bamboo splints sliding under my fingernails

Friday, May 22nd: 9:37 a.m.
I am an abject failure. . . . this has been THE worst year of my professional life. I have been useless, pointless, ineffective. I can't relate very well to my students, nor they to me. I have, quite frankly, given up . . . their utter disrespect for the value of an education, lack of respect for teachers & teaching has worn me down and worn me out.

Friday, May 29th: 8:40 a.m.
I refuse to ENABLE . . . I do not believe you are doing anyone a favor by letting them "slide by " or get over . . . A diploma should not be a Certificate of Attendance.
On June 10th I interviewed at the Urban Assembly School for Design and Construction, a 400-student high school on

West 50th Street. One of our former Brown MATs, Rachel Bello (who had been the Principal of Brown Summer High School during my tenure as "Czar"), had notified me of *two* Social Studies/History openings at the school and said she thought I'd like working there. By Monday, June 15th I had an offer. At the end of that week, I accepted.

I sat through the final Panels at *ESA* and listened to *every* student of one of my colleagues present *the exact same script* (which I KNOW *the teacher* had written), so they could pass. I sat through a Graduation ceremony where I watched students *I KNEW* were *not* literate get diplomas and receive praise from our Principal. I was aware of "bleeding-heart liberalism;" *Essex Street Academy* exhibited what could only be described as *hemorrhaging-heart* Social Services, to the detriment of the students, as I saw it.

I left my Brooklyn apartment on July 1st and moved into my old neighborhood on the Upper West Side, happy to start a *final* Chapter of my teaching career with a clean slate at a new place.

Chapter 31

Resurrection

The Upper West Side of New York City *feels* like home to me. There is something about the neighborhood, Broadway, Amsterdam, West End Avenue, that feels *comfortable* in a way no other place ever has. In July of 2009, when I moved into a one-bedroom on West 82nd Street, right off Broadway, I felt like I was home. Combined with having a job a relatively short subway or bus ride away, it was a sweet set-up and stood in high relief to what I had endured only one year earlier. Questions remained, however. Was my year on the Lower East Side the "exception that proves the rule," regarding my ability to *teach?* I certainly hoped so, but only being back in the classroom with students would establish whether I was, in fact, a pretty good teacher or I had actually lost my touch.

Back on The Upper West Side (cue Beatles, *Back in the USSR* as b.g. music)

New York City has a population of over 8 million people. They all live in very distinct *neighborhoods*, some for generation upon generation. Each neighborhood has its own unique culture, its own landmarks, its own claims to fame. I was born in Brooklyn but only lived there in 2008-2009 (technically, I also lived there from 1949 to 1951, but you really don't retain memories from ages 0 to 2). Having already discussed my (lack of) neighborhood on Spencer Street, you can understand my delight in returning to the Upper West Side. One of my oldest, and best, friends, "Uncle Jay" Fasold, (aka: Puddin'head) lived on West 70th St. and it was great to be able to see him regularly. By late August, I established a solid relationship with my local Cleaners (a *must* in NYC), and still stop in to visit Mr. Lee and Kimberley whenever I'm back on West 82nd St. It was easy to find a doctor (*literally* two doors down) and a dentist (right around the corner on 83rd, off West End Ave.). As far as grocery shopping went, unlike my predicament in Brooklyn, this part of the UWS was *rife* with meat, seafood, and produce. *Fairway* ("Like No Other Market"), *Citarella's* (*excellent seafood*, and they expanded to open a butcher shop), the famous *Zabar's*, as well as scores of other food stores within easy walking distance. Also, as I noted in my essay about *Big Nick's*, "between 72nd St. and 86th St., up Broadway and down Amsterdam Avenue, there are seven diners." As one who *loves* diners this neighborhood was *heaven*. Even though *Barnes and Noble* drove *Shakespeare & Co.* out of the neighborhood (see *You've Got Mail* with Tom Hanks and Meg Ryan for the Hollywood version. *It was* filmed in our *real* neighborhood), it *is* a great book store and affords one a chance to catch *free* lectures from the likes of the late Pete Hamill on a random Tuesday night.

The *Upper West Side* is actually *several* neighborhoods. Some folks would mark the beginning of the UWS at Lincoln Center, and I'd say the LC community runs from

66th to 72nd (two stops on the #1 train). 72nd to 86th, in my estimation, is another discrete community, just as 86th to 96th is. The Streets noted are major *crosstown* thoroughfares, as well as being Subway stops. That combination allows folks to mark their territory. 96th up to 116th Streets has its own array of distinct, smaller neighborhoods and then, at 116th you have Columbia University (and Barnard), running up to 125th and the southern edge of Harlem. All of this, happily, is bordered on the west by Riverside Park (starting at 72nd Street and running to 125th Street)and Central Park, over the same area, on the East. I spent many hours in Riverside Park, not only with my dogs, but also playing tennis on the red clay *public* courts at 96th Street! Aside from the numerous theatrical and arts venues at Lincoln Center, Upper West Side denizens also have the *Beacon Theater, Second Stage Theater,* and *Symphony Space,* offering an array of music, drama, comedy, and so on. *Stand-up New York*, a popular comedy club, is right near the corner of 78th and Broadway. There are also a plethora of small bars and clubs that provide *live music* on a nightly basis. While I mentioned grocery stores and diners, there are, of course, countless restaurants all over the neighborhood. It is, in essence, a city unto itself — and I *loved* being back.

The Urban Assembly School of Design & Construction

The Urban Assembly is a non-profit organization, started in 1990, whose mission is to create and maintain high quality small (junior and senior high) schools throughout New York City. Each school has a theme/focus and is engaged with public and private *partners*, providing students with a real-world experience and support network not only when they are *in* secondary school but beyond. That sounds idealistic of course, but after spending five years at the UA School of Design and Construction, I can vouch for the efficacy of the model.

I had interviewed with Matt Willoughby, the Principal at SDC, and we hit it off. Rachel Bello had undoubtedly put in a good word for me and, since she was a stalwart on the staff, it probably increased the odds of my securing a position. Whatever the case, Matt had a decent sense of what school reform looked like and he also was willing to give me some latitude, regarding methodology and assessment. My department chair was Jonathan Davis, a very bright young guy (who would soon leave to get his doctorate) and my colleagues, Meredith Matson, Anna Tabet, and Martin Regan (also a "new hire"), were young, bright, experienced practitioners. It was a good team and I felt much better in my first few days at SDC than I had during my *entire* year at *Essex Street.*

SDC was serious as a heart attack about preparing its students to go to college. While realistic (no one was claiming we were going to fill the Ivy League), there seemed to be a clear "eye on the prize" commitment from the Administration and Staff, as to what it would take to move our students (*"this population,"* as my former Principal referred to them; a term I *never* heard in my years at *SDC*) to being genuinely prepared to *not only go* to college, but to succeed. (Don't buy anybody's hype about how many of their graduates are *accepted* at colleges. There are colleges out there that will *accept* a barely-breathing corpse! Find out how many of a school's *graduates* not only go to college but also *complete* a year, two years, three years and graduate.) What impressed me from the get-go was that *SDC,* unlike *ESA,* had created a *culture* that could, in fact, help its students achieve and succeed.

Park West Educational Campus

525 West 50th Street was once a *huge* comprehensive high school, housing between 2500 and 3500 students during any given year. When I arrived in August of 2009, the four-story building was divided between five small schools (350 to 500 students each), each with its own administration, staff, and its own *identity. Food and Finance High School,* New York City's *only* culinary high school, occupied the first floor. There was a glass-walled industrial kitchen that allowed visitors to watch the students working with their chef instructors as they walked in. The second floor was *Facing History High School,* based on the Brookline (MA) historical inquiry project approach to teaching/learning. Floor three was *Manhattan Bridges High School,* designed to transition Spanish-speaking students through the education system, graduating not only English-speakers but student scholars in four years. *Manhattan Bridges* is consistently one of the "Top 50" High Schools in New York City. The fourth floor was divided between the *High School of Hospitality Management* and our *UA School of Design and Construction* The mission of those schools is self-evident in their titles. With the exception of *Manhattan Bridges*, none of the schools screened their applicants, relying on students to actually *seek* admission ("choice") to fulfil enrollment. At *SDC*, we always had a number of students on a waiting list. Our student body was 400 to 425 students the years I was there.

I cannot emphasize enough the success of all five of these small schools, and how their success *reinforces* the *Coalition's* call for small schools where students are *known*. To truly appreciate it, you need only consider the *New York Post* headline from March 28, 1999: *Park West H.S.: Prep School for Prison; SEX, DRUGS, CRIME RAMPANT.* The article about

Park West reveals "students were the victims of 9 robberies in the last 16 days — one at knifepoint. . . . One recent assault victim was a pregnant student who was beaten and dragged down a flight of stairs by a student who snatched her bracelet . . . . Another recent victim was Principal Frank Brancato, who was punched by a student when he tried to break up a melee." It goes on, citing staff who had criminal records and administrators who were uncertified, noting how Park West's graduation rate was far below the city average but their drop-out rate was almost double that of other high schools. One veteran teacher is quoted as saying "The effort that's put forth to deal with these children is criminal." The school was shut down in 2004 and the five small schools were quickly moved in, renovating the culture in short order.

The five schools share a cafeteria, library, and gymnasium, but competitive interscholastic sports teams are fielded as cooperative ventures. There is surprisingly little conflict between the schools (there are *strict rules* forbidding any "excursions" from one school to another during the school day). Two things that made the New Park West a safe environment and a place that actually achieves academic success are #1) metal detectors and great Public Safety Officers who *know* the kids. (It's like TSA screening, as students and their bags pass through metal detectors and x-ray machines every morning) #2) An administrator from each school collects *all* electronic devices (phones, iPods, iPads) from students, returning them at the end of the school day.

NOTE: I learned there is a "cottage industry" of Step-vans, lining the streets of schools where electronics are left by students during the school day. These vans, and some local deli's, provide a "safe-keeping rental

*service" for the day — if students do not want to turn
their devices over to school officials, for whatever reason).*

A third item, which I believe established a very conducive
academic culture at *SDC* is that we had a *Dress Code*. Not uniforms. Students had to be in "professional dress:" shirts with
collars, pants with belts, shoes, not sneakers, for boys. Skirts /
dresses(of "acceptable length") or pant-suits and dress shoes for
the girls. In case a student arrived *out of* Dress Code, the Deans
had an office with, literally, a wardrobe closet and shoe rack.
It was not the most fashionable attire. In fact, if students had
to borrow a Dress Code outfit for a day, it was usually the *last*
time they forgot to arrive with their own, proper attire.

SDC seemed a world away from my experience at *ESA*
and, as my years there went on, it proved to be a very good
place to finish my career.

Chapter 32

Redemption: Part One

It's easy to look back from the comfort of 2020 retirement and say that my five years at *SDC* were wonderful. Overall, they were, but that doesn't mean there weren't tough patches. In fact, toward the end of my third year (2011-2012) I flirted with changing schools and even interviewed at a couple of places. Happily, neither proved a good fit and my last two years at *SDC were* very successful. The reason for that was the fact that I had *known* (taught) the last two groups of Seniors since they were freshmen, yet again reinforcing that *Coalition* principle of *knowing students well.* Another factor was that I now had *total* control over the 11th grade United States History program and instituted, as I had at Blind Brook High School way back when, *AP for ALL!* If you were an 11th grade U.S. history student, you were an *Advanced Placement* U.S. History student, no ifs, ands, or buts. In September, when the students arrived in class and I told them it was an *APUSH* class, some would invariably say, "But I didn't *sign up* for A.P." and I'd smile and say, "No, *you* didn't, but *I* signed you up for it!"

Skeptical at first, students quickly accepted the situation (as students do) and, while we didn't set the AP Test on fire, we did *annihilate* the New York State U.S. History Regents exam every June.

SDC: 2009-2014

Arriving at *SDC* in August 2009 to work with staff, my first observation was not *how young* everyone was (I had already experienced that at *Essex Street*) but how *smart* they were. I already knew Rachel Bello from Brown but now I met her English colleague (and fellow *Harvard* graduate) Rebekah Shoaf. While they were stars in the Department, their colleagues (Chad Frade, Nina Silva, and, later, Bryce Klatsky) were equally impressive. Our support people, Deans Eric Burnside and Axel Taveras, Counselor Rebecca Dransfield, IT guru Jeff Martinez, the *entire* Special Education corps, were *top-notch* educators and great with students. Across the Departments, in fact, was one good, young teacher after another. Added to that was a fabulous Art and Design group, led by Guy Roger, who really set our students on track for architecture and construction futures. While I had some ups and downs in my "transition" back to being in a "real" classroom teacher (I *did not* count my time at *Essex Street* as "teaching"), I was surrounded by energetic, idealistic, and committed young professionals everywhere I turned. Hallelujah!

The student body at *SDC* came from all five New York City boroughs (we had *one* student trek from Staten Island each day, and another from City Island), many of them taking long subway rides from the outer boroughs (Queens & Brooklyn). They were, on the surface, not much different from "the population" at *Essex Street Academy* but the metal detectors and the *Dress Code* were just the beginning of a completely different *school culture*. Unlike the *ESA* Panels, which, to my mind, were the phoniest Exhibitions I had ever seen, *SDC* students had to complete an original *public* project in front of *real experts,* starting freshman year. This involved teams of three students, in *Design* class, building a model of a bridge (they were given several choices and shown "how to," regarding principles, design, and so on). They had to stand in front of a panel of *three* architects (from our school's partner firms) who would assess their work and provide feedback. It doesn't get more *real world* than that! It also sets high *standards* starting freshman year, with the *expectation* that students *will* publicly present work, defend it, explain it, and learn to hear constructive feedback to improve performance. By sophomore year, when presenting "shelters" (houses, office spaces), they were seasoned presenters and the work was outstanding.

In the same way, I was *thrilled* to learn that *SDC* students knew what *Socratic Seminars* (see Endnotes) were. Employed extensively by the *Coalition*, the Socratic Seminar (created by Mortimer)

Adler and popularized by Dennis Grey), is a wonderful vehicle for introducing students to close reading, critical thinking, and thoughtful writing. Often executed in a fishbowl (an inner circle of discussants with an outer circle of observers, who, after a time, switch places), there are *rules* to a seminar and it introduces students, in a very active, engaged way, to intellectual discourse. The "text" the discussion focuses on can be anything from a piece of literature to a clip from a movie to a song/rap lyric. The purpose is to delve *deeply* for *meaning* while *listening* to each other (respectfully). *Socratic Seminars* had been my stock-in-trade when recruiting for the *Parker School,* so it was really fun to be working at a school where I wasn't looked at like I had two heads (as I was at *Essex Street*: "You *can't do that with this population."*) when we would arrange our desks in concentric circles.

What also made SDC enjoyable was the chance to do interdisciplinary work. I actually taught a freshman English class one year and, when Rachel left for several months on maternity leave, I took over her 11th grade English classes (who were also my APUSH students!). While I loathe *The Great Gatsby,* I taught it and, thanks to Chad Frade, we not only went down to one of the huge multiplex theaters on 42nd Street to watch the Leonardo DiCaprio version of it, but also did a Gatsby Scavenger Hunt around the city; where students had to not only find landmarks from the novel (like the Plaza Hotel) but also create and photograph a *tableaux* for presentation in class over the following days. The Gatsby experience opened the door to another fabulous opportunity for me. I proposed an elective course on New York City History and actually got Eric Burnside to team-teach it with me. Aside from getting our students to research NYC History, we went out into the City to explore. None of my students, for example, had ever been inside the NY Public Library on 42nd Street! We got to spend a long afternoon there, exploring its wonders and, for them, seeing things like a Gutenberg Bible for the first time. It was satisfying, fun, and made me feel like I was really a teacher again.

During the Gatsby project Rebekah Shoaf told me about The Cullman Center at the NY Public Library.

The Center conducts one-week Institutes for New York City area teachers each summer. The Cullman Center Institute for Teachers provides opportunities for teachers to enrich their understanding of the humanities in The New York Public Library's landmark building at Fifth Avenue and 42ⁿᵈ Street. Leading our seminars are scholars and writers who have won Cullman Center Fellowships and pursued their excellent work using the research collections of this Library. (www.nypl.org/ events/cullman-institute-teachers.)

There was a simple application process and, in the course of my time at *SDC*, I got to do *two* Cullman Institutes: one with *New Yorker* writer Ian (Sandy) Frazier and one with graphic artist and (Emmy award-winning) set designer Gary Panter. The Institute with Frazier resulted in an essay about *Big Nick's Burger Joint* while Panter's led to my creating several *graphic art* stories. As with the NEH Seminars I did in the 1980s, the camaraderie with other teachers, combined with tutelage from consummate professionals, proved highly rewarding.

The summers between teaching at *SDC* were not only occupied by *Cullman Institutes*. One was spent doing yet another a two-week NEH Seminar as well as taking a one-week Gilder-Lehrman Teacher Seminar. Both were held at Columbia University, a short *M-Eleven* bus trip up Amsterdam Avenue. The NEH Seminar was facilitated by the *Theater for a New Audience*, a Brooklyn-based Company specifically focused on producing the works of Shakespeare. In the course of the Seminar on the Bard we actually got to see (and page through) Columbia's *First Folio* editions of Shakespeare's plays. We were also able to look through Holinshed's *original Chronicles of England*, Shakespeare's historical *source* for many plays. Aside from doing close readings of various works, we got to act and direct scenes, under the guidance of scholars and professional actors/directors. As usual, the NEH experience was energizing and educative.

The Gilder-Lehrman Institute was a week with Ken Jackson, an eminent U.S. Historian who teaches at Columbia. I had known Ken for years because his wife, Barbara, was the head of English Department at Blind Brook when I first started teaching there. Ken's seminar was on *New York in the Gilded Age* and, like the Cullman Institute and the NEH Seminars, featured a fine array of educators. We did quite a bit of touring around NYC (including a walk across the Brooklyn Bridge) and heard from a number of scholars in the field, all of which contributed to developing my *NYC History* course for SDC. The summer experiences not only made me more of an inveterate New Yorker but also renewed my energy and focus as a teacher, while making my *SDC* experience extremely positive.

Chapter 33

Redemption: Part Two

We all know that three basic needs for any happy human are:
1) an adequate supply of food; 2) a decent shelter: and 3)a
sense of belonging to a community. At Essex Street Academy,
during the WORST year of my professional life, I came up
short in all three categories. A factor that made my final years
working at the *School of Design and Construction* particularly
satisfying was *meeting* those basic needs.

Food

Grand and Essex Streets proved not much better than my
"food desert" neighborhood when it came time for lunch.
When I started working at *ESA*, Chinatown was stretching
down into what used to be the predominantly Jewish Lower
East Side. While *Noah's Ark Original Kosher Deli* was down
the street on Grand (it's now closed), it was expensive and certainly not a place for *daily* eating. A couple of blocks over, on
Eldridge Street, was *Vanessa's Dumpling House*, which served

a wide variety of great dumplings but, again, not something you'd eat every day. Directly across the street was a Chinese take-out joint which actually made *very good*, quick Chinese dishes. To cater to our student population, they also served hundreds of pounds of fried chicken wings *and* French Fries each week. Since we didn't have a cafeteria, students would grab their take-out fries and wings and come back to eat in a classroom, where a teacher was also eating (Lunch Duty). By the end of my year at *ESA* I developed a hatred for, and repulsion to, *ketchup!* My students would *cover their fries* in the red condiment to such a degree you *couldn't tell* what was under the unctuous red sauce, and the aroma, the *smell*, was stomach-turning. When a half-dozen or more students would arrive in my classroom to eat, I would *lose my appetite* and, to this day, have *never* used ketchup on anything, ever.

The only notable place to eat (I ate the Chinese take-out pretty regularly) was also on Grand Street, just about a block from the school: *The Doughnut Plant* had great coffee with artistic (*artisanal*) doughnuts the New York Times called "Doughnuts of the Gods." It's no wonder I put on some pounds eating on Grand Street. But even those heavenly doughnuts couldn't be consumed *daily*, so my school days, like those in my neighborhood, were conspicuously barren regarding decent food. Not so when I got to *SDC*.

On 10th Avenue, between 49th and 50th Street, there were two delis, a pizza place and a pretty good Chinese take-out establishment (you could call ahead). On the west side at 50th was the omnipresent *Subway* shop. There was even a *DINER* on the southeast corner of 10th and 51st! Within a couple of weeks, I was enough of a regular at the diner and at the 48th & 10th Deli, that I'd get a friendly greeting the moment I walked in. If I happened to have a day with extra time for lunch, I'd trek around to 51st and 9th, where there was an excellent *Gourmet* deli (they made pizza *and* burgers) to get a specialty sandwich (pastrami with cole slaw and Russian dressing). Between the school neighborhood, and living on West 82nd St., with its myriad grocery stores and diners, I was now "living the life," as far as food was concerned. I was one happy camper.

Shelter

A predicament I had at *ESA* was being a "traveling" teacher. This meant I wheeled a cart with all my books and materials, traveling from one classroom to another: five classes in three different rooms with no home base. The only desk I could call my own was in the Faculty Room, which was always teeming with students (If you have your own classroom there are times, particularly before and after school, when you can close *and lock* your door, achieving some semblance of peace and quiet). Having no "oasis" contributed to the recurring nightmares I had that year.

SDC provided me with a classroom that was mine, and mine alone, which was great, but in my first two years it proved highly problematic. When I got there, in August of 2009, the only available classroom space for me was a Science Lab, which was *tiered* and had a huge, black *lab table* up front. As one who likes to move desks around — into concentric circles for Socratic Seminars, into tables of four for group work — this was *challenging*, to say the least. Added to that situation was a much graver problem, and one I battled for *two years*. The thermostat for my room was broken and apparently *unfixable* by *anyone* who worked for the New York City Board of Ed! The room always felt like it was 75 to 80 degrees (F), leading one to believe we had been transported to Arizona. Did I mention that the room had *NO WINDOWS?* My students, god bless them, dealt with it as best they could, as did I. Even though I *constantly* requested a room change ("As soon as one's available, you'll get it") we *baked* in that *sauna* for two years.

When Jonathan Davis left to start his doctorate, a *real* classroom became available and I spent my last three years in *my own room*, with my own desk, my own posters on the walls, and *movable desks* for my students. My *SHELTER* prayers were finally answered!

Community

The lack of *community* at *Essex Street Academy* was palpable. I not only felt like an old man with my students, but also with my colleagues. I was appalled, sitting at staff meetings, watching them *on their phones*, clearly not paying attention to whatever Alex was talking about, *or texting each other*, commenting on it! Their seeming indifference to setting standards and demanding that students meet them was a sore point I kept raising. *ESA* was a classic bad-fit. *SDC* proved quite the opposite. While I may not have been seen as a wise old elder, I *was,* at least, *respected* as a veteran teacher. The staff was serious about preparing students for the next level, be it college, junior college, the military, or the work world. *The School of Design and Construction* created a sense of belonging *between* staff and students, *among* the student body and *within* the Faculty. Some activities were small, and certainly not unique to *SDC*, while others were school-wide and public.

For example, there was a yearly contest to design a mural, with the winning entry being painted on a wall of the school by a team of teachers and students. Another wall, in the Main Hallway, was used to post the entire faculty's photos, with each teacher's college and graduate school listed. Students were encouraged to talk to us about our college experiences, to ask about what it was like to go to the schools we did. In the same fashion, our annual *Alumni Day* saw former *SDC* students, now in college or working in the Design or Construction fields, come back to talk and answer questions. All of this was a *community-wide* effort to make our claim of being a *college preparatory* high school a reality, and it definitely pulled us together.

Another way the staff worked toward ensuring students were ready for the next level occurred during Departmental Meetings. At *SDC,* teachers worked together creating standards, using Tuning Protocols, a method first developed by Joe McDonald and David Allen for the *Coalition,* ensuring that grading, within a Department, was consistent and *criteria-based,* based on a *standard* and not *personal whimsy.* Using a *rubric,* we shared our students' work and *collectively* assessed it, making sure we, as a Department, were being *fair* and *consistent.* This process created *genuine collegiality* as well as respect. The sense of *collective* work toward a mutual goal was professionally satisfying and clearly reflected a commitment to the school.

A common problem shared by New York City high schools is *attendance* and *tardiness.* (There are reams of research about schools opening too early for the adolescent brain) We combatted those issues by designing a schedule where school started with "X" Block. This was a first period where *NO* classes met while teachers were in classrooms, available for extra help, counseling, or whatever students wanted or needed. Starting school around 8:45 or 8:55 improved our attendance and our more conscientious students certainly benefitted from the early morning support. In a similar fashion, I got a chance to feel more like an integral member of the school when Principal

Matt Willoughby asked me to *mentor* Keith Mendak, our Art teacher. Keith was part of a New York City certification program and needed guided (and documented) observation/practice. I was already friendly with Keith (who is a *brilliant* artist) so it was a fun assignment. What was *educational* for me was seeing our students (some of whom I taught) in a *completely* different environment, working on tasks that were unlike anything they would do in "academic" classes. It sparked my own thinking about methods and assessment, and I think I offered some constructive advice to Keith. Because our Art and Design classes were on the lower floors of the building (as were the cafeteria and library. The gymnasium, oddly, was on the fifth/top floor) it was good to observe a part of the school that was integral to our students while alien to those of us teaching upstairs.

On the whole-school front there were several events, programs, and on-going activities that also created a strong sense of community. One of these was *Poetry Out Loud:*

> *a recitation contest sponsored by the National Endowment for the Arts and the Poetry Foundation. About 200,000 high school students take part in this competition. They recite poetry of all kinds from memory. (wiki)*

Every student at *SDC*, and *every* English teacher (as well as several *Social Studies/History* teachers, and others), *memorized* a poem, stood in class and recited it, *without notes*. (This is *exactly* like an "Exhibition" Ted Sizer uses as an example of student-centered work in *Horace's School).* Ultimately, about 10 students were competing to be our representative to the National Contest. Our Finals were held in the auditorium. I recruited two judges, getting Sara Nolan, a former Brown student, poet, and education activist, and one of my all-time favorite Blind Brook High School graduates, Joe Levy. After writing for, and later editing, *The Village Voice*, Joe was an editor at *Details* magazine and then the Executive Editor at *Rolling Stone*. When I asked Joe to be one of our judges, he was editing *Maxim* magazine and our students were appropriately impressed. I was extremely happy to contribute to an event that clearly brought our school together, unlike anything in my *ESA* experience.

All schools, not just urban schools, struggle with *discipline*. There are always *bad actors* around and the question is: "How do we deal with them?" I was never a fan of detention (I believed it was a Club in most schools, because the *same* kids met *after* school each day, often with a particular teacher — a Club Advisor, as I saw it. If the *same kids* were there all the time, it seemed the punishment, *detaining them*, really wasn't working.). *Suspension* and *expulsion* didn't seem to remedy problems either. Kids were acting out because there was something they didn't like about being in school: so let's give them *days* off (suspension) or throw them out altogether? No, we needed to find a system that more effectively worked at not only modifying behavior but also making students responsible for their actions. Luckily for us, that's when Erin Dunleavy arrived at *SDC*.

Erin Dunleavy was a whirlwind of an educator, who introduced a *crucial innovation* to our community. Erin brought us *Restorative Justice* and we bought in right away because it seemed *right* for our school.

The concept of restorative justice, which has only gained widespread attention in the past decade, seeks to address youth justice in a more holistic way. Restorative justice aims to shift the conversation away from

*how a punitive legal system can enact retribution on
an offender and instead looks to help the offender
make reparations to their community, usually through
justice mediation, counseling, or even reparations.
This often results in more community-based support
for the delinquent, stronger relationships within the
community, and a deeper sense of remorse.*
(SocialSolutions.com)

Restorative Justice *became* our disciplinary program and
it was impressive how quickly *both* teachers and students took
to it. With Erin's guidance (she is now a Restorative Justice
Coach & Equity Consultant at NYU) the program became an
integral and formative element of our community. Students
were no longer assigned detention or given suspensions.
We had student/teacher panels of mediators/arbiters (all
prepared for their roles) who listened to cases and meted out
judgments, often in the form of community service or some
other reparations activity. *Restorative Justice* took the weight
of discipline off the teachers and administrators, making it a
community responsibility.

What you can see in these examples is a consistent focus
on making students engaged and responsible members of the
school *community*. It wasn't a weekly Town Meeting, like *Essex
Street*, which was artificial and forced. Yet even our best efforts
could not combat tragedy, and that befell *SDC* the weekend
of March 9, 2013. As reported in numerous news outlets on
Sunday morning, March 10th:

*Two plainclothes police officers shot and killed a
teenage boy late Saturday night on a Brooklyn street,
after he pointed a handgun at the officers, the police said.*

Kimani Gray was a sophomore at *SDC* and the news of his death and *how* it happened was a shock that reverberated throughout our school.

By 2013 I was only teaching Juniors and Seniors at *SDC* so I never had Kimani in class and can't claim to have known him. But *everyone* who knew him, students and staff, was *devastated*. And, to a person, *no one* believed he was carrying *a gun*! What appeared in the papers, several days later, was a picture of a rather antique *revolver* and, while I know I watch too much *Law & Order*, it certainly looked like a "drop gun," the kind police plant at a scene where a *bad shooting* occurs. Within days, there were questions about the "incident." Touré, the political commentator for *MSNBC*, wrote:

> *If that's true then it's a justified killing. But some doubt that story. Some eyewitnesses say Gray did not have a gun. I'd like to see if his fingerprints are on the gun found at the scene. Officers say they yelled "don't move," but others say they did not identify themselves as NYPD and Gray may have thought he was being robbed. What was Gray doing to attract police attention? Standing on a corner. When they approached, he walked away and grabbed at his waistband. Cops zeroed in.*

There was a great deal of conflicting information. By March 28th the *NY Daily News* published this report:

> *A Brooklyn woman who witnessed the fatal police shooting of 16-year-old Kimani Gray in East Flatbush in 2013 has testified under oath that the teen had his hands up and did not point a gun at cops as they claim*

he did, according to court papers. "On cross-examination, I asked King a few questions about the shooting, and she testified that (Mourad and Cordova) shot Kimani Gray while he had his hands up and that, at no time, did Gray point a weapon at the defendants King gave the same account to the Daily News three days after the shooting, insisting that Gray did not have a gun in his hand and was backing away from the officers when he was shot.

Finally, we learned this from our local *CBS* news outlet:

Kimani Gray, 16, was shot and killed March 9, 2013, by two officers in East Flatbush, Brooklyn. Autopsy results showed he was shot seven times in his shoulders, arms and legs, with wounds to the front and back of his body.

We held a Memorial for Kimani within about ten days after the incident and his Mother addressed the entire school, thanking students and staff for their outpouring of support. This woman's strength and composure, in light of the egregious personal tragedy, was stunning. My students were not unfamiliar with violence (one of my favorite students had lost her older brother to gun violence) but this killing of a child made no sense to any of us. We tried to offer comfort to Kimani's mother. The cloud of Kimani's killing hung over us for the final months of that school year, bringing the school together as only a shared tragedy can.

We were able to finish on a bit of high note that Spring because of a tradition that had begun several years earlier, *The Iron Designer Challenge.* Taking a cue from the popular *Food Network* show, *Iron Chef* (a Japanese import which pitted two chefs in a competition based on a *mystery* ingredient) the *School of Design and Construction* devised an architectural competition that also used a *mystery* element. Set on the roof of the Park West Campus, a vast area where we also held a School Carnival each Spring, teams of students, paired with several young architects from our partner firms, were given a month to prepare the construction of some basic architectural item — like a portal or a shelter. Each team was given the same building materials and *one hour* to construct their assigned item but *one-half hour in*to the competition, a *mystery* element was introduced to the challenge ("You have to use *roofing tiles!*"). Outside judges would walk around, with their *written criteria* (Teamwork, Using all Required Elements, Creativity) and then confer, declaring a winner. There were prizes for the winners. The event was also a fund-raiser for the school, with a silent auction of donated gifts (Yankee tickets, bottles of wine, cruises). Hors d'oeuvres and canapes were served and it was a great *community* event, involving students, parents, staff, outside guests and our school partners.

My contribution to the *Iron Designer Challenge* was, once again, my ability to recruit *judges.* One year I got my Yale classmate, Duncan Hazard, the Managing Partner of Ennead Architects (formerly *Polshek Partnership*), and several of his colleagues, along with a high school classmate, Robert (Bob) Marino, a wonderful architect who not only has his own firm but also taught at Columbia, to serve as our arbiters. Another year I got Pulitzer Prize winning architectural critic Paul Goldberger, a Vincent Scully acolyte and Yale schoolmate, to be a judge. As the old guy on the staff, my *connections* were appreciated for events like *Poetry Out Loud* and *Iron Designer Challenge.* I was more than happy to contribute and it made me feel I was an integral part of our school *community.*

Chapter 34

A Rumination

A Side Street

Before completing this story, it's important to put the school reform crusade in context with a metaphor I find historically apt. Around the time Horace Mann was trying to systematize America's public schools (early 1840s), organized baseball began in the United States (according to Wikipedia: *"The first team to play baseball under modern rules was long believed to be the New York Knickerbockers. The club was founded on September 23, 1845."*). As schools developed, so did our national pastime. Both were formalized around the turn of the 20th century (*The committee of Ten* report in 1892-93 & the merger of the National & American Leagues in 1903). By the 1920's the public-school system *and* professional baseball were not only an inherent part of *American culture*, they were crucially important for *assimilating* hundreds of thousands of new U.S. immigrants and their families. Obviously, the school did it through teaching "reading, writing, and 'rithmetic" and baseball provided an easily understandable sport with home-town heroes (whose last names were *ethnically* identifiable in a variety of *white* communities). Just as New York was a very inviting city for newcomers (you can *always* find your way around a *numbered grid*), baseball, played in its summertime *parks* for cheap admission, was also a natural for the emerging world power. After World War II, baseball led the way in Civil Rights, with Jackie Robinson breaking the color barrier April 15, 1947. By then, the strong regional identities of teams were established and, like the schools, were part of the *cultural glue* that held American society together.

The biggest difference between baseball and the schools has to do with standards and *assessment.* And this is where *school reform* enters the picture. From the outset, we knew how to gauge *who* the outstanding baseball players were, based on *performance.* Even though a batter's success rate might only be 30%, that made him *one of the best* in the business (incredibly *high standards!*). Pitchers who could strike out a high per-centage of batters and win lots of games were also valuable. *Schools* have yet to learn this simple lesson: *performance-based standards* provide clear, known measurements of success and *clear targets* for students! (And, yes, there have been "cheaters," *spitball* pitchers, corked-bat hitters, and, of course, all those *PED-users* in the 1980s/1990s. While they may have altered some records (I'll always recognize Hank Aaron as the Home Run King) none of them *changed the standards*) I could go on about how following the westward movement of baseball teams after World War II — from 16 teams clustered *East* of St. Louis, to *30 teams* spread across the width and breadth of the continent — reflects demographic and economic shifts in our nation, but I won't. I'll only offer a simple essay about *baseball,* a sport that is played for about 180 to 200 days a year (just as most public school years are a mandated 180 to 200 days) and, like schools and school change, has a subtle beauty to it, when viewed with the right perspective.

An Excursion

One of the benefits of my years consulting was the opportunity to visit cities with Major League Baseball teams. As a result, I saw games in a wide variety of ballparks and stadiums around the country. As one who grew up playing baseball and rooting for his home team starting in the 1950s, it's part of my DNA. When I was eight years old, the Brooklyn Dodgers announced they were leaving the Borough and moving to (gasp!) Los Angeles. My parents, both born and raised in Brooklyn, were die-hard Dodger fans. I don't know how my Dad did it (we were *working-poor*, at best) but he managed to get *two box seat tickets* for the last Labor Day doubleheader at Ebbets Field in Flatbush, against the Philadelphia Phillies. While I can't recall the outcome of the games, I'll *never forget* my first walk through the dark, moist tunnel leading to the field. Almost blinded by the sunlight and the vast expanse of *green*, I *do* remember blinking furiously and gasping for breath. It was *The. Most. Beautiful. Sight.* I had ever encountered in all of my eight years! I still get that childhood rush when I see the beautiful, manicured outfield grass extending forever. Consulting gave me the opportunity to experience that thrill in parks across the country and it was always a special pleasure.

On various Education junkets, I had the opportunity to see games in Toronto (on artificial turf, which really *does* detract from the game but, hey, it's *Canada*), the old Kingdome in Seattle (the *absolute worst* artificial turf *and* the *worst lit* ballpark I've ever been in. It was like watching a game in someone's *cellar!*), the then-new Seattle SafeCo (now T-Mobile) Field (nicest ballpark I've been to, making up for the past sin of the Kingdome), PetCo Park in San Diego (built to accommodate an old warehouse in Left Field,and a beautiful venue), the Oakland Coliseum (a football stadium used for baseball), the (relatively new) *Nationals* Park in D.C., and, most notably, *Wrigley Field* in Chicago, the 2nd oldest extant ballpark in the country. Consulting with two of my best friends, Joel Kammer and Steve Cantrell (*"Trust the Process" Consultants*), we actually went to Jacobs (now *Progressive*) Field two nights in a row to enjoy Indians games. Before I started consulting, I had been to the *original* Yankee Stadium, as well as the renovated (and uglier) Yankee Stadium, and Shea Stadium in New York. Living in Boston, I visited Fenway Park (the *oldest* ballpark) numerous times, including the 1986 World Series against the Mets.

On my own, separate from the consulting, I've managed to see games in Philadelphia (with my brother, which is always a treat) as well as a number of ballparks with the Lovely Carol Marie. In the spring of 2015, on an extended road trip to Miami and back (from Norwalk, CT) we caught a Yankees/ Rays game at Tropicana Field in St. Petersburg. We enjoyed that so much, we actually *planned* a vacation around seeing baseball games in 2016. We flew to San Diego, catching games at PetCo Park *and* Dodger Stadium (the 3rd oldest ballpark) and then drove north to the Bay Area to see the Athletics at the Oakland Coliseum and the Giants at AT & T (now Oracle) Park. Luckily for me, the Lovely Carol Marie is not only a brilliant and dedicated school reformer but also an avid baseball fan — and a *knowledgeable* one as well (her son, Mark, pitched *professionally*). We took a weekend trip to Baltimore, just to experience Oriole Park at Camden Yards in the spring of 2018. And we're not averse to seeing Minor League games on *Staten Island* (the Yankees). I've also seen Minor League teams in New Britain, Connecticut (the Rock Cats), Norwich, Connecticut (Norwich Tigers), Coney Island, Brooklyn (the Mets/*Cyclones*) and Tacoma, WA (the *Rainiers*). Last summer, visiting friends in Chapel Hill, I caught a Durham Bulls game in their beautiful, newly renovated park.

While living in Providence, I was only a few miles away from McCoy Stadium and can't count the number of games I saw the Pawtucket Red Sox play over the years. I was *always* accompanied by Ed Abbott, the best classroom teacher I've ever known and the finest Mentor teacher in Brown's teacher prep program. We sometimes arranged for field trips with our UTEP/MAT groups, to watch games at McCoy (I even saw a Bob Dylan concert there). It's a wonderful little ballpark and going with Mr. Abbott always made it special. A dyed-in-the-wool Red Sox fan, he and I would spar about the Yankees/Red Sox rivalry while observing the finer points of baseball during a PawSox game. Pure pleasure.

I know there are (many) people who find baseball boring and can't stand watching it. The action of NFL or NBA games is more satisfying. That makes sense to me, particularly in our video-game, digital culture because baseball is, indeed, a throwback to another time — *just like our schools*! Professional baseball started 150 years ago, shortly after the *Civil War* ended! It took a while to develop the version we know today but it is remarkable how *stable* the sport has been. By that I mean, the baseball we watch in 2020 is essentially *the same game* that spectators in 1920 watched. No added *3-point lines* or widening of the foul lane; no moving the goal posts and hashmarks in and out, back and forth. Yes, the distance to the fences periodically changes and the addition of the *Designated*

Hitter in the American League in 1973 seemed *revolutionary* to purists, but the *basic* game *has not changed.*

And that's what makes baseball interesting to me. No matter how much bigger, faster, stronger athletes get (even *without* performance-enhancing drugs), *no player* can outrun a hard-hit ball to shortstop (if it is fielded cleanly). Somehow, the 90 feet from base-to-base is *perfect* for humans (and human evolution). The 60'6" distance from the pitcher's rubber to home plate seems *exactly right* for someone trying to hit a round ball with a round bat (*the single most difficult athletic skill*). In what profession does a 30% Success Rate put you at the *TOP* of your field? And, because baseball's dimensions have remained constant, we *can* compare .300 hitters from one generation to another. Sure, there have been tweaks to the game (the evolution of *relief pitching*, for example, or travel schedules and their effects on performance) but, overall, *baseball is baseball* and it's a beautiful game. It *is the* Summer Game. As George Carlin noted, you go to "the park" and the players wear a cap (not a *helmet*). In Carlin's words, where football "is directed by a field general marching his troops down the field with pinpoint bombs while avoiding the blitz," baseball players are just "trying to get Home." Comic, but insightful. It's a wonderful game any kid can start playing at an early age.

I got my first baseball mitt on my 7th birthday and, from that point on, had a catch with my Dad in our backyard almost *every* summer night after dinner until I started playing Little League at age 11. It's why the final scene in *Field of Dreams* will *always* bring a tear to my eye (and I'm sure I'm not alone). Kevin Costner's character, Ray Kinsella, asks his Dad (John Kinsella, brought back as a spirit thanks to the *Field of Dreams*), "Hey, . . . Dad . . . do you wanna have a catch?" It's just *so*

American. And that's what baseball is. James Earl Jones's character, Terrence Mann, sums it all up in his final soliloquy:

> *The one constant through all the years, Ray, has been baseball. America has rolled by like an army of steamrollers. It has been erased like a blackboard, rebuilt and erased again. But baseball has marked the time. This field, this game; it's a part of our past, Ray. It reminds us of all that once was good, and that could be again.*

I agree with that (and particularly like the blackboard connection to school) and it's why baseball parks, and the game itself, will always be near and dear to me. As Spring training begins in mid-February, *baseball* revives our hopes (Spring is on the way), as the players begin their marathon schedule in April (and even late-March now) we unfailingly root for our home team, something a non-baseball fan finds curious and mysterious.

Eileen Landay, my dear colleague at Brown, could *never* understand the allegiance Larry Wakeford and I had to our New York Yankees. To Eileen it seemed primitively *tribal* and irrational (she was, after all, an *"East"*). We, of course, totally dedicated to our hometown heroes, tried to explain to her the *importance* of cheering for your team and *suffering* during their losses. For us, both lapsed Catholics, it was as close as we would ever get to religion. You live and die with your team.

> *(I remember coming home from South Bay School in Babylon, when I was in first grade in the fall of 1955, finding my mother in front of the television set, something she never did during the day, with an ironing*

board in front of her, ironing our clothes, as she watched the Brooklyn Dodgers playing the New York Yankees in the World Series. It was 1955 and Brooklyn fans were famous for saying "Wait 'til Next Year" because they had never won the World Series — and often lost to the Yankees — 5 out of 5 at that point in time. As it turned out, 1955 was the "next year" Brooklynites had been waiting for. They won their one and only World Series Championship in Brooklyn, before leaving for the West Coast in 1958. They did return to the World Series in 1956 but, of course, lost to the Yankees!)

Like religion, it is very difficult to explain to a non-believer like Eileen. For those who "root, root, root for the home team," there's nothing like it!

That *allegiance* to one's home team has always been part of my make-up, making an unquestioned *commitment* to support a team/teammate, a cause, a friend, through thick-and-thin. Just as I have remained a loyal New York Yankees fan for 62 years, my dedication to trying to reform/change schools has also been a *commitment*, a cause, I've been dedicated to for a half-century. Even though I'm "out of the game" now, this book, about a career spent tilting at windmills, is an attempt at creating a record of what it's like to find one's passion and pursue it, through the ups and downs, the hot streaks and losing seasons, the championship seasons and the down years. Looking back, it's been a good run and, in the end, only my teammates, my colleagues and my students, can judge what was accomplished. All I know is that I can honestly say, *"I left it all on the field."*

Chapter 35

Final Report Card

"Don't remind me of my failures, I had not forgotten them."

Jackson Brown, *These Days*

I started writing this memoir on February 22, 2019 as a simple reflection. Originally, it was supposed to be a look at what I believed were the *formative texts* that shaped my teaching career. But the narrative grew and now, two months later, it's several hundred pages chronicling a forty-five-year journey. Teaching is an odd profession because, historically (before widespread social media), the young people you work with leave your sight/care by the time they are 18 and you never see them again. Even if you teach college or graduate school, they turn 22, 23, 25, whatever, and "poof!" they're gone. I have been fortunate, throughout my years in teaching, to maintain contact not only with those colleagues whose friendships I have valued, but also with scores of former students. It is gratifying to have them (some in their *late 50's*) tell you they think you were a *great teacher*. Truth be told, few remember *anything* you taught but they do seem to remember that your class was fun, interesting, engaging, and they were challenged to *think*.

When preparing students to become teachers, I remember telling them to think about *that teacher* they admired, revered, loved, in high school (mine was Harold Anderson, my 9th grade English teacher). My guess was that what led to their choice was that the teacher *never* talked down to them, *always* expected high-quality work, and clearly took his/her job *seriously*. I shared with my students that, as a teacher, I *always* wanted to be *that* teacher for my students. What I reminded them was: *wishing doesn't make it so*. As a teacher, you have to know *yourself* and *never* be a phony with the kids. Finding who *you* are in your classroom is the key. Once you are comfortable with *how* you will work with/talk to kids (*honestly*), *what* you will expect from them (*their best*), and make a total *commitment* to your profession, everything else falls into place. My belief in this was based not only in personal experience but also from having read two stories, one by Andy Rooney and another by Fred Hechinger, documenting the work of great teachers. I still have the yellowed, Xeroxed copies of the articles — one from the *NY Daily News* (Rooney) and one from the *New York Times* (Hechinger). Neither has a date but I remember clipping them years ago, when I was still a young classroom teacher.

Both articles note that a revered teacher had passed away. In Rooney's column (*His Subject Was English But He Lived, Taught Life*) he begins by relating how he was shocked to read about that death of Herbert Hahn, 75, in an obituary and laments never having called to tell him what an important influence he was. Hahn had been Rooney's high school History teacher in the 1930s, before moving to "a good private school in New Jersey" where he became an English teacher. As Rooney notes:

> *It didn't really matter what Mr. Hahn's class was*
> *called. He taught life.*
>
> *When we were 13 and 15, he talked to us as though*
> *we were human beings, not children. He talked about*
> *everything in class, and just to make sure we knew he*
> *didn't think he was omnipotent, he often followed some*
> *pronouncement he made about government or politics*
> *by saying, "And don't forget, you heard it from the same*
> *teacher who predicted in 1932 that Hitler would get*
> *nowhere in Germany."*

I remember reading this column (I believe I was still teaching at Blind Brook — because my dear friend and colleague Del Shortliffe mentioned he went to prep school with Rooney's son) and thinking, "That's the kind of teacher I'd like to be." There were a couple of other quotes about Mr. Hahn I related to.

> *He didn't do a lot of talking, but when he talked*
> *he was direct and often brilliant. He exuded wisdom,*
> *concern for the world and quite often a bad temper. Id-*
> *iots irritated him and it annoyed him when teen-agers*
> *acted younger than he was treating them.*

I believe I let my students know my concern for the world (my politics were *never* a secret!) and, especially in my early years, students (particularly my poor basketball teams) suffered the wrath of my bad temper when patience ran out. For all of that, I hope (to this day) that my colleagues and students would see me in the light Rooney paints Mr. Hahn in: *"He was the kind of person who gave teachers the right to be proud to be teachers."* If nothing else, I was *always* proud to be a teacher

and worked hard at helping my students reach *their* poten-
tial. I was never unaware that their incredibly sharp eyes *never*
missed a detail of what you wore, how you spoke, what *little*
mannerisms you brought into your room (if you want a great
mirror, watch a student impersonate you, as I did, more than
once in my career. It's frightening in its accuracy). Indeed, in
Rooney's article, he mentions *"I even remember that he had only
two suits."* Even at Albany Academy in the 1930s the students
remembered *what* their teacher wore. It's a harsh spotlight and,
as a teacher, you have to remember you are *always* a role model
— for good, you hope, and, not too often (you also hope) for ill.

The Hechinger article (I tracked it down through *Google*:
November 10, 1987) details the work of Theresa Ross, a 60-
year teaching veteran who passed away at 83. She had spent
43 years at the Dalton School and the point of Hechinger's
article is simple:

> *It has been said that education is what you re-
> member when you have forgotten what you have learned.
> Often, that means remembering one's great teachers
> more vividly than any particular lesson. Anyone who
> has never had at least one such teacher is truly deprived.
> To expect many is unreasonable. I remember three.*

Unlike Rooney, Hechinger does not detail his great
teachers but uses Theresa (*Tessie*) Ross as a *case study*. As he
says: *"To write about her is not to celebrate a person but to try
to define some qualities of exceptional teaching."* Reading that in
the fall of 1987, as I was just beginning my Bronxville journey,
made me sit up to see if I was checking the correct boxes in my
desire to be a great teacher. What made *Tessie* one, according
to Hechinger, was that *"Great teachers are strong enough to*

dare being unconventional, even controversial . . . Tessie's idea of progressive education was, like Dewey's, that the school should function like a well-ordered, fair community." Certainly, my work with the *Coalition* coincided with that model — and the Student-Faculty Legislature (SFL) at Bronxville, as well as the Community Congress and Justice Committee at Parker, attempted to create a "well-ordered, fair community."

At the same time, Hechinger notes, "*She could be tough. . . . 'Children must learn that any act has consequences' . . . She considered it absurd to teach ethics separately from other subjects . . . She never prejudged children, never thought of them as being below grade level. She looked at their progress.*" Those were *all* qualities I aspired to throughout my career. You can only hope you achieve those goals to some extent.

Finally, Hechinger notes: "*One test of great teachers is how long their influence lasts.*" As mentioned earlier, I've been lucky enough, even before the advent of *Facebook* and social media, to stay in touch with many of my former students, from the high schools I worked at, as well as numerous colleagues who were students in Brown's preparation program. In fact, one of my former Brown MAT's sent me an email saying I must have felt pretty good about what Kathryn Bertine had written about me in the Introduction to one of her books. I knew Katy (now Kathryn), a Bronxville graduate who went to Colgate, had pursued a professional athletic *and* writing career, but was unaware of the piece Tim mentioned. The introduction to her book *The Road Less Taken: Lessons from a Life Spent Cycling*, discusses a letter I had the seniors write in her Advisory group at Bronxville in the spring of 1993. I asked them to compose a letter to themselves (I learned this from Margaret Metzger, a legendary English teacher in Brookline, MA) that I would *not* read and would send to them in *ten years*. Kathryn starts her introduction discussing that assignment (after receiving the letter in 2003). She then says:

> *Bil Johnson was the man. The dude. The cool teacher. The one with the ponytail, the hip wardrobe, and a passion for teaching accented with a slight, un-spoken disdain for the syllabi and structures that steered students toward test-score prowess instead of an educa-tion based on truly absorbing the lessons of the world. . . .*
> *I wrote this (book) for the Bil Johnsons of the world, who send mirrors masked as letters and use words to help us take a look at ourselves.*

To say that such a testimonial is gratifying would be a gross understatement.

I have often said I've had a very *fortunate* life, always seeming to be in the right place, at the right time (my Mother, of course, attributes it to *"Fate,"* but she's Sicilian). All the stops along the way (with the exception of *Essex Street* Academy) made my school reform journey an exciting *and* enjoyable trek. The students were always my focus and one only hopes to get the kind of feedback Kathryn documents in her In-troduction. Equally significant, is the relationship you have with your colleagues. I can't even begin to list all the won-derful teachers and teacher-educators I have had the honor to work with over the years. I learned a great deal from those colleagues and only hope they gleaned some wisdom from me, too. When I left Brown, Carin Algava, the always-thoughtful and hyper-efficient Teacher Prep Program Administrator, put a book together, a collection of notes from colleagues, students, and former students. Eileen Landay, the Director of English Education, the founder of the Arts/Literacy program, author, and all-around amazing *Educator,* had to miss the *going-away* party but wrote this:

> *Bil, you are brash, outspoken, a whirlwind of energy. At the same time, you are intuitive, sensitive and deeply caring. You are also efficient, and you work very, very hard. Most important, you are deeply serious and committed to the work you do, something I hope this university recognizes and acknowledges. Bil, you ARE A TEACHER and I have been privileged to learn from you.*

High praise, indeed, particularly coming from a colleague I have so much respect for — and one who put up with my endless teasing and sarcasm for twelve years! I include this not to "blow my own horn" but more to reinforce, for myself, that all the work was not in vain, that people along the way "*got it.*"

Many years ago, when I was teaching at Blind Brook High School and avidly reading the Village Voice, they ran a sketch of Sherlock Holmes with this quote:

> *My mind rebels at stagnation. Give me problems, give me work, give me the most abstruse cryptogram, or the most intricate analysis, and I am in my own proper atmosphere . . . I abhor the dull routine of existence.*
> *I crave for mental exaltation.*

I cut out the sketch and quote and taped it up in my classroom. I took it with me when I moved. It went to Winchester, and Bronxville, then Brown, and Parker, and Yale, and Essex Street, and, finally, *SDC.* It's still in a file folder in our home office. I have always found those inspiring words not only a quote to live by but also to *teach* by. It made me particularly pleased when, as I researched writing this memoir, I ran across a letter from November of 1986. It was written by Howard Stein, the Chairman of the Oscar Hammerstein Center for Theater Studies at Columbia. I had worked with Howard in the summer of 1986 with a National Endowment of the Humanities fellowship. As a follow-up to the summer program, Howard wrote letters to the Principals of the 15 high school teachers he had worked with. In describing my work that summer, Howard said: *"His mind jumps to analogies and associations and as a result he shared with us many such private and illuminating moments. He ventured out into the city for as many unconventional and conventional theater going experiences as he would find. He has an alive mind which yearns for challenge and adventure. . . . I thought you should know."*

If I could choose my epitaph, one that I *hoped* represented who I was as a teacher and person, it would be Howard's *"He has an alive mind which yearns for challenge and adventure."* It's right up there with Conan Doyle's quote about Holmes. Maybe that's why I still have that clipping.

PostScript

One Last Thought

As this book was being re-written, New York City's Mayor and School Chancellor proposed doing away with "Gifted and Talented" programs, as a strategy to de-segregate the nation's largest school system. While applauding their initiative, the results are predictable. After much ballyhoo, the proposal will be abandoned and the city will continue to wrestle with a system that clearly does not serve its African American and Latino students very well. (The proposal, by the way, left the "Select" high schools— Stuyvesant, Bronx Science, et al— untouched, insuring the "high achieving" Asian and CaucAsian test geeks would have a "safe space.") If I sound unduly cynical it's only because I am.

After nearly a half century of trying to reform education, after working with some of the most brilliant people in the field, after being part of the creation of two very successful *progressive public high schools*, the larger system remains veritably *unchanged*. I'm guessing students attending Bay Shore High School in the early 21st century are getting a tech-updated version of the *same education* I received there in the mid-1960s.

This only reinforces Herndon's and Sizer's view that the public school in America is a *secular church*. It wouldn't be so distressing me if there had been a larger and more successful *Protestant Reformation*! That's what I thought was transpiring, starting with the New Haven High School in the Community in the late 1960s, the no-walls Blind Brook Jr./Sr. High School of the 1970s, the Coalition of Essential Schools participants of the 1980s and 1990s, and the creation of *The Francis W. Parker Charter Essential School* and *Blackstone Academy* in the 1990s and early 2000s. As it turns out, those are all *outliers*, existing in their own atmosphere, distant planets having nothing to do with that larger, stultifying system that New York's Mayor and Chancellor hope to reform.

This is not to say I regret one moment of my journey. The Citadel of Schooling in the United States was constructed in the late 19th century, when America was a blatantly apartheid nation, wrestling with a growing immigrant population and increasing its Global Power militarily, as well as in industry and economics. Maybe it's foolish to think you can topple such a Beast but, when you believe your Cause is just — particularly because its goal is to bring equality and social justice to those who have been oppressed — you *have to* try. And that's what we did.

Despite today's bleak landscape, I am still an optimist at heart, particularly regarding *education*. It *is* a great equalizer when implemented properly and, even though history weighs against the notion that the system will change, it doesn't mean we can't continue to work at it and maybe, just maybe, bring about a genuine *revolution* across school systems around the nation. There are thousands and thousands of dedicated teachers working hard, every day, to do the best for their students — and they, as much as their students, deserve a system that works *for* them, not against them. Surely, that's an ideal worth believing in, and working toward, isn't it?

Bibliography

Dante Alighieri, *1265-1321. The Divine Comedy of Dante Alighieri: Inferno, Purgatory, Paradise. New York: The Union Library Association, 1935.*

DeLillo, Don, *The Day Room*, New York, Alfred A. Knopf, 1986

Freire, Paolo, *Pedagogy of the Oppressed*, New York, Continuum, 1970

Herndon, James, *How to Survive in Your Native Land*, New York, Simon and Schuster, 1971

Herndon, James, *Notes from a Schoolteacher*, New York, Simon and Schuster, 1984 hooks, bell. *Teaching To Transgress: Education As The Practice Of Freedom*. New York, Routledge, 1994. Print.

Jacobs, Heidi Hayes, (ed.), *Interdisciplinary Curriculum: Design & Implementation*, ASCD, Alexandria, VA, 1989

Johnson, Bil *The Performance Assessment Handbook, Volumes 1 & 2*, Princeton, N.J. Eye-on-Education, 1996

Johnson, Bil *The Student-Centered Classroom Handbook*, Larchmont, NY, Eye-on-Education, 2003

MacInerney, Jay, *Bright Lights, Big City,* Random House, N.Y. 1984

Mailer, Norman, *Why Are We in Vietnam?* New York, J.P. Putnam's Sons, 1967

Mailer, Norman, *Armies of the Night,* New York, New American Library, 1968

Meisner, Sanford, & Dennis Longwell, Sydney Pollack, *Sanford Meisner on Acting,* Vintage Books, NY, 1987

Oakes, Jeannie, *Keeping Track,* Yale University Press, 1985

Postman, Neil, and Weingartner, Charles *Teaching as a Subversive Activity,* New York, Delacorte Press, 1969

Reich, Charles, *The Greening of America,* New York, Random House, 1970

Rogers, Carl R., *Freedom to Learn,* Columbus, Ohio, Charles E. Merrill, 1969

Roszak, Theodore, *The Making of a Counterculture,* University of California Press, 1969

Sizer, Theodore R. *Horace's Compromise.* Boston Houghton Mifflin Co., 1984

Sizer, Theodore R. *Horace's School,* Boston Houghton Mifflin Co, 1993.

Slater, Philip, *The Pursuit of Loneliness,* New York, Random House, 1970

Spolin, Viola, *Theater Games for Rehearsal,* Northwestern University Press, 1985

Thompson, Hunter S., *Fear and Loathing in Las Vegas*, New York, Popular Library 1971

Wheelock, Anne, *Crossing the Tracks,* The New Press, 1993

Wolfe, Tom, *The Electric Kool-Aid Acid Test,* New York, Farrar Straus Giroux, 1968

Endnotes

- *The New Haven High School in the Community is still in operation — I even placed Yale student-teachers there when I was the Field Supervisor for the Teacher Preparation Program in 2007-2008. Here's a quote from the High School in the Community's website:*

Welcome to the website for High School in the Community, the small school for students who want to do big things. Our goal is to help all students grow into the leaders our families and communities need and we have an increasing track record of success in accomplishing this task. Our students serve as leaders of their own learning both here at HSC and in off campus courses through our neighboring colleges and universities. They gain experience working with dozens of nonprofits and organizations right out our doors in downtown New Haven. They start their own campaigns and efforts to solve local problems, travel to foreign countries to examine global issues from new perspectives and collaborate side by side with staff daily to design and build a school fit for the 21ˢᵗ century.

HSC has a unique relationship with the New Haven Federation of Teachers, which serves as the operator of the school and provides management oversight and broad support towards our mission. Our teachers are passionate, empowered to make decisions as professionals that move the work of the school ever forward. Their voice and ethos animates what we do here as they strive for greatness in their teaching craft and for success for all students.

It is a unique school and, while it now has many characteristics of a "traditional" school, it is still quite distinct because of the Teacher/Community governance and its use of community resources.

Coalition of Essential Schools
Common Principles

Learning to use one's mind well

The school should focus on helping young people learn to use their minds well. Schools should not be "comprehensive" if such a claim is made at the expense of the school's central intellectual purpose.

Less is more: depth over coverage

The school's goals should be simple: that each student master a limited number of essential skills and areas of knowledge. While these skills and areas will, to varying degrees, reflect the traditional academic disciplines, the program's design should be shaped by the intellectual and imaginative powers and competencies that the students need, rather than by "subjects" as conventionally defined. The aphorism "less is more" should dominate: curricular decisions should be guided by the aim of thorough student mastery and achievement rather than by an effort to merely cover content.

Goals apply to all students

The school's goals should apply to all students, while the means to these goals will vary as those students themselves vary. School practice should be tailor-made to meet the needs of every group or class of students.

Personalization

Teaching and learning should be personalized to the maximum feasible extent. Efforts should be directed toward a goal that no teacher have direct responsibility for more than 80 students in the high school and middle school and no more than 20 in the elementary school. To capitalize on this personalization, decisions about the details of the course of study, the use of students' and teachers' time and the choice of teaching materials and specific pedagogies must be unreservedly placed in the hands of the principal and staff.

Student-as-worker, teacher-as-coach

The governing practical metaphor of the school should be "student-as-worker", rather than the more familiar metaphor of "teacher as deliverer of instructional services." Accordingly, a prominent pedagogy will be coaching students to learn how to learn and thus to teach themselves.

Demonstration of mastery

Teaching and learning should be documented and assessed with tools based on student performance of real tasks. Students not yet at appropriate levels of competence should be provided intensive support and resources to assist them quickly to meet standards. Multiple forms of evidence, ranging from ongoing observation of the learner to completion of specific projects, should be used to better understand the learner's strengths and needs, and to plan for further assistance. Students should have opportunities to exhibit their expertise before family and community. The diploma should be awarded upon a successful final demonstration of mastery for graduation: an "Exhibition." As the diploma is awarded when earned, the school's program proceeds with no strict age grading and with no system of "credits earned" by "time spent" in class.

A tone of decency and trust

The tone of the school should explicitly and self-consciously stress values of unanxious expectation, of trust, and of decency (fairness, generosity, and tolerance). Incentives appropriate to the school's particular students and teachers should be emphasized. Families should be key collaborators and vital members of the school community.

Commitment to the entire school

The principal and teachers should perceive themselves as generalists first (teachers and scholars in general education) and specialists second (experts in but one particular discipline). Staff should expect multiple obligations (teacher-counselor-manager) and demonstrate a sense of commitment to the entire school.

Resources dedicated to teaching and learning

Ultimate administrative and budget targets should include student loads that promote personalization, substantial time for collective planning by teachers, competitive salaries for staff, and an ultimate per-pupil cost not to exceed that at traditional schools by more than 10 percent. To accomplish this, administrative plans may have to show the phased reduction or elimination of some services now provided to students in many schools.

Democracy and equity

The school should demonstrate non-discriminatory and inclusive policies, practices, and pedagogies. It should model democratic practices that involve all who are directly affected by the school. The school should honor diversity and build on the strength of its communities, deliberately and explicitly challenging all forms of inequity.

The Socratic seminar is a formal discussion, based on a text, in which the leader asks open-ended questions. Within the context of the discussion, students listen closely to the comments of others, thinking critically for themselves, and articulate their own thoughts and their responses to the thoughts of others.

— Readwritethink.com

Teaching Internship Greenwich HS 1972 (wMike Maguire)

Mini-teaching at Colgate June 1972

Steve Jones & Me 1975

Bronxville Basketball Coaching

BBHS Girls Volleyball coaching

Blind Brook Basketball Coach
1975-76

1980 Blind Brook Punk Day
wJim Spano

1984 world Series at Fenway wthe Harrison Family

Wichester Proctoring

BBHS prep room wEliza McFeely

Blind Brook Classroom
wCouncilman John Perone

Winchester Coach of the
Year 1987

olume XLIV, No. 2   80 Skillings Road, Winchester, Ma. 01890 Winchester High School   November 1984

Johnson brings a new style to WHS

Mr. Johnson, a new English teacher at Winchester High, possesses an interesting method of instruction.

Photo by Scott Olivieri

By Scott Olivieri

As students, you and I often view school as a tedious chore which holds little purpose. We often neglect to see the meaning in attending school and its relevance in our development as people. Many classes in the high school involve minimal participation on the part of the students, and include endless lecturing on the part of the teacher. Even though we must realize that certain classes cannot revolve around student participation, this lack of student involvement is what makes many classes seem boring.

Mr. Johnson, a new edition to the Winchester High scene, is well aware of the lethargic approach many students take toward their classes and concerns himself with excitement toward education. He feels that students should "learn why they need education" and that education is "centered around the students" so they should become a major part of the class. This philosophy entails lengthy group discussions involving a particular novel or

a critical analysis of a movie, depending upon the class. He teaches his T.V./Media classes to question the decisions of the director of a movie and to think up ways that they themselves may have altered the script or screenplay. In American literature Mr. Johnson's students often create small student discussion groups in which they discuss symbolism and meaning in novels.

Mr. Johnson makes certain that all his classes become aware of the "artistic elements" involved in studying literature. The purpose of education, as Mr. Johnson sees it "is not just to make you literate, but to make you aware of the fact that life can be enjoyed on all different levels." He is confident that this can be achieved by analyzing other people's works. By seeing other viewpoints one can "broaden your scope" and eventually get some "insight to oneself." Analyzing a movie or novel, as he sees it, is like learning to repair an automobile: "To learn about literature you must take it apart and put it together

Cont. on p. 8

Winchester School Paper Nov. 1984

Yearbook Dedication Bronxville 1992

Blue Marlin Venezuela 1987

Venezuela fishing

Venezuela fishing

BSHS Observation

1992 Harvard Model Congress wBronxville students

Parker Staff Meeting 1994

Parker Planning Staff 1994

Parker Opening Day (news photo)

Parker School Year One

Howard Luke Academy Fairbanks ID card

2004 Fairbanks, Alaska target practice

Alaska dogs & snowmobile

Fairbanks Snowmobile

Jack in Alaska

Jack at a Conference.jpeg

Jack - Karl Dominey's Portrait of him.jpeg

AlCan Highway.jpeg

Sign Post Forest - Watson Lake .jpeg

Sogn Post Forest Canada.jpeg

Professor Johnson
at Brown 2006

SDC photo

Original Teacher Ed Team

LAST UTEPMAT group

Ed Abbott me Leaving Brown

List of Credits

Material in Chapters Four and Five originally appeared in somewhat different form in *The Student-Centered Classroom Handbook* (Eye-on-Education, 2003).

Acknowledgments

A book that spans a half-century is naturally going to entail a long list of people to thank. Because this book follows my journey in education from Yale in the late 1960s to New York City in the 20-teens, the best way to acknowledge all those who contributed to this venture is to proceed chronologically.

I've been lucky enough to maintain friendships with a group of contemporaries from my years at Yale — and they have all contributed to my personal and intellectual growth since the late-1960s. Jay Fasold, John Lissauer, Roger Schactel, Karl Pavlovic, Jay Bryan, and Jim Moyer all pitched in, each in his own way, to keep me thinking and working. The incomparable teachers at Yale who left a lifelong impression were Bill McFeely, Vincent Scully, Charles Reich, and Mark Rose — with the late Steve Kellert and Michael Lerner also steering me in important directions.

My experiences at Colgate (getting my Master of Arts in Teaching) and first fulltime teaching experience at Blind Brook Jr./Sr. High School in Rye Brook, New York, laid the strong foundation for my entire teaching career. Steve Jones, my Colgate housemate and Blind Brook colleague, has been there on every step of the journey, right up to the present. Right next to him is Del Shortliffe, another Colgate M.A.T.

and Blind Brook veteran, who remains a trusted friend and colleague to this day. At Colgate, the late Bill Moynihan's mentorship provided crucial guidance and the late David Schein's leadership as Principal of Blind Brook made sure I navigated thoughtfully and passionately. Other Blind Brook colleagues who expanded my horizons were Peter Tarshis, Jim Spano, Jim Alloy, Tom Pandiscio, Roger Smith, Bill Mendlesohn, and the late Cora Lattanzio.

My move to Boston, and then New York, teaching at Bronxville High School, as well as becoming an active member in the Coalition of Essential Schools saw another group of people adding to my knowledge, vision, and aspirations. In Boston, another Colgate alum, Jamie Jacobs, along with Charlie Berg, and Craig Lambert, provided invaluable support intellectually as well as serving as companions in numerous adventures. The summer of 1986 introduced me to Howard Stein and Marilyn Elkins, both of whom challenged me to think more deeply and creatively, particularly about teaching literature. At Bronxville, Anthony Angotta's collegiality and good humor, along with Judy Codding's and Sherry King's leadership, ushered in my work with the Coalition of Essential Schools. John Chambers, Maureen Grolnick, Grant Wiggins, and Heidi Hayes Jacobs all advanced my work at Bronxville, while Ted and Nancy Sizer inspired me to increase my school reform efforts, introducing me to luminaries like Deborah Meier and Dennis Gray. I met another set of spectacular colleagues as part of the Coalition's National Re:Learning Faculty, incomparably led by Paula Evans, Gene Thompson-Grove and Faith Dunne. Outstanding educators there were Michael Patron, Cheri Dedmon, and Dot Turner as well as Steve Cantrell, Joel Kammer, Jennifer Prileson, and the Lovely Carol Marie Bjork (my wife). It was during this period that I also started a doctoral program at Columbia Teachers College where I was fortunate enough to work with Linda Darling-Hammond, Maxine Greene, and Ann Lieberman. That ultimately led me to Brown and the founding of the Parker School.

Regarding Parker, the co-founders, Kathleen Cushman, Laura Rogers, and John Stadler, along with early staff members Jed Lippard, Elizabeth Fieldstone Kanner, Matt Smith, Deb Merriam, Dave Berkley, Heather Douglas, Keith Grove, Suzy Becker, Clare Ringwall, Mary Wren Van der Wilden, and Dawn Crane all made the adventure of creating a progressive model *of what school could be* a pure joy — even it if was a crazy amount of work.

After Parker, the work at Brown provided some of the most enjoyable and productive years in my career. That was thanks to Department Chairs Cynthia Garcia-Coll, Tom James, and Reg Archimbault. I can't even begin to express the gratitude I still feel for working with Eileen Landay, Larry Wakeford, Romi Carillo, and Polly Ulichny during those years. The support from Yvette Nachmias-Baeu, Carin Algava, and Ann D'Abrosca helped make it all possible. I'd be remiss if I didn't mention the Providence teachers who made our program second to none. First among equals was Ed Abbott, one of the finest teachers (and human beings) I have ever known. Orah Bilmes, Elma Shannon, Scott Barr, Ruth Macaulay, and Bill Meyer produced a level of mentoring and cooperating teaching that was, quite simply, superb.

After leaving Brown for Yale, and then New York City, I "re-built" my professional support network, relying on my brother, John Johnson, Steve Jones, Del Shortliffe, and Carol Bjork. Jay Fasold, along with John and Lillian Lissauer, always reminded me there was theater and music to be seen and heard in the Big Apple.

I apologize to any folks I have failed to name here, not to mention the hundreds of students who always made my job as an educator challenging, inspiring, and gratifying.

Finally, I have to thank Stevan Nikolic and Adelaide Books for making this work possible.

About the Author

Bil Johnson was born in Brooklyn, New York in 1949 and grew up on Long Island, where he became "Mr. Bay Shore" at his high school after quarterbacking an undefeated football team and serving as captain of the basketball squad. He graduated from Yale College in 1971 and, after a semester of substitute teaching at his old high school, began a Master of Arts in Teaching program at Colgate University in upstate New York. After receiving his degree from Colgate, Johnson started his teaching career in Westchester County, N.Y. He finished teaching in New York City in 2014,. That October he married the Lovely Carol Marie Bjork, in Norwalk, CT, where they live, enjoying the arts in New York City, and painting, playing music, writing, playing tennis, and sharing their ideas about school reform with all who care to listen.